EDDIE WOULD GO

XXXXXXXXXX

THE STORY OF EDDIE AIKAU
HAWAIIAN HERO

Photo by LeRoy Grannis

Jeff Hakman and Eddie paddle out at Waimea in 1966.

PUBLISHER:
MindRaising Press
P.O. Box 11391
Honolulu, Hawai'i 96828-0391
(808) 732-5460

www.eddiewouldgo.com

Library of Congress Catalog Card Number 20022114004
ISBN: 0-9706213-7-X
Hard cover trade edition
Printed in Hong Kong
First trade edition, October 2002
Cover image: Robert B. Goodman
Cover Design: Michel Le
Design & Production: MacKinnon Simpson/Noreen Valente

EDDIE WOULD GO

THE STORY OF EDDIE AIKAU
HAWAIIAN HERO

by
Stuart Holmes Coleman

MINDRAISING PRESS

DEDICATION

***Mahalo* to my family and friends**
who told me to follow my star
and helped me find my destination.

TABLE OF CONTENTS

Master navigator Nainoa Thompson scans the sea ahead as Hokule'a crosses the channel from O'ahu to Lana'i.

Sailing in Eddie's Wake

"Here lies one whose name was writ in water."
– John Keats

Sailing out of Honolulu Harbor in darkness, I am standing on the deck of a twin-hulled voyaging canoe called *Hokule'a*. The canoe was modeled after the ancient Polynesian vessels that brought the first settlers to the Islands of Hawai'i more than twelve hundred years ago. Now, a crew of mostly Hawaiian sailors is taking the canoe to the Island of Lana'i as part of a statewide educational sail. We have been asked to take off our watches, turn off our cell phones and leave the modern world behind. It's the middle of the night, and all is quiet, except for the sound of waves lapping against the hulls. The city is asleep under its own constellation of burning lights, which makes it hard to see some of the stars. But the further we sail from Honolulu, the clearer they become. Nainoa Thompson, the captain, is teaching the crew how to navigate a course by mapping out the night sky and its guiding lights. He points out the Southern Cross, the North Star and Hokule'a (Arcturus), Hawai'i's zenith star. Hokule'a means "star of gladness" because it once guided Hawaiian voyagers home from their distant journeys across Polynesia; and now centuries later, that voyaging spirit has been reborn in this canoe.

Nainoa has invited me as a guest on the canoe to retrace the last voyage of Eddie Aikau, the Hawaiian surfer and lifeguard who was a crew member on *Hokule'a* in 1978 when she capsized, and he was lost at sea. We are sailing on a similar course through the Islands, though ours is only a 12-hour sail to Lana'i while theirs was to be an arduous 30-day journey to Tahiti. As the navigator on the doomed '78 voyage, Nainoa still feels partly responsible for Eddie's loss, and it's difficult for him to talk about what happened. Although it was a tragic event in his life, Nainoa also recognizes that it marked the beginning of a new era in voyaging, one that was guided by safety and education. He wants me to experience the mystical power of sailing on *Hokule'a* so I can better understand Eddie's dedication to the canoe and what it represented. With its V-shaped sails, long wooden hulls and large steering paddle, the vessel looks like it sailed right out of Hawai'i's past. Watching her glide across the blue water, I can see why Eddie believed the canoe was a symbol of his people's heritage and pride.

About an hour and a half into the sail, we see the sun rise over the peak of Haleakala on the island of Maui, where Eddie was born. The last stars dissolve in the daylight. An 'iwa bird hangs in the air, directly over the center sail, as if tethered to the mast. In the distance, whales spout and leap out of the water like giants playing in an endless sea. As O'ahu fades on the horizon, I see the islands of Maui, Moloka'i and Lana'i slowly emerge from the sea like turtles. During the course of the sail, I stare at the rhythmic ocean swells and remember when I first learned about Eddie and the *Hokule'a*. It was 1993, and I had just moved to Hawai'i and started teaching at Punahou School. Knowing I was a writer, a fellow teacher named Marion Lyman-Mercereau asked me if I would help edit an article she had written about the voyage in 1978. Marion told me how she and Eddie had trained together on the *Hokule'a* in preparation for an epic, 2500 mile voyage from Honolulu to Tahiti. But on the day of departure, the canoe set sail at night in stormy weather, and the voyage ended in tragedy. Eddie tried to rescue the crew but was never seen again.

I was mesmerized by Eddie's story, but there were still many unanswered questions about his life, death and enduring fame. I began asking people about Eddie, and this started a chain reaction of introductions and connections. I met big-wave riders Peter Cole and Fred Van Dyke, who had also taught at Punahou years before. They shared incredible stories of surfing the biggest waves at Waimea Bay with Eddie and going to wild, drunken luaus at the Aikau home in the Chinese graveyard. They told me about some of their former students who had surfed and competed against Eddie, including surf legends like Fred Hemmings, Jeff Hakman and Gerry Lopez. I had grown up seeing these guys in old surf flicks and magazines and greatly admired them, and they in turn admired Eddie for his courage as a surfer, lifeguard and sailor.

Peter Cole then introduced me to Clyde Aikau, Eddie's brother. When I first met Clyde in Waikiki near the Duke Kahanamoku statue, I was a little intimidated by his intense gaze and aura of power. I could tell Clyde was fiercely protective of his brother's memory, but he was also eager to talk about Eddie's accomplishments. Sitting by the beach where he and Eddie had first learned to surf when the Duke was still alive, he opened up and shared vivid memories about Eddie that gave me chills on a hot, spring day. Clyde told me about how he and Eddie were best friends and how their lives revolved around the ocean. They had surfed some of the world's biggest waves at Waimea Bay and saved countless lives as lifeguards on O'ahu's treacherous North Shore. Through Clyde, I met his sister Myra and brother Sol at the graveyard where they grew up. Though it was painful digging up the past, they shared stories about their brother that made him come alive for me. Wanting to know more about Eddie, I spoke with scores of people, including fellow surfers, lifeguards and sailors. I interviewed former governors, boat-builders and Hawaiian activists. I got to know his ex-wife and closest friends who told me funny, heart-breaking and inspiring details about his life, and our conversations were often punctuated with laughter, tears and mystical revelations. I gradually filled five spiral notebooks with their stories, and these became the foundation for this book.

The event that originally made me want to write Eddie's story took place on New Year's Day, 1999. That morning, I drove out to the North Shore for the Quiksilver in Memory of Eddie Aikau Contest being held at Waimea Bay. The waves were huge, bigger than I had ever seen, and thousands of people had come to watch the event. The crowds gathered on the cliffs and on the beach stared in awe as the surfers rode the huge waves. Six-time world champion Kelly Slater was there, along with some of the world's best surfers, lifeguards and watermen. But more than just competing against each other, they had come together in memory of Eddie Aikau, whom they had honored during the annual blessing at Waimea Bay prior to the contest. Seeing all the surfers, friends and fans gathered around his memorial at the Bay, I began to understand the depth of Eddie's life and legacy. His story was also the story of modern Hawai'i. Though he had disappeared twenty-five ago, his spirit refused to die.

"All of the guys in this event have such respect for his family, big waves and Eddie himself," Kelly Slater told me recently. We were standing on the beach at Waimea during the finals of the "Eddie" Contest in January of 2002, minutes before they announced that he had won. "When we're out in the water, he's present in everyone's mind," Kelly said. "It's amazing the impact he had on the surfing world and Hawai'i. It goes beyond surfing—it touches the community at a grass-roots level. And this event perpetuates that feeling." That's partly why Eddie's legacy has only grown larger since his disappearance. "I think most of us wish if we had a chance to die a certain way, it would be doing something great like he was doing. Obviously, it was a sad way to see him go but almost a fitting end to the way he lived his life. Being lost in the ocean is tragic, but it's also romantic at the same time."

Standing on the deck of the *Hokule'a*, I stare into the shimmering sea and think about Eddie. The swells are small, the winds are light, and as we sail along, I watch the parting wake of the canoe. We are about twenty miles south of the island of Lana'i, which looks like a shadow on the horizon. Nainoa looks out over the vast expanse of water and tells me we are approaching the area where the *Hokule'a* capsized in 1978. He looks anguished as he tells me how terrible the conditions were that day as the stranded crew clung to the hulls of the overturned canoe. Howling winds and stormy seas. Sick sailors and no sign of rescue in sight. Unable to watch his fellow crew members suffer, Eddie volunteered to paddle his surfboard to the island of Lana'i for help. Nainoa vividly remembers holding his hand and staring into his eyes for a few moments before Eddie paddled out of sight and into the maelstrom.

Later, Nainoa tells me, "At a deeper level, Eddie tried to rescue not only the crew of the *Hokule'a* but the symbolism and dignity of the canoe because he knew it carried the pride of his people. Twenty-five years later, he's still navigating all of us in the voyaging community. He reminds us what our destination is and why we continue to sail. In the end, Eddie's story is about hope and healing."

Nainoa's words remind me of a story Eddie's friend Bill Kapuni once told me. A big Hawaiian man with a warm smile and a hearty laugh, Bill said he had been sailing on a vessel similar to *Hokule'a* when he suddenly saw a large shark rise up near the hull of the canoe. "The shark turned sideways, and you could see his eye. Eddie's cousin Carl was sitting next to me, and I told Carl, 'That's Eddie! Eddie came up to show us he's okay.'" Lost in the memory, Bill wiped the tears from his eyes as he described how the creature swam beside the canoe and then went away. "All of a sudden, the shark just dropped down and disappeared. He showed me, a close brother, his 'aumakua (ancestral spirit or guardian)." For Bill, there was no doubt that Eddie's spirit lived on in the form of the shark, and he found comfort in that belief. "If you believe in 'aumakua like the Hawaiian people do, he was okay. He was the caretaker of this water." Watching Hokule'a's hulls cut through the sea, I realize we are sailing in Eddie's wake.

A special shrine at Eddie's Memorial at Waimea Bay during the Quiksilver In Memory of Eddie Aikau.

The Spirit of Waimea Bay

"Greater love hath no man than this,
that a man lay down his life for his friends."
—John (15:13)

January 1, 1999. New Year's Day at Waimea Bay, the North Shore of O'ahu. In the darkness before dawn, just before the moon sets and the sun rises, a strange calm settles over the Bay. It is interrupted periodically by the thunder of waves and whitewater in the distance. How big the swells are and what they look like is still unclear due to the darkness. But many believe today will be the day they run the Quiksilver in Memory of Eddie Aikau Contest, the largest and most unusual big-wave competition in the world. The "Eddie" can only take place when the surf reaches at least 20 feet by Hawaiian standards, which means the wave faces are 40 feet high from top to bottom. (Metereolists measure surf heights by estimating the vertical distance from the wave's peak to its trough.) Inaugurated in 1987, the contest has only been held twice in the last twelve years, but many believe today could be the day.

During the winter, the true *mana* or spiritual power of Waimea Bay can be overwhelming when massive swells suddenly rise up on the horizon and come crashing down against the shoreline. Like a fickle god, the Bay can be moody and violent: one day it is calm and peaceful, and the next it is angry and deadly, threatening to crush those who enter its waters. Only the best big-wave riders in the world are invited each year to compete in the "Eddie," including former world champions like Florida's Kelly Slater, Australia's Tom Carroll and Hawai'i's Michael Ho. Along with the 24 competitors and a list of alternates, there are two honorary invitees, Mark

Foo and Todd Chesser. These big-wave riders perished in a pair of tragic accidents that shook the surfing world. Mark Foo died in a highly-publicized wipeout at Maverick's, a newly discovered offshore break located in Half Moon Bay, California on Dec. 23, 1995. Todd Chesser drowned at a North Shore break called Outside Alligator Rock on Feb. 13, 1997. Both pro surfers seemed invincible in big waves, but in the contest between man and ocean, the ocean often wins.

Though disturbed by the loss of Foo and Chesser, the competitors in the "Eddie" have not stopped riding big waves. They take comfort in the fact that at least their friends died doing what they loved. Most of the invitees come from families who have been surfing together for decades, forming well-known surf tribes from around the world. Each winter, they make an annual pilgrimage to O'ahu's North Shore, the Holy Land of surfing. As wildly different as their backgrounds are, they are spiritually connected by an almost fanatical love of the ocean, their open-air cathedral. Because Eddie is the closest thing to a martyr in the surfing world, these surfers and competitors gather together each December around his memorial at Waimea Bay to honor the man and his memory. Many of the younger pros didn't know Eddie, but they can tell by the serious tone of the speakers and the ceremony that he deserves respect. Each year, this opening ceremony begins the three-month holding period for the contest, as the competitors wait for the biggest waves and the best conditions. But it's been nine years since the last event in 1990, and they are getting restless.

With his 10'6"spear-like surfboard strapped to the roof of his SUV, Brian Keaulana pulls into the parking lot at Waimea Bay. His headlights cut across the darkness, revealing figures gathered by the shore looking out to sea. Son of legendary Hawaiian waterman Richard "Buffalo" Keaulana, Brian is a respected big-wave rider, former Lifeguard Captain and Hollywood stuntman. With his dark skin, rugged build and easygoing smile, Brian resembles a younger version of Eddie. The Aikaus and the Keaulanas are well-known clans in Hawai'i and the surfing world, and the two families have been good friends for years. In the 60's, Eddie and his brother Clyde used to watch Buffalo compete in the Makaha International, the first world surfing contest. Then, in the '70's, Brian and his brother Rusty watched Eddie and Clyde compete in the Duke Classic. "As a young kid," Brian says, "Eddie was one of my heroes."

Brian has been waiting years to surf in the contest, and today he is confident it's going to happen. "I already had the feeling from the night before that the swell was going to be huge," he says solemnly. "It was slowly rising through the night. As any knowledgeable surfer knows, you can feel the energy in the water. Every year I surf the last wave of the year and the first wave of the new year. I paddled out at 11:45 pm and surfed until 12:15 am. And just feeling the energy of Makaha—all that power and the waves washing across the road—I already had the gut feeling, 'It is on!'" While most people were out shooting fireworks, drinking and celebrating, Brian was paddling his surfboard into the roaring darkness and getting thrashed by the big waves. Rell Sunn, the Queen of Makaha, took part in this ritual each New Year's Eve, until she passed away from cancer the previous year. It was a mystical experience for Brian: surfing by the dim light of the moon and the car headlights on the beach, he could hear the waves and fireworks exploding all around him. He could also feel the presence of departed friends who had once shared these waves.

Looking out at the ocean in the faint light of dawn, Brian can barely glimpse massive walls of whitewater exploding in the distance. He can feel their primordial power. "Your senses are heightened to a whole new level," he says. "You don't really see clearly yet, it's still dark, but you can feel it. It sounded like *Jurassic Park*: all of the sudden the dinosaurs come by and go boom, and the ground starts rumbling. You can hear the boulders in the Bay clashing and the sand kind of screaming. At first, all you see is foamy whitewater. As soon as the light starts to break through, you have an idea of how much power and energy are generated out there." Waimea is a natural power plant, and it's been said the energy in these waves could light up the city of Honolulu for a week.

Brian looks for George Downing, the gray-haired contest director, to find out if the event is on. George was one of the first big-wave riders in Hawai'i and a champion surfer in his day. Known for his courage in huge surf and his cunning in competition, he is an intensely private man with deep-set eyes and glasses. He stands on the beach next to Brian and the other surfers, scanning the horizon for the larger sets he has predicted will be arriving soon. After being married to the ocean for almost 60 years, he has an innate feel for its moods. He combines intuitive wave knowledge with a scientific understanding of meteorology and weather patterns.

For months, George has been studying weather charts and buoy readings for signs of swell activity. For the best and biggest waves at Waimea

Bay to break, low pressure systems and ferocious winds need to whip the North Pacific Ocean into a frenzy. Swells are generated by wind, wind is generated by storms, and some of the meanest, most perfect storms are generated in the cold, forsaken sea off Japan and the Aleutian Islands. Like earthquakes, these storms send out shock waves that move across the sea, building in power and size. George noticed that the buoys have been registering swells of over 20 feet for the last twelve hours. After travelling thousands of miles across the open ocean with no continental shelf to slow them down, these giant swells suddenly jump up to almost 40 feet when they hit the reefs just off the shore. Reaching their peak, they finally pitch over in an explosion of water and energy, as they reel across the Bay.

There are temporary lulls in the surf this morning, but Downing tells Brian and the other surfers on the beach that buoy readings say the swells are on their way. "The Bay calls the day," he says, sounding like an old prophet of the sea. An ocean of responsibility and pressure rests on Downing's shoulders. The surfing world awaits his word, and so does an international media network of photographers, writers and TV reporters. Besides the $55,000 first prize, surfers from around the globe have extended their annual migrations to the North Shore just for the honor of competing in the contest. When Northern California charger Peter Mel received word that the contest was on the previous night, he jumped on the last plane out of San Francisco on New Year's Eve to fly to O'ahu. After flying all night and taking a $100 cab ride to the North Shore, Peter shows up on the beach this morning jet-lagged and groggy but ready to compete. Despite the lull in the surf, Downing repeats his prediction that "the 'Eddie' will go."

At 10:00 am, giant waves start pouring over the horizon, as if on cue. Downing announces that the contest is on, and news of the event spreads rapidly over what locals call the "coconut wireless" or word of mouth. Soon people from all over the Island begin driving to the North Shore to witness the event. By 11:00 am, thousands of locals and tourists are gathered on the cliffs and the beach to watch, and traffic is backed up for miles in either direction of Waimea. Shaped like a natural amphitheater, the Bay offers one of the greatest shows on earth. "Waimea is like a huge arena, and you can feel the power of the place," Brian says. "It's heavy being in the epicenter of all that power and energy. It's kind of like when the gladiators go into battle in the coliseum. You can hear the crowd cheering and ooo-ing and aah-ing."

The sun is out, the waves are heavy, and the surfers are pushing themselves to take off on the biggest and steepest waves. Helicopters fly overhead as cameramen film the surf, while lifeguards race across the Bay on jet skis to rescue fallen surfers. The competitors scramble for giant waves, and spectators in bathing suits and bikinis watch from the shore. Like a mantra, the words "EDDIE WOULD GO" keep repeating themselves on T-shirts and bumper stickers and in the minds of the surfers. "The saying from the bumper stickers sticks in your head when you're at the Eddie Aikau Contest," Kelly Slater says. "You think, 'If Eddie was in this place that I'm in right now, would he take this wave?' And pretty much every time the answer is going to be Yes. I'm sure that accounts for all the people who take off late and surf really big waves."

With 24 invitees in all, there are four heats of six surfers, and each competitor gets to surf in two rounds. When the swells rise up on the horizon, the crowd starts hooting and screaming as these ant-sized surfers drop down the faces of the massive beasts. People peer through binoculars and gasp, while cameras zoom in on the action and click away. Some swells are too big or steep, and the surfers back off at the last minute, afraid of being run over. These waves look like massive locomotives steaming across the Bay, leaving a smoke-like mist in the air. Along with epic rides and maneuvers, there are some epic wipe-outs. The crowd groans in mock pain as surfers free-fall almost 20 feet before being slammed into the water and churned inside a rolling mass of whitewater more than two stories high. Many of the spectators hang around the judges' tower to get a glimpse of the surf pros and the Aikau family.

Eddie's surviving siblings—Clyde, Sol and Myra—join George Downing in the VIP area to get away from the crowds. Like George, the Aikaus are intensely private people, and they generally don't like talking to the media about their brother because it's still too painful. Wearing "Eddie Would Go" T-shirts, they can't help but stare at the orange lifeguard stand where Eddie worked for years. Clyde is older now, and his dark hair and mustache have been touched with gray, but he can still vividly see his brother keeping watch over the Bay. He restlessly follows the event, wishing he were out there surfing. Some of the most memorable moments of his life happened at the Bay. He remembers standing on the beach as a teenager during the epic swell of 1967 and watching Eddie catch some of the biggest waves ever ridden at Waimea. His heart raced as his brother screamed across the giant waves, and it sank whenever he fell. He and Eddie later surfed and competed with each other in the biggest contests of the day. They both lifeguarded at the Bay, and Clyde watched his older brother bring dead men back to life on the beach. But when Eddie disappeared at sea in 1978, it left a hole in Clyde's life. Looking out at the Bay, he can't help but recall the emotional moment almost ten years later when he won the first Quiksilver contest—at that moment, he felt like they were reunited.

After winning in 1987 and reaching the finals in '90, Clyde has decided to retire from the contest this year to give a younger surfer his slot. At 49, he is almost twice the age of many of the competitors, but he is still in good shape and ready to compete in the big waves (in fact he would later compete again in the contest). Though envious of the younger surfers, he enjoys being a spectator for the first time. "What's really exciting is that when the waves break, they break so big and strong that the actual ground shakes. Feeling the wind come down from the valley, with the *heiau* (temple grounds) on top of the mountain and with the big waves pounding and so much energy, it's a real special thing just to be there and be a spectator." As one of the last and most powerful *kahunas*, or priestly leaders, Clyde's great ancestor Hewahewa once watched over the Bay from the *heiau* above.

Out in the water, the competitors are charging in the spirit of Eddie and pushing themselves to catch the most dangerous swells. Having survived deadly wipeouts at the Bay, surfer Brock Little says surfers have to overcome their fears and natural tendency to panic. "You gotta be relaxed and believe it's mind over matter. But we're all human, and it gets to the point where your mind realizes that there's too much matter out there." Brian Keaulana remembers how one wave threw him onto the bottom and held him down until his lungs were screaming for oxygen and his legs felt like Jell-O. Scared to death like any other mortal, Brian says he was also strangely excited. "Wipeouts are actually like the highest point of your life—dealing with death, trying to survive, trying not to panic." He finally made it to the surface, gasping for air. His confidence took a beating during the wipeout, but he still manages to enjoy the thrill of riding and surviving such huge waves. He describes surfing at Waimea with an almost religious reverence for its power. "It's kind of like being in a big cathedral. Everything is just magnified, and you can feel the spirit flowing through you." Being in such huge waves might be a spiritual experience for Brian and other big-wave riders, but for most people, it would be hell.

"It's important that all the riders are physically, mentally and spiritually ready to endure these waves," Clyde says. "If you're physically in shape but not spiritually ready, I'd say you're in trouble." During a massive swell on Christmas day ten years earlier, a surfer named Titus Kinimaka was surfing at Waimea when the lip of a huge wave broke right on his leg. The force of the wave not only broke his board, but it snapped his femur in half. "I reached down to feel my leg," Titus recalled later, "and it was gone. Then I had to dive under another wave, and when I came back up, something was hitting me in the back of my head, and I looked back, and it was my foot!" Most surfers would have panicked or gone into shock, increasing their chances of drowning, especially with huge waves still rolling toward them. But Titus was in good physical and mental shape, and he remained calm until lifeguards came and rescued him.

Always concerned with safety, Brian struggles with conflicting feelings about competitive surfing and lifeguarding. As a competitor, he strives to be the best. But as a lifeguard, he is constantly looking out for the other surfers. Like Eddie, he enjoys pushing his limits in big waves, but he also knows that safety is more important than anything else. As a young kid, he was inspired by stories about Eddie's heroic rescues. After becoming a top lifeguard himself, he went on to win the Quiksilver Aikau Waterman Award in 1991 for his contributions to ocean safety. "Eddie was a true waterman. For me, a waterman is someone who has great respect for the ocean. The ocean is my educator, teaching me many things." That's why Brian is dedicated to the spirit of Eddie and the contest bearing his name. "For me, the whole competition and the money are secondary," Brian says. "It's really important to represent who Eddie was and what he did. Eddie's whole Hawaiianness is like dropping a rock in a pond, creating ripples that affect everyone around the world. Our culture is about protecting life." Since his disappearance, Eddie has re-emerged as a heroic figure in Hawai'i and the international surfing community.

As his youngest brother and closest friend, Clyde has the most to say about Eddie. He is Hawaiian to his core and proud of his family's heritage. A businessman and unofficial ambassador of aloha, he owns two beach concession stands in Waikiki and travels all around the world, promoting surfing and Hawaiian culture. But more importantly, he seeks to honor his brother's legacy. He has a tendency to stutter when talking about serious or emotional issues, but he speaks from the heart. When it comes to the contest, Clyde says, "I think the image of Eddie, what he stood for—to give your life for somebody else—has come through the event. I feel very honored when the younger surfers really recognize what he was about. To help someone in need and not expect anything back was what Eddie was all about."

As part of the opening ceremonies for the contest, Clyde, Brian and all the other competitors gathered at Eddie's memorial at Waimea. Fans and photographers hovered near the tan, muscular surfers. Standing in front of their long, sharp boards, they looked like a tribe of warriors. They circled around the memorial's large, volcanic boulder, decorated with ferns, flower leis and blown-up pictures of Eddie. In one famous photo taken in 1967, he races across the face of a huge wave at the Bay that is almost five times his height. In another picture, one of the last ever taken of him, he is standing on the deck of the Polynesian voyaging canoe *Hokule'a*. It was shot on the fateful day of his departure for Tahiti in 1978.

During the ceremony, the *kahu* or pastor said that the event was not about competing against each other but about honoring Eddie's memory. He wore a traditional Hawaiian robe and spoke to the competitors before blessing them with *ti* leaves dipped in salt water from the ocean. "You surfers come not so much to win money or fame but to grasp at this time who you are and the love you have for the memory of this man and all the good he lived for and the beauty you see in this Bay. Your achievement will come out of this love and let the money and medals fall where they may."

Asked to say a few words, Brian took the stage and addressed the crowd in front of the memorial. After mentioning that Eddie was his hero as a kid, he said that as Hawaiians they didn't have a lot of money growing up. "But we were rich in culture, rich in knowledge, and those are the kinds of things we share. Eddie shared a lot with my family over the years. When I look around and see the young kids looking at their idols standing here before them, I see Eddie's heart and soul. Everybody here carries around part of Eddie's soul."

On the memorial behind Brian, there is a bronze plaque that tells the cryptic tale of Eddie's tragic loss. "'Greater love hath no man than this, that a man lay down his life for his friends.' (John 15:13) Eddie Aikau disappeared at sea on March 17, 1978, while trying to get help for the crew of the Polynesian Voyaging Society's double-hull canoe *Hokule'a*....Eddie Aikau is gone, but his name will live in the annals of heroism of Hawai'i."

These words give only the faintest glimpse of his life, but they say nothing about his dreams as a boy or his final moments as a man. For Brian and all those who knew Eddie, they can't help but wonder what happened to him during that last day, as he struggled to paddle his surfboard across miles and miles of stormy waves and raging seas.

As the sun sets behind Ka'ena Point, dusk descends on the North Shore. The contest results have been announced and the prizes awarded. Noah Johnson, one of the youngest and smallest of the competitors, took home first place and a check for $55,000 after catching the biggest waves of the day. The crowds have dispersed, and a strange calm comes over the beach, except for the thunder of surf in the distance.

An orange lifeguard tower stands on the beach at Waimea, seeming to glow in the twilight. This is where Edward Ryan Aikau made some of the most dramatic rescues ever seen on the North Shore. Friends, family and fellow watermen say his spirit still presides over Waimea Bay, and a few say they have even seen visions of Eddie and spoken to him in their dreams. Songs and chants have been written about him, and his memory lives on through the contest, as well as the countless T-shirts and bumper stickers that proclaim, "EDDIE WOULD GO." Yet few people know the intimate details and tragic events that transformed a shy local boy into an enduring cultural icon. The man has become a myth. So who was Eddie and what made him go? The answer lies in his unique relationship with his family, his people and the ocean he called home.

At the 1967 Duke awards ceremony, a shy 21-year old Eddie accepts his trophy from his hero, Duke Kahanamoku.

CHAPTER 1

The Life of the Land

*"Man is merely the caretakeer of the land that maintains
his life and nourishes his soul. Therefore, the 'aina is sacred.
The church of life is not in a building, it is the open sky, the
surrounding ocean, the beautiful soil…"*

— *George Helm*

With the sun setting over the Wai'anae Mountains, Waimea Bay
looks like a blue jewel carved into the jagged coastline of O'ahu's North
Shore. Looking down from the *heiau* on the cliffs above the Bay, you can
see a crescent moon of white sand encircling its darkening waters. For most
of the year, the Bay is quiet and calm like a sleeping giant, but each winter
it awakes in a violent assault of huge waves. Large rock formations stand
like warriors at each end of the Bay, clashing with the incoming swells in
explosions of whitewater. From the landing of the first Western ships to the
bombing of Pearl Harbor, the history of Hawai'i is reflected in the water of
the Bay and its changing temperament.

Walking among the stone ruins of the *heiau* above the Bay, you can
feel the presence of the people who once worshipped and prepared for war
here. Eddie's story is intricately tied to the history of his people and the life
of the *'aina* or land. He wandered through the same hills where his ancestor
Hewahewa once roamed. In the early 1800's, Hewahewa ruled over the
entire valley as the chief *kahuna*, just as Eddie would later watch over the
Bay as the head lifeguard. Though generations apart, they both saw Hawai'i
go through enormous changes with each new wave of immigrants flooding
its shores. One saw the demise of his culture, while the other saw its revival
a century and a half later.

In the orange light of late afternoon, the *heiau* overlooking the Bay and the green valley behind it appear timeless and pristine. Except for a few emblems of modern civilization—the square tower of St. Peter and St. Paul Mission on the eastern cliff, a few houses on the point and a lone lifeguard stand on the beach—you can almost imagine what it looked like more than two hundred years ago when Captain Cook and the first Westerners 'discovered' what they called the Sandwich Islands in 1778. When his ships landed in Hawai'i, Cook marveled at the tropical beauty of this remote island chain in the middle of the Pacific and the thriving civilization he found there. He had heard chants in Tahiti that mentioned these mystical islands, but he didn't know if they really existed. When Cook encountered the native people, he asked for provisions in the language of the Tahitians and was amazed how they welcomed him and understood his requests. Cook was confounded by how many similarities they shared with the natives he had encountered in Tahiti and throughout Polynesia. They were big people, some over seven feet tall, with the same dark features and many of the same words and food staples. The physical, linguistic and cultural similarities led him to believe that these people had migrated across the Pacific and formed the "most extensive nation on earth." But it was unclear to him how they could have traveled such vast distances across the world's largest ocean in their small sailing canoes. It seemed impossible without large ships or Western instruments like the compass, quadrant and timepiece. How did they ever arrive and settle in Hawai'i? It was a mystery he would never solve.

Throughout their travels in the Pacific, Cook and his men were surrounded by thousands of natives who swam, sailed and paddled their canoes to visit the foreign ships. He realized that these people practically lived in the ocean, depending on the sea for their food, transportation and play. Most Europeans of the time could not swim and feared that the ocean was full of dragons, but for these people it was home. He witnessed such rare sights as canoe surfing, but only in Hawai'i did the riders stand up on boards and "walk on water," as the later missionaries would describe it. Watching a native ride the waves in an outrigger canoe, Cook had once written in his journals, "I could not help concluding that this man felt the most supreme pleasure while he was driven on so fast and so smoothly by the sea."

With his pale skin and tall ships, Captain Cook may have been mistaken for the Hawaiian god Lono when he first arrived in Hawai'i, but his divine aura quickly diminished when he began trading and dealing with the locals. After held a Big Island chief ransom for some items that had been stolen from his ship, the chief's warriors attacked and killed Captain Cook, along with four of his men. Fearful of a native uprising, Cook's badly shaken crew quickly set sail for Oʻahu, stopping to rest and recover in Waimea Bay's seemingly tranquil and peaceful waters. Four years later, one of Cook's officers returned to Waimea. When Captain Vancouver's ship, the *Daedalus*, landed at the Bay in 1793, bringing another wave of *haole* explorers, a skirmish erupted between the sailors and the natives on the shore. Two crew members were killed and supposedly sacrificed by warriors at the *heiau*. Having established a more powerful presence in the Islands, Vancouver then demanded the killers be punished. Two Hawaiian natives, most likely not the culprits, were brought on board the ship and immediately shot. After this fateful collision of worlds, Hawaiʻi would never be the same.

Like the huge swells that roll into Waimea Bay each winter, waves of Westerners began landing on Hawaiʻi's shores. With the help of *haole* advisors and their guns, the great warrior chief Kamehameha I conquered Oʻahu and united the Hawaiian Islands in 1795. Pleased by his conquest, the new King gave his *kahuna nui* (chief advisor) Hewahewa dominion over the Waimea *heiau* and the lush valley that stretched from the mountains to the sea. Hewahewa had been in charge of honoring and appeasing the war god Ku and enforcing the *kapu* system, the set of ancient laws and taboos that governed Hawaiʻi's people. But with each wave of *haole* sailors and merchants from America and Europe, the infusion of alcohol, guns and germs violently transformed Hawaiian culture. The ruling chiefs began to question the old ways and structure of their society. After the death of King Kamehameha, his widow Kaʻahumanu, his favorite of 21 wives, and his son Liholiho took control and decided to abandon the old gods and social *kapus*. They had seen how the Westerners were not affected by their *kapus*, like those that forbade men and women from eating together or restricted their interaction with the *aliʻi*. In one of the most incredible coincidences of Hawaiian history, they ordered the *kahunas* to destroy the *heiaus* and burn all the wooden idols, just months before the first Christian missionaries arrived. This created a spiritual void that the new religion would soon fill. It is said that Hewahewa complied because he could foresee the coming of the missionaries. He even sent a messenger to the royal family's home near the shore, saying, "O heavenly one, the new God will soon land yonder."

Supposedly gifted with the power to see the future, Hewahewa believed it would be useless to fight the onslaught of Western forces and the white man's God; so he embraced the new ways and shunned the practice of most ancient rituals. The powerful *kahuna* even tried to become a Christian and wrote a chant in honor of the missionaries when their ship, the *Thaddeus,* arrived in 1820. In the chant, he told his people, "Pray, with reverence to Jehovah,/ As a mighty kahuna of the island." When Ka'ahumanu and many of the ruling chiefs converted to Christianity not long after, the *kapu* system and the *kahunas* eventually gave way to Western laws and missionary influence. But Hewahewa later became disillusioned with the Christian priests and their lack of magic, apparently disappointed the missionaries could not cure the sick or raise the dead. He saw his people embracing the new religion and the Western ways while losing their land and customs. This was the twilight hour of Hawaiian culture, and legend says Hewahewa predicted the dawn of a new age when a renaissance of traditional values and culture would awaken in his people. When he died, his bones were hidden deep in the valley where no one would disturb them.

During the 1800's, O'ahu and the other Hawaiian Islands were overrun with foreigners from all over the world, including sailors, merchants, whalers, missionaries, businessmen and migrant field hands. During the Great Mahele of 1848, King Kamehameha III was persuaded by *haole* advisors to let the Islands be divided and sold into private ownership, a concept that was completely foreign to most Hawaiians. In their culture, there was no such thing as ownership of any part of nature because it was sacred—people could live on the land and take care of it, but they could not own it. That would be like claiming the sky or the ocean. The kingdom was divided among the monarchy, the *ali'i* and the common people. But eventually wealthy businessmen and planters bought most of the land at dirt-cheap prices, and the natives were often evicted from their native soil. Many Hawaiians became homeless in their own homeland, forced to eke out a living on plantations, settlements or in the city. Sugar and pineapples became the cash crops, as plantations spread across the Islands like a dark shadow.

As the *haole* planters and businessmen gained more power, they began exerting increasing influence over the Hawaiian monarchy, while pushing for American annexation of the Islands. King Kalakaua decided to reassert his royal powers by building the costly 'Iolani Palace, where he held Hawai'i's first coronation, which was followed by two weeks of elaborate celebrations. Known for his lavish style and love of the arts, King Kalakaua was called the "Merry Monarch" because he helped start a revival of Hawaiian music and dance. He and his sister Princess Lydia Lili'uokalani were talented musicians and songwriters, and her song "Aloha 'Oe" became Hawai'i's most popular anthem. Both were loved by the Hawaiian people but resented by the Western establishment of educators, missionaries and powerful planters. In 1887, an armed insurrection led by a *haole* political group forced the King to sign what came to be called the "Bayonet Constitution," severely limiting the monarch's powers and the rights of the Hawaiian people. He lived for a few more years as a royal figurehead, hosting grand balls and parties, and then died on a trip to San Francisco. Hawai'i's last king was followed by his sister, who became the kingdom's last monarch.

When Queen Lili'uokalani came into power, she was committed to restoring the power of the monarchy and the rights of the Hawaiian people. The Queen tried to regain political control of the Islands by creating a new constitution, but she was soon overthrown by a group of wealthy, American businessmen, many of whom were descendants of the original missionaries. Backed by 160 U.S. Marines, the anti-royalist and pro-annexation forces launched a bloodless coup in 1898. They established a provisional government and later formed a Republic, with planter and missionary son Sanford Dole as its president. Hawai'i's last Queen was forced to abdicate her throne and later put under house arrest at 'Iolani Palace, where she wrote, "I yield to the superior force of the United States of America to avoid any collision of armed forces and perhaps the loss of life." Her later attempts to convince Washington to return her kingdom proved futile.

The Republic was eventually annexed as a territory of the United States. But generations later, Eddie's grandparents and parents would not learn this version of history in school—like most Hawaiians, they were taught that the Queen had voluntarily given up power to the new Republic. By this time, Hawaiians were not allowed to speak their native language in school, and their chants and customs were looked down upon. (Ironically, though the missionaries had helped suppress many native traditions, they also helped preserve much of Hawai'i's oral history by creating a Hawaiian alphabet and recording the people's stories, genealogies and myths.) Many locals were ashamed of their culture and wanted to be American, with all the wealth and rights that entailed. Meanwhile, the number of Native Hawaiians had dwindled to a fraction of their original population, due to the onslaught of foreign diseases and chronic health and social problems. It's estimated that there were more than 800,000 Hawaiians in the Islands when Captain Cook arrived, but by the next century, they had dwindled to less than 40,000. Like many of the indigenous plants and animals that had become extinct, the Hawaiian people seemed to be a dying breed. Waimea's once thriving valley had been almost completely abandoned by the mid-twentieth century.

Because of its strategic location in the middle of the Pacific, Hawai'i became a key military post for the U.S., as well as a playground for the rich and famous. Most of the Pacific naval fleet was stationed at Pearl Harbor, and American G.I.'s and tourists could mingle with movie stars and corporate tycoons down at Waikiki Beach. As battles raged in Europe and Asia, isolationist groups in America were determined to stay out of a world war. But all that was about to change. In their book *Waikiki*, Paul Berry and Edgy Lee write that "On the evening of Saturday, December 6, 1941, military officers were having a Christmas party at the Royal Hawaiian," the luxurious pink hotel at the center of Waikiki. Meanwhile, "Offshore a Japanese submarine hovered close enough to hear the music." Early the next morning, Japanese planes descended on O'ahu in one of the most devastating surprise attacks in history. With the bombing of Pearl Harbor on Dec. 7, 1941, Hawai'i suddenly became the center of the Second World War's raging battles in the Pacific Theater. The sleeping giant had awoken, and many Hawaiians like Eddie's father Sol eagerly joined the call to fight for their country—even though they were not considered official U.S. citizens. Struggling with their conflicted identity, they were torn between their Hawaiian roots and American dreams. Into this spiritually divided land, Eddie was born just after the war.

Conceived during the last year of World War II, Edward Ryan Makua Hanai Aikau came into the world during the first year of peace. He was born in Kahului, Maui on May 4, 1946 to Solomon and Henrietta Aikau. His father Sol was a strong Hawaiian man with a husky voice and a commanding presence that made him seem much taller than his 5' 9" frame. Henrietta was shy by nature, but there was a quiet strength beneath her soft, comforting features. Sol had been a private first-class in the Army when he met Henrietta, who said he remained a private because he was always getting into fights. When they first started dating, it caused a rift between the two families because she was a devout Catholic of mixed Hawaiian heritage and he was a Mormon of pure Hawaiian blood. But when Henrietta became pregnant with their first son Freddie, they decided to get married and start their own family. Sol converted to Catholicism, and they were wed by the priest in the local church. They settled down in a small house on a dusty road near the Kahului Railroad Company, where Sol worked as a driver and stevedore. Shortly after their son Frederick was born, he and Henrietta had a girl named Myra. Within six years, they had had four more boys—Edward, Gerald, Solomon III and Clyde. The Aikaus lived on a dirt road in a small compound of houses across from the Kahului Harbor called Rawfish Camp, which has since been replaced by expensive condos. They lived near the ocean and in the shadow of Haleakala, the majestic volcano whose name means "house of the sun." When the sun rose behind the cloud-covered volcanic peak each morning, the Aikau household would erupt with the sounds of six young kids.

Stern at times, "Pops," as he came to be called, raised Eddie and his siblings with all the discipline of his Army days. He marched them to church, inspected their outfits and yelled at the boys if they picked on Myra or fought with each other. But Pops also had a lighter side, and he was passionate about watersports. He loved playing in the ocean with his kids, who learned to swim soon after they could walk. In contrast to her husband, Henrietta hardly ever raised her voice with her kids, but a disapproving look from her kind eyes was enough to set them straight. She enjoyed their outings to the beach, but she was a little afraid of the ocean. Music was her passion, and she would often play the ukulele and sing for her children, lulling them to sleep with old Hawaiian songs.

The third of six children, Eddie was small like his father and quiet like his mother. But he was an active boy and soon became the unofficial leader of the troop. Growing up in a family obsessed with watersports and music, Eddie was the first to start surfing and playing the guitar, and the others quickly followed his lead. Myra learned to sing and play the ukulele from her mother. A slightly pudgy boy with a big heart, Freddie was not as musical or athletic. As the oldest, it was his duty to watch over his younger brothers, who used to gang up against him in play-fights. Gerry, Sol and Clyde struggled to keep up with Eddie. Describing him as "the leader, the Elvis Presley of the gang," Clyde says Eddie loved playing games. Whether they were chasing each other along the beach or racing in a swim contest,

Eddie pushed himself the hardest and usually won. This may have been compensation for the fact that he was also the smallest of the boys and the darkest. He was always self-conscious of the fact that his brothers had called him "popolo," referring to the dark-colored *popolo* berries and the Hawaiian term for Negro. Though the Islands were known for their ethnic diversity and intermingling, there was still an underlying racist hierarchy, and blacks were just below Hawaiians on the social and economic ladder. Though he had hardly ever seen a black person, Eddie didn't like being called *popolo* and was acutely aware of his dark skin color. Being a dark Hawaiian was not a source of pride for many local families who had been influenced by the prejudice of the day. Many of the more powerful Hawaiians were those with fairer skin who had married into the white establishment.

Despite the teasing and competition, there was not a lot of animosity between the brothers, mostly because Pops forbid it. Each month Pops would gather everyone together for a family meeting to work out any disagreements or resentments. This was a tradition in Hawai'i called *ho'oponopono* (to make right), and no one could leave the table until the matter had been hashed out and resolved. Whenever arguments or sibling rivalries arose, these meetings helped the family deal with the divisive issues, bringing them closer together. "I think that's the key," Myra says. "You've got to talk with each other. I think that's why it works so well in our family. My dad had that meeting every month since we were five. We'd say our prayers and then, boom, we'd talk." If the brothers picked on Myra, they would have to apologize or face their father's wrath. But if 'outsiders' teased or offended one of the family members in some way, making fun of their dark skin or old clothes, the Aikau boys were more than ready to 'beef it out' with them. No negotiations. Like their father, the Aikau boys established a reputation as tough scrappers, generally peaceful but with short tempers.

As a stevedore, Pops operated heavy loading equipment and was considered one of the better drivers on Maui. He unloaded shipping containers, hauled sugar cane and helped construct the telephone and electric lines up the slopes of Haleakala. He was a jack of all trades, but he barely made enough to feed his growing family. In spite of their poverty, Pops managed to send his kids to St. Anthony's Catholic School. Though Hawaiians were often looked down upon, he raised them to be proud of their heritage. A descendant of *kahuna*, he resented how his people had been reduced to third-class citizens in their own land. The social hierarchy could clearly be seen in the organization of the plantations that were run by the "Big Five," a group of interlocking business interests which owned (and still control) most of the private land in Hawai'i. These *haole* businessmen and their extended families were at the top of the pyramid. Many were the descendants of missionaries who came to Hawai'i 'to do good' and ended up 'doing very well' for themselves. Below them were the Portuguese overseers and managers who watched over the field hands. Most of Hawai'i's major ethnic groups originally migrated here to work on the sugar and pineapple plantations, coming from China, Japan and the Philippines. The owners often pitted the different groups against each other to prevent them from organizing a labor union. With each wave of new immigrants, the previous ethnic group moved up a little higher, while the Hawaiians languished near the bottom. But Pops was determined to make something of his life and do better for his kids. Like the Hawaiians of old, Pops turned to the ocean for comfort, food and a glimpse of their former glory. It was there that his ancestors had demonstrated their remarkable skills as sailors, fishermen and surfers.

On weekends, Pops would take the family down to the ocean to go diving, fishing and surfing. Looking like a centipede, all six kids would help lug his heavy, old 16-foot redwood surfboard to the beach. With a gentle push from Pops, Eddie and the older boys caught their first small waves on this barge-like board, yelping with excitement as the whitewater pushed them along. Surfing had always been a traditional sport in Hawai'i, and the Aikau boys learned to ride the waves from their father, a local rite of passage like learning to ride a bike. Pops also taught the boys how to fish and cast a net, while Momma Aikau and Myra picked *opihi* from the rocks and seasoned the little snail-like creatures. They would gather driftwood to start a fire on the beach, cook the catch of the day and then "talk story," as the locals say.

These family outings established an enduring relationship with the ocean, and any financial problems or domestic pressures were usually washed away in its clear, blue waters. Eddie spent as much time as he could in the ocean, swimming, diving and exploring the silent world below the surface. He would see sea turtles, eels and all kinds of fish. Thin needlefish, fat pufferfish and colorful butterflyfish. Each spring during their mating season, he would see humpback whales breaching off the coast of Maui, playfully leaping out of the sea and landing in an explosion of water. Occasionally, Eddie would see sharks ominously cruising in the distance, but he was taught not to be afraid of them or any other creatures in the sea. The water's warm, sensual embrace was as soft and comforting as a woman's touch, and it was the beginning of Eddie's lifelong love affair with the ocean.

In 1958, the year before Hawai'i became the 50th state, Pops debated whether he should move the family from Maui to O'ahu. Though the Islands remained a U.S. Territory, O'ahu was rapidly being transformed from an agricultural backwater into a crucial economic center because the business community, the military and the tourism industry were all concentrated there. The Aikaus enjoyed living on Maui, where they had relatives and good friends, but Pops was barely making enough to support his family. Hearing of better economic opportunities on O'ahu, he decided to apply for a job as a stevedore down at Honolulu's shipping yards. It would be a big change, leaving the rural lifestyle of Maui for the city life of Honolulu, but he felt the move would be worth it. Myra was devastated and cried for weeks about leaving her friends and grandparents behind. The Aikau boys didn't seem to mind moving because they were best friends and would remain together.

With their six children in tow, Pops and Henrietta packed up their meager belongings and boarded an inter-island ferry called the *Maui Queen* to start a new life in Honolulu. Having never left Maui before, the kids were anxious yet excited about the move. As the ferry pulled away, they took one last look at the sugar cane fields waving in the distance. Maui had been a magical place to grow up, an hourglass-shaped island where Eddie had spent the first fourteen years of his life. A rural land of rainbows, waterfalls and volcanoes. As they crossed the rough waters of the channel, Eddie watched the cloud-covered peak of Haleakala fade behind them as O'ahu's green-covered mountains and city skyline came into focus. Staring hypnotically into the wake of whitewater rushing by the side of the boat and the deep blue water beyond, the quiet fourteen-year-old boy probably wondered what kind of future awaited him on the new island.

Their first year on O'ahu was rough as the family tried to find a permanent place to live and adjust to life in the city. Social and political changes were reshaping the landscape. On March 12, 1959, Hawai'i finally gained statehood. The local parades and celebrations were soon followed by an infusion of federal funding for new roads, schools and buildings. Honolulu was fast becoming a major metropolitan city with a population of almost half a million. Most residents celebrated statehood and the ensuing economic development, but some Hawaiians felt like their culture would be lost in the general rush to become "Americanized." Reverend Dr. Abraham Akaka expressed his people's concerns in a sermon given the day after Hawai'i became the 50th state. In front of a packed congregation at the historic Kawaiha'o Church, the charismatic preacher said, "There are some of us to whom statehood brings great hopes, and there are some to whom statehood brings silent fears. One might say that the hopes and fears of Hawai'i are met in statehood today. There are fears that statehood will motivate economic greed toward Hawai'i, that it will turn Hawai'i into a great big spiritual junkyard filled with smashed dreams and worn-out illusions."

Many of the fears Rev. Akaka mentioned were deeply rooted in a lingering resentment of how Hawaiian culture had been co-opted by outside forces and influences. To most Americans on the mainland, Hawai'i was still more of a tourist destination and military outpost than a state. Life in the Islands evoked romantic images of hula girls and grass huts, and the tourism industry promoted these popular stereotypes. Ukuleles, Hawaiian music and aloha shirts became the rage on the mainland. Visitors flocked to Waikiki for vacation, looking for a fabricated image of some exotic paradise. But life for most locals was much harder and more complex. Still, local Christian families like the Aikaus embraced the change and the promise of the American Dream. Rev. Akaka summed up their feelings at the end of his sermon. "Since the coming of the missionaries in 1820, the name of God to our people has been aloha," he said. "In other words, aloha is God. Aloha is the power of God seeking to unite what is separated in the world—the power that unites heart with heart, soul with soul, life with life, culture with culture, race with race, nation with nation."

In spite of their poverty, Pops worked hard to make sure his family had enough to eat and a decent place to live. He secured a free residence next to a Chinese graveyard in Pauoa Valley, in exchange for working as the cemetery's caretaker. A lush piece of land filled with mango, banana and guava trees, the Chinese graveyard was surrounded by beautiful views of Punchbowl Crater in front and the Ko'olau Mountains behind. With their brood of rambunctious kids, Pops and Momma Aikau brought new life to the graveyard. Moving from a small, rural area of several thousand to a large city with more than half a million people had been traumatic for the family. They had never seen so many cars, traffic lights and tall buildings. But the cemetery was hidden back in the valley, away from the city, and soon became the family's sanctuary, their own little piece of country in town.

For the first few months, the kids were frightened about living in a graveyard, surrounded by death, with old tombstones sticking out of the grass like crooked teeth. But they eventually grew accustomed to their new surroundings. Sitting in the graveyard more than forty years later, Eddie's brother Sol has fond memories of that time. A large man with gray hair pulled back in a ponytail, he has two tattoos on his thick brown arms that say, "Eddie Boy" and "Chale," the names of his two sons who died. Speaking in a raspy voice from years of hard living and constant smoking, Sol remembers playing in the cemetery with his siblings. "At first it was kinda scary, but then over the years it became like living next to a playground or a big park. Besides being brothers and sister, we were all best friends and did everything together. I remember when we were kids in the graveyard and we would play hide and go seek at night, and Eddie would make like one of the stones, and we wouldn't see him. Or he would climb in the mango tree, and he was so dark it was hard to see him." Eddie could hide better than anyone, and as hard as his siblings searched, they couldn't find him.

As they grew older, the boys began to work in the cemetery, cutting the grass and tending the graves. Their childhood games turned into adolescent chores and pranks. Death became part of the daily business of living. "We were the caretakers, and we had to maintain the graveyard and keep it looking nice," Sol says. "Maintaining of the graveyard was rent. The Yee King Tong Society owned the place. After so many years, Chinese tradition is that you dig the bodies out of the ground and put 'em into the crocks inside the mausoleum. People would clean them up and put them into crocks inside the bone house, which is like their temple. It's a building with shelves, and on the shelves are the crocks, and in the crocks, there's the bones. And as kids, we would go in there and play with them. We would take the skulls out and scare each other with them. We would always play tricks like carry each other's beds into the bone house so they would wake up in there; or we'd carry their bed and put it in the middle of the graveyard." Imagine waking up from a disturbing dream and seeing a skull at the foot of your bed or headstones all around you in the darkness.

The Aikau compound was centrally located between the four centers of activity in the family and the community. Blessed Sacrament, the Catholic church where they attended Mass each Sunday, was right down the hill. Papakolea, the Hawaiian homestead land where friends lived, was just up the street. Roosevelt High, where the kids went to school, was a long walk down the road. And of course, Waikiki Beach was just a few miles and a short drive away. Waikiki was their favorite place, and the family spent countless hours camped at the beach where they would swim, surf and fish.

During the first years of statehood, times were financially tough for the Aikaus, but they were happy and thankful for their new home in the graveyard. Since then, Clyde has gone on to become a successful business-man with his beach concession stands in Waikiki and other ventures. In fact, he recently bought two new homes in Waimanalo on the other side of the Island, one for his wife and son and one for his sister. But he frequently returns to their old home in the graveyard, which the family still takes care of. No one lives in the silent, run-down houses on the property, but they stay there occasionally and gather there for family meetings. Though no longer poor, Clyde recalls the lean times of his youth with nostalgia. "We come from a real poor family. All we had when we were kids was rice, sugar and cream. That was our diet. We had no money to buy meat, hamburgers, hotdogs, nothing. In the morning, it was two slices of bread and that's it. We used to eat lunch by climbing the trees and eating coconuts and mangos and guavas, and we were happy. I've got some money now, a couple of houses I own, but I'll tell you those years when you got nothing seem to be some of the happiest. How much money do you really need to make you happy?"

"We were brought up very poor," Myra says, but the family stuck together and made the most of their situation. Like her brothers, she turned to the beach for work and play. An ocean recreation specialist for the City and County of Honolulu, Myra teaches swimming, surfing and lifeguard training to local kids. She looks like Sol and has the unmistakable features of an Aikau: dark skin, wavy hair, a solid build and a husky laugh. Myra chuckles at the memory of how poor they were and how her mom once told her that a can of soup or sardines was enough to feed the entire family. But like the multitudes at Jesus' Sermon on the Mount, they had faith that they would always be fed. She remembers a time when one of her brothers brought home a friend for lunch, and there was not enough food to go around. So Pops just did without, saying he had to get back to work. But Myra knew how hungry her father was and looked outside the window to see him eating fruit from a tree. She says taking care of guests and feeding the hungry were important parts of their culture and Christian upbringing. "My parents were very religious. We went to Mass every Sunday, whether we wanted to or not. We did everything together. My parents always wanted to keep us together." Pops raised the family with a combination of religion, discipline and a deep respect for Hawaiian culture, including surfing, music and luaus. But work at the graveyard always came first.

Digging graves was a welcome chance to earn some cash for the family. Sol says the Yee King Tong Society would sometimes "hire people from the mortuary to bury their members or dig them up again." Often, Chinese families would have their relatives' bones disinterred and shipped back to their ancestral homeland. "We wanted the job because we were poor," Sol continues. "When we were younger, we would bury people for extra money. We would dig the hole, my dad and all of us boys, and then on Sunday when they came, we would bury them. We put 'em to rest. My dad would get paid a few hundred dollars, and that went a long way for the house. We did that quite often when we were little. That was a lot of money, $400 or $500. After that, Dad would buy barbecue—that was a big treat. Sometimes, we had to bury people when the surf was up, and that was torture." Leaning on their shovels on a bright Sunday afternoon, the boys would stand a respectful distance away and watch the grieving family and friends gathered around the pit they had dug. Sweating in the heat, their minds drifting away like the prayers and incense of the Chinese burial service, they would dream of surfing the cool, blue waves of Waikiki only a few miles away. When the service was finally over and the last limousine had pulled away, Eddie and his brothers would quickly start shoveling dirt into the pit. They desperately hoped to make it down to the beach for a few late afternoon waves before the sun sank below the horizon.

"Growing up, my parents were always very strict with us," Myra says. "We all had to do our chores before we could do anything else. If the boys didn't do their chores, they didn't go to the beach. Even if they knew the surf was going to be huge, Pop wouldn't let them go until they finished their chores." In the early days, the Aikau boys had to use crescent-shaped sickle blades and work all day in the hot sun to cut all five acres of grass in the graveyard. Later, when they were able to afford a lawn mower, they could do the job in less than half the time. Myra says when the waves were really good, "What Eddie would do is get up at 2:00 am, turn on the car headlights, mow the lawn and work through the night so he could go surf in the morning." Pops could be very disciplined and deadly serious with the kids, but once all the work was done, it was time to have fun.

After church and chores, the whole family would go to the beach. Eddie and his brothers began *paipo*-boarding at the Wall in Waikiki. Unable to afford surfboards, a valuable commodity in those days, the Aikau boys and most local kids created their own homemade plywood boards. Loosely modeled after the carved, wooden planks the Hawaiian commoners used to ride, these *paipo* boards were the early precursors to the spongy Morey Boogie Boards which would eventually become the most popular in the world. In the 60's, *paipo*-boarding was the rage, and Eddie became hooked. After kicking to catch the waves, he would ride them on his stomach, trying to stay just ahead of the crashing whitewater. As he got better, he rode them on his knees, and eventually, he stood up. "If you could stand up on a *paipo* board, you were the king, and Eddie mastered that in six months," Clyde says. After becoming experts in the art of *paipo*-boarding at the Wall, Eddie and his brothers were ready to start surfing at Queens, just up the beach in Waikiki. This was the birthplace of modern surfing. After nearly fading out of existence in the 1800's, the sport had enjoyed a robust revival at the turn of the century.

Prior to Western contact, surfing had been one of the most popular sports in the Islands. Almost everyone took part in what they called *he'e nalu* or wave-sliding: men and women, young and old, chiefs and commoners. During the best swells, almost all work stopped as the people headed to the beach to ride the waves. The ruling *ali'i* excelled at the sport, and they had their own special beaches and wooden surfboards, some of which were more than sixteen feet long. Unburdened by the daily labor of fishing and farming, they were free to surf as often as they liked. King Kamehameha and his wife Ka'ahumanu were said to be excellent canoe paddlers and surfers who loved being together on the ocean. One of their favorite games and contests involved catching waves in an outrigger canoe and then jumping with their heavy boards onto a cresting wave, which they would then ride to the shore. According to anthropologist Dr. Ben Finney, this was quite a feat, as their boards often weighed over one hundred pounds. "They were a majestic aristocracy, often taller, broader, and stronger than the commoners. Their status as leaders depended, in part, on their strength and stamina."

After epidemics of measles and small pox decimated the Hawaiian population, many cultural practices like surfing went into decline. To add insult to injury, the missionaries also condemned the sport's lack of "modesty, industry and religion." They preached against the immorality of men and women surfing and competing together in such "scanty costumes," condeming the sexual freedom and betting practices associated with the sport. Surfing's popularity took a nose dive over the next century. By the time Mark Twain visited the Islands in the 1860's, only the most dedicated natives still surfed in Waikiki. Like most visitors, Twain was intrigued with the sport and wanted to give it a try. But he wasn't so lucky. "I tried surf-bathing once, subsequently, but made a failure of it," he wrote in his humorous description. "I got the board placed right, and at the right moment, too; but missed the connection myself. The board struck the shore in three-quarters of a second, without any cargo, and I struck the bottom about the same time, with a couple barrels of water in me." After nearly drowning that day, Twain concluded, "None but the natives ever master the art of surf-bathing thoroughly."

By the beginning of the 20th century, there was renewed interest in the sport. When Jack London first went surfing in Waikiki in 1907, he was hooked. Calling it "a royal sport for the natural kings of earth," he wrote about the Hawaiians' agility in the waves and how the best surfers were either *ali'i* or at least treated like royalty. London published his accounts about the wonders of surfing in a widely read journal of the time. Soon after, the sport's popularity began to surge again, and watermen like Alexander Hume Ford and George Freeth put on popular surfing events in California. But no one was more influential in promoting the sport than Hawai'i's Olympic swimmer Duke Kahanamoku, "the father of modern surfing." Known as the fastest swimmer in the world, he was equally famous for his surfing feats. During one of the biggest swells to hit the South Shore, it was said he caught one of the longest waves ever ridden. Standing on his big redwood board, he rode a wave almost a mile long. It was the stuff of legends, and local kids like Eddie and his brothers would argue about how big the wave was, where he caught it and how long he rode it.

Duke and his five brothers had helped make Waikiki famous, and they personified the spirit of the place. They met visiting celebrities and tourists down at the docks, welcomed them to the Islands with leis and showed them the best Hawai'i had to offer. Good looking and outgoing, these Hawaiian watermen taught their guests how to surf and paddle outrigger canoes during the day and then escorted them to scrumptious luaus at night. Stationed on the beach in front of the Moana Hotel and the Royal

Hawaiian, the oldest and most elegant resorts in Waikiki, these beach boys acted as local hosts, tour guides, musicians and evening escorts for visiting VIP's. Many became lifelong friends with their wealthy guests who took them on trips around the world. In fact, Sam Kahanamoku even became the paramour of Doris Duke, the world's richest woman. He had been the caretaker of her Diamond Head mansion called Shangri-la, and she later bought him a house nearby. The wealthy tobacco heiress and the local beach boy became the talk of the town, from New York to Honolulu.

By the time Eddie and his brothers started surfing, Duke and his brothers were already old men, decades past their prime. But they were still legendary figures, surfing, paddling and sailing in the waters off of Waikiki. Though he was just a poor Hawaiian kid, Eddie hoped that eventually he and his brothers would become well-known watermen like the Kahanamokus. What they lacked in money, they would earn in respect.

When the Aikau boys graduated from *paipo*-boarding to surfing, they evolved from riding the waves on their stomachs and knees to standing face to face with the wave. They rented surfboards from an infamous beach boy named "Steamboat" Mokuahi. Steamboat and the other beach boys were known for their flirtatious ways and funny antics. Like most kids, the Aikaus got a kick out of their outrageous stories about seducing wealthy divorcees and getting drunk with celebrities. These "perpetual adolescents," as Michener once referred to them, dominated the scene at Waikiki, and the beach was their stage where they surfed, sang and played. These colorful characters showed uptight mainlanders how to enjoy the laidback lifestyle of the Islands. Waikiki was one big party to the beach boys, but Eddie and his brothers were more interested in surfing all day than drinking all night.

Along with surfing, the Aikau brothers raced in six-man outrigger canoes in Waikiki. These canoes were the oldest method of transportation in Polynesian culture, and sports clubs like Outrigger and Hui Nalu had reintroduced them in racing competitions. Paddling for Healani Canoe Club, Eddie and his brothers enjoyed the challenge of testing their strength and endurance, qualities their ancestors had prized. During the summer, the different clubs would stage big regattas in Waikiki. Hundreds of tourists and locals would gather to watch the intense competitions as the paddlers fiercely stroked their canoes across the water. Like the Kahanamoku brothers, the Aikaus enjoyed competing and making a name for themselves. It was an exciting time, and the boys drank in the carnival atmosphere of Waikiki.

They flirted with *wahine* (girls) from the mainland and taught them how to surf. They would show the girls how to make the shaka sign, with their thumb and pinky extended like horns, a popular gesture among Hawaiians and surfers. Occasionally, while surfing or paddling in Waikiki, they would see Woody Brown's sleek catamaran, the *Manu Kai*, whipping across the sea. Modeled after ancient Polynesian voyaging canoes, the twin-hulled catamaran was considered the fastest sailboat in the world, and Eddie was intrigued with her speed and beauty.

Eddie and Clyde began surfing regularly at two Waikiki breaks called Canoes and Queens, whose gentle waves were ideal for beginners and experts alike. Squatting on his knees, Eddie would paddle his rented Styrofoam and fiberglass board out into the lineup, where the surfers gathered together to catch the incoming swells. They would then sit on their boards and wait for the next set of waves. As the ocean undulated beneath him, it felt like a living, breathing mass of energy. He would watch the shearwaters gliding effortlessly across the waves, their black-tipped wings riding the currents of wind and water. He could see streams of sunlight radiating toward the ocean floor as fish darted below him. When he saw a long bump rise up on the horizon, Eddie would start paddling toward shore to catch it. When he felt the lip of the wave rise up and propel him forward, he would jump to his feet. As he dropped down the glassy face, he had to turn the board to stay just ahead of the breaking curl and rushing whitewater. The wave would hurtle him toward the shore, his board skipping across the water like a magic plane, his heart racing with excitement. There was nothing in the world like surfing. After each great ride, Eddie knew this was the best that life had to offer and that he would surf until the day he died. He belonged in the ocean.

Just like today, scores of surfers of every rank gathered in Waikiki to compete for the same waves. The seasoned veterans usually surfed the bigger outside waves, while the beginners rode the smaller waves on the inside. Paddling out into these crowded surf breaks, Eddie and his brothers quickly established themselves as talented, up-and-coming surfers. But they never lost the enthusiasm of their early days. Like most surfers, Clyde vividly remembers his own first ride at Waikiki. "I caught my first wave out here at Canoes, going left, and I was so amazed by how fast I was going and how fast the water was moving by me. The feeling was so exhilarating that I never stopped after that." The rush of that first ride was revived each time they caught a good wave. As they struggled to their feet and stood up on the board, it felt like the whole ocean was lifting them up and carrying them forward on a chariot of water.

The Aikau boys were hooked on surfing and decided they had to have their own boards, no matter how much they cost. Selling newspapers and shining tourists' shoes, Eddie and his brothers managed to save enough money to buy their first boards, which became prized possessions. Sol and Gerry surfed too, but Eddie and Clyde were clearly the most dedicated. As they grew older and more accomplished, they started competing in amateur contests and winning trophies. They graduated from Queens and began surfing in front of the marina at Ala Moana Bowls, where the waves were faster and hollower because of the shallow reefs. On weekends and afternoons, the family would often camp out at the beach. They came to be known for their aloha, generosity and family spirit. Local surfers like Sammy Lee, Ben Aipa and Gerry Lopez remember how the Aikaus took care of the boys and their friends after surfing. "We had a lot of good times at Ala Moana when we were young," Gerry says. "Mom and Pops would be in the parking lot, and they would always have food and soda." Whenever the South Shore was breaking, the Aikaus were there on the beach, cooking food and watching their sons surf.

Yet even as a teenager, Eddie was not satisfied with the smaller waves of the South Shore. He kept yearning to ride bigger and more challenging waves. One night the family went to an outdoor amphitheater called the Waikiki Shell to watch a new surfing movie by Bud Browne, the first serious surf cinematographer. Lying out on the lawn under the stars, Eddie was hypnotized by the footage of a big-wave rider named Kealoha Kaio taking off on a huge North Shore swell. He watched in awe as Kealoha dropped down the face of the wave that was three times his height as it peeled across the large screen in slow motion. It was beautiful to see this big, graceful Hawaiian gliding across such a huge wave, so at home in the roaring surf. The crowd whistled and shouted in excitement. Staring in wide-eyed wonder, Eddie looked at his parents and said, "I'm going to catch the biggest waves ever ridden and make our name famous in the surfing world." He was in his teens at the time, Myra recalls, "and he loved surfing. And it all came true." Eddie was determined to make his dream a reality.

Already a surf addict, Eddie began cutting school to go to the beach. In just one year, he went from being an A-student to failing the tenth grade.

When Pops found out about it, he was furious. Despite their poverty and the temptation to make his kids work instead of attend school, he had insisted his children get an education. His siblings did fairly well, but Eddie just couldn't see the relevance of his boring classes, especially when it came to learning the literature and history of the white people on the mainland. Why not study about his own people? The stifling torture of being inside a hot classroom all day could not compare to the thrill of surfing and being in the ocean. In class, he would draw pictures of peeling swells in his notebook and daydream about riding the perfect wave. A restless sixteen-year-old, he felt trapped in the stuffy confines of school and church. Having fallen in love with the sea, he longed to be in it all the time. For a waterman like Eddie, the ocean could teach him more about *mana'o* (thoughts and ideas) and *mana* (spiritual power) than any teacher or priest.

"Pops said, 'If you're not going to school, then you're going to work for a living," Myra recalls. So at the age of sixteen, Eddie dropped out of Roosevelt High School and joined the working world. He found a job at the Dole Cannery, where his older brother Freddy was a forklift operator. It was not far from where Pops worked as a stevedore down at the waterfront. Eddie traded in his books for a timecard and gave up graduation for a paycheck. He did mind-numbing work at the Cannery, where tons of pineapples were processed each day and shipped out all over the world. The huge metal pineapple that served as the Cannery's water tower had once been one of the tallest structures in town, casting its shadow far and wide over the city. While his siblings and friends sat in class and played sports at school, Eddie was operating heavy machinery and moving endless crates of canned pine-apple. It certainly wasn't glamorous work, but at least he could help out his family financially and earn a little extra spending money. He gave most of his earnings to his parents. He eventually saved enough to buy a new surf-board, a guitar and a used car.

One day, Eddie saw a bright red board in the front window of the Hobie Surf Shop, and he told his brother, "Oh, Clyde, I got to get that board." It was a beautiful, 11-foot long, Styrofoam and fiberglass board, shaped by Dick Brewer, who would become one of the most influential designers and shapers in the business. With a thick, wooden stringer running through its length, it had a rounded nose in front, a squared-off, woodblock tail in the back and a large skeg or fin on the bottom to keep the board from sliding out on big waves. Although the family couldn't really afford it at the time, Pops went down to the shop and talked to the shop manager Jack Shipley. He somehow convinced Shipley and the owner to give him a good deal because Eddie was already making a name for himself in the surfing world. He made them realize it would be good for the shop to have his son riding their boards in the future. Little did they know that Eddie would become famous riding this red surfboard across the mountainous waves at Waimea. Though he had fallen in love with surfing, he had only ridden the smaller swells on the South Shore. Nothing could have prepared him for the dangerous and seductive beauty of the waves on the North Shore whose power was so mighty they made the ground tremble. Only the 'natural kings of earth' dared to confront such a fierce force of nature.

Eddie and Jose drop in together at Waimea Bay in 1966.

CHAPTER 2

A Brotherhood of Surfers

"Men of the sun and the sea
Those men who ride mountains
Bend to the wind
Top to bottom, side to side
Looking for the ultimate ride."
—Israel Kamakawiwoʻole

In the 1950's, the North Shore was a wild and mysterious place, sparsely populated by a few farmers and fishermen. Most of the surf breaks were considered unrideable because the waves were too big, the take-offs too steep and the water too shallow and dangerous. Jagged coral reefs lay right under the surface. But in 1955, a small band of Californian transplants and Hawaiian locals led the first modern surfing expeditions to the North Shore. These daredevils became some of the biggest names in surfing. Growing up, Eddie knew them all by reputation, but he would soon come to know them as mentors, friends and fellow big-wave riders.

During those first expeditions to the North Shore, men like John Kelly, George Downing, Greg Noll, Pat Curren, Peter Cole and Fred Van Dyke would drive across the Island in their old jalopies, camp on the North Shore and surf pristine and unridden breaks that had yet to be named. Of course, they suspected that the ancient Hawaiians had probably ridden these waves, but it seemed impossible with the long, heavy planks of wood they used to ride. And without skegs on the bottom, there would be no way to avoid sliding sideways down the wave. Innovating all the time, these modern surfers designed, cut and laminated their own boards. They experimented with skeg designs and used various kinds of lighter wood at first but eventually switched to using Styrofoam and fiberglass boards, which were much lighter and easier to shape. They called their long surfboards 'elephant guns' and 'rhino-chasers,' and they thought of themselves as big-game hunters roaming around on the rugged North Shore, trying to bag the biggest and wildest waves of the day.

Others in the group playfully likened themselves to characters from the King Arthur myths. Like the Knights of the Round Table, they confronted the North Shore's monstrous waves, armed only with their long, spear-like boards and bare courage. Big-wave rider and board shaper Pat Curren (father of future world champion Tommy Curren) even tore down a wall of the beach house he rented to build racks for all of their many surfboards and a long, wooden table where all the surfers could gather for meals. They christened the place "Meade Hall" and lived out their "round table" fantasy until the landlord found out about their crazy antics and sent them all packing. Though the Arthurian myth was a humorously grandiose illusion they entertained, this eccentric band of young wave-warriors would soon become legends in their own right. Strong, handsome and daring, they had left mainstream America and the post-war boom behind and moved to these remote and exotic Islands in the Pacific. They rejected lucrative jobs and corporate conformity for a more adventurous way of life. In the early days, many of them lived like Bedouins on the beach, surfing all day and partying like Beatniks late into the night. The ocean became their playground for surfing, diving and fishing. Though they came from the mainland, they embraced Hawaiian culture enthusiastically and were warmly accepted by local families like the Aikaus.

Known as the 'country' because it was so rural and sparsely populated, O'ahu's North Shore was less than thirty miles from Honolulu as the shearwater flies. But it might as well have been a different world. Because there were no freeways, surfers had to take back roads through endless cane fields and pineapple plantations as they cut across the center of the Island. It took two hours to get there, yet it was so undeveloped that it was like going back in time to the Aikau's home on Maui. Rides to the North Shore were difficult to find, but Pops was determined for Eddie to get there. So when he discovered that veteran surfer John Kelly made regular surfing trips across the Island, Pops decided to ask John to give his son a ride. Though Pops had heard rumors that Kelly was a Red sympathizer, he enjoyed meeting outspoken and colorful characters. Eddie didn't care if he was a radical Communist or a conservative Republican and was more intrigued by his fame as a big-wave rider and dedicated waterman.

A gentle music teacher by trade, John was a fierce waterman and reformer at heart. The only son of mainland artists who came to Hawai'i in the early 1900's and created well-known portraits of native Hawaiians, John loved the Islands, their people and their closeness to nature. He had learned to surf, fish and dive from native Hawaiians so he was eager to return the favor to locals like Eddie. During this time, in the mid-60's, John became a social and environmental activist, and he was blackballed as a Communist at one point and fired from his job as a choir director. He founded a group called Save Our Surf (S.O.S.) and organized rallies and marches to stop development of Hawai'i's coastlines. John's cause made a lot of sense to Pops, who was generally not a political person by nature. But as the father of four surfers, he wanted to make sure his sons' favorite surf breaks and beaches were not replaced with more marinas and hotels. Besides supporting S.O.S., Pops also respected John's work on behalf of the Hawaiians and was grateful for his interest in Eddie. Seeing that Eddie had the potential to become a big-wave surfer, John offered to take him and another local boy named Sammy Lee on a trek to the rugged North Shore. With no sons of his own, John took Eddie and Sammy under his wing when he saw what promising surfers they were.

Eight years older than Eddie, Sammy was a protégé of John Kelly's and remembers the day they went to the Aikau's home at the graveyard. "I was introduced to Eddie by John Kelly. John and I would carpool to the North Shore from time to time. One day he picked me up and said, 'By the way, we're going to stop by the Chinese graveyard over by Papakolea and pick up this young Hawaiian guy,' who I had never heard of or seen before. So we stopped down there, and he loaded his board on." It was a long drive, and the talkative veteran would entertain the quiet rookies with stories from his past. As they drove by Pearl Harbor, John would share grim memories about being strafed by bullets on the day of the bombing and seeing all the dead bodies floating in the harbor. As they bounced through endless pineapple fields, stirring up clouds of red dust in their wake, he would tell them about how the Hawaiians lost their land; how a few rich *haole* families had divided it into plantations, housing developments and tourist resorts. In this way, he taught them about land, politics and power, lessons Eddie would remember later in his life.

As they got closer to the North Shore, John shared tales about being amongst the first modern people to surf in Makaha—"Ours were the only footsteps in the sand." Stories about discovering new breaks on the North Shore and naming the huge waves after mountain ranges—"I said the waves were as big as the Himalayas, and the name just stuck." And memories of epic surf sessions—"I caught sixteen beautiful rides that day, and the waves were humongous." Sitting in silence, occasionally asking questions, Eddie and Sammy listened to John's stories and wondered what adventures awaited them on the other side of the Island. How big would the waves be and could they handle them?

Driving across the pineapple and sugar cane fields, they could see the big, blue ocean stretching below them. The two mountain ridges that run the length of O'ahu rose up on either side of the horizon, the dry Wai'anae range to the West and the green Ko'olau range to the East. Mount Ka'ala loomed on the left, the tallest mountain on the Island, sloping down to the sea. The view of the valley and the ocean below was beautiful. Long lines of whitewater rolled in and a thick mist from the waves hung over the green pastures and tree-lined shore. Signs of big surf. After driving through the small town of Hale'iwa and around Waimea Bay, they finally reached Sunset Beach. The three surfers lugged their long fiberglass boards down the beach and studied the way the waves were breaking. Then, they paddled out through the channel into double-overhead surf.

It was Eddie's first time, but he seemed fearless as he turned and paddled for a large wave. When he felt it suddenly rise up beneath him, he jumped to his feet in a low crouch as the board shot straight down the face of the wave. There was so much more power in these waves than the ones on the South Shore. Turning at the trough of the wave, he pushed his long board back up the face of the wave and angled it to stay just in front of the crashing whitewater. It was like racing a sports car along a winding road. When he wanted to accelerate, he leaned forward on his board, and when he wanted to change lanes, he leaned back and turned with his feet. Driving up and down its face, Eddie rode the wave until it finally petered out in the deep-water channel. When he paddled back out, John and Sammy congratulated him on his ride. They hooted for each other whenever someone got a good one. Eddie ended up catching some of the biggest waves and riding them all the way to the inside section. "I mean, he blew everyone away at Sunset that day," Sammy recalls. "Eddie was a natural: he just took to the waves and everybody was saying, 'Who the hell is this guy?!' He was easy to like, a humble guy. And certainly his talent was immense and noticeable right away. Because of his skills, he quickly established his reputation."

Sammy started surfing big waves with Eddie and hanging out at the graveyard on occasion. "Over time I became friendly with the family and eventually ended up spending a lot of time with them," Lee says. "I admired that family for their cohesiveness. And I got to know the father really well, and he became a personal friend of mine. He was easy to talk to, and he had a lot of aloha. The father was a really charismatic man. He wasn't educated in the book sense but he was a charismatic individual, and he appealed to people from all walks of life, people from this country and other countries as well. You either loved the guy or you hated him. He was very blunt but very generous. His generosity knew no bounds if he liked you." Pops welcomed Sammy into his family like a son because he was like an older brother to Eddie and the boys, taking them to the beach and looking out for them.

Pops was also grateful to Sammy for introducing his sons to famous surfers like Fred Van Dyke and Peter Cole, who had taught Sammy (and his fellow surfers) at Punahou School. Like John Kelly, these men were champion big-wave riders and gods in Eddie's eyes. For Sammy's 25th birthday, Pops threw a party for him and invited Kelly, Van Dyke and Cole to join the festivities down at the graveyard. Along with well-known surfers, Pops also invited talented local musicians who performed for the crowd. Though the party took time and money to put on, Pops knew it would be worth it. With several of the boys working now, the family wanted to share their earnings with their friends. It was the Hawaiian way to share everything. The party was a hit, with good music and delicious food. "We put up a tent and got a side of beef," Lee recalls, "and it went on and on like the Aikau parties would do. The old man was famous for his *swipe* [a powerful, homebrewed concoction made with fermented pineapple juice], and there was always plenty to drink and music and people coming and going. The Aikaus had a wide circle of friends that at its peak ranged from the Mayor to criminals, surfers and socialites—I mean everyone wanted to know the Aikaus or be around them. They were a real force, a social force."

Looking back at that time when Eddie started surfing on the North Shore, Sammy modestly says he would have made it on his own. "Pops was always grateful to us for many years, and he would verbalize this over a few beers, saying, 'It was you and John Kelly who really gave Eddie his first break,' which wasn't true. Eddie would have succeeded on his own anyway. He certainly didn't need John Kelly and I—we had nothing to do with it. We just happened to be his taxi that day." But Pops knew that meeting John and Sammy was a turning point for his family, because they had introduced his family to a whole new sector of society, educated and important people such as Fred Van Dyke, Peter Cole and others who excelled in their various fields. Though he never graduated from high school himself, Pops instilled in his kids the value of education, common sense and social connections. "My dad was the true teacher of us all," Clyde says. "If there was a degree given in common sense, my dad would have had a PhD, even though he only went to the 6th grade. We were very dear friends with the best minds in Honolulu, the best lawyers, the best doctors, the best whatever, but when it comes to common sense, I give my father a lot of credit for doing what he could for us."

After Eddie's first trips to the North Shore with John and Sammy, Pops and the family began driving up there on their own. They would ride in the beat-up, old telephone truck that Pops had converted so they could lie down inside the tool compartments. The family would camp out on the beach for the weekend. The boys would surf all day and then go fishing or diving for dinner. Whatever they caught would end up on the grill, and Momma Aikau and Myra would help Pops prepare it. After eating a delicious meal, they would sit around the fire, drinking, talking and singing their favorite Hawaiian songs. It was a peaceful life, and the family enjoyed these weekend outings. If it rained, they would sleep inside or under the truck. When it was clear, they would stay outside. As Eddie and his brothers lay on the beach watching the fire die down, they would swap stories about the legendary big-wave riders who had first surfed unknown breaks like Sunset Beach and Waimea Bay. Eventually, the music of the waves would lull them to sleep. Like most young surfers, they probably dreamed of slow-motion rides that seemed to go on forever. Then, they would get up early the next morning and try to live out their dreams. They would literally surf all day and into the twilight. When they finally came in, it would be dark. Because they could barely see the swells coming, the brothers had to use their intuition and instinct to ride their last waves back to shore in the darkness.

Occasionally, the Aikaus would run into Peter Cole at Sunset Beach, and he would invite them to his home for beers, barbecue and *pupus* (appetizers). Peter and Fred Van Dyke had been two of the first surfers to settle down on the North Shore. Peter and his wife Sally built a simple two-story wooden house right on the beach at Rocky Point, just down from Sunset Beach, where he could surf every day after work. The first freeways had been built about this time, along with a newly paved road through the pineapple fields, so the time-consuming commute to the North Shore had been cut in half. After driving out from town and surfing until the sun went down, the Aikaus would join the local surf crowd over at Peter's house. It would be a fun evening of drinking Primo beer, playing music and talking story. Eddie and his brothers were "shy and introverted in a way and didn't impose themselves on people," according to Peter. The boys didn't say much at first, but the more they drank, the more they opened up. Besides, they just felt more comfortable communicating through their music. "They played great slack-key," Peter says, recalling the unique sound and tuning style of the Hawaiian guitar. "When they played music, my beer-drinking quotient went way up. Some of my best nights were just having a small gathering out here after we'd surfed all day."

The young Aikau brothers were shy, but the older surfers loved to talk and had plenty of stories to tell. Fred Van Dyke was the local raconteur, and he would tell tales about surfing giant waves with Peter and other big-wave pioneers like Greg Noll. Peter would warn the crowd that Fred always exaggerated his stories, especially when it came to wave heights. As a math teacher, he had figured out a formula for determining the accuracy of his tall tales: you had to add up everything Fred said, divide it by two and subtract one. Fred would counter that you couldn't completely trust Peter's judgement either because he was half-blind (due to a surfing injury to his right eye) so the waves always looked half the size. Their banter always made people laugh.

With the Aikaus and other friends sitting around, Fred and Peter would share stories about how they had met years earlier in California and then moved out to Hawai'i. A star football player in college, Fred had been working as a coach and teacher near Santa Cruz. He was surfing by himself in the frigid waters of Northern California when he met Peter Cole, a tall, lanky swimmer who was studying at Stanford. Peter was a national swimming champion who had grown up surfing in Malibu. They soon became good friends and started going on surf trips up and down the California coast. Before Santa Cruz surfer Jack O'Neil invented the first wetsuits, the two die-hard surfers wore wool sweaters taped to their bodies and put Vaseline on their skin to endure Santa Cruz's numbingly cold water. Sitting out in the lineup with their teeth chattering, they dreamed of the big waves and warm waters of Hawaiʻi.

Peter would talk about how surfing was still considered a cultish sport for renegades and oddballs back then. But with the release of the novel *Gidget* and the blockbuster movie that followed, everything changed. Surfing suddenly found its way into American pop culture, and the crowds swarmed to the theaters and to the beaches. Overnight, Hollywood turned this marginalized sport into a 'hip and happening scene' for young people, and they churned out a series of silly surf flicks. Surfing suddenly became part of the free-wheeling, Southern California lifestyle, as well as a symbol of youth, sex and freedom. Tapping into the sport's new popularity, the Beach Boys exploded onto the scene, singing songs like "Catch a Wave" and "Surfin' U.S.A." But for die-hard surfers like Peter and Fred, there were already too many muscle-headed posers and Gidget wannabes on the beach, and they were looking for a way to get away from the trendy California scene.

Restless and yearning for adventure, Fred says he saw a picture in the newspaper one day at school that changed his life forever. The AP photo showed three surfers (Buzzy Trent, Woody Brown and George Downing) dropping into a perfect wave at Makaha on Oʻahu's West Shore. The image sent shock waves of excitement down the California coast. After studying the front page picture, Fred decided at that moment to move to Hawaiʻi. The birthplace of surfing. Home of the greatest waves on earth. A place where surfing was a noble sport, not a popular trend. So he quit his teaching job in Santa Cruz and found a new one at Punahou School in Honolulu the next year. Within a year and a half, he recruited Peter to come to Hawaiʻi and work at the prestigious private school, which had been established by missionaries in 1848. Fred taught English and other subjects in the middle school, and Peter taught upper-level math. Though Punahou was stereotyped as a breeding ground for rich *haoles* and Asian kids, the Aikaus respected the fact that Peter and Fred worked at such a good school whose beautiful campus was just a few miles from their home.

Though Eddie had quit school, he was an avid student of the sea, and he learned a lot from Peter and Fred. "Talking story" was a natural part of Hawaiian culture, and Eddie loved listening to their stories about the early days of big-wave surfing, as well as their observations about waves, weather and ocean dynamics. He also admired their love of nature and dedication to surfing which bordered on the fanatical. For them, surfing was more than just a sport; it was a complete lifestyle, an artform and a spiritual experience. As a student at Punahou, Gerry Lopez remembers Peter giving a talk during chapel once and telling the students that he had seen God in the barrel of a tube while surfing at Sunset Beach! "Peter was talking about how he rode that wave, how everything was glowing afterward and how it was the most religious experience he had ever had. I thought it was pretty blasphemous, but I was impressed."

When the waves were really epic, Fred says, he and Peter used to call in sick or pay a substitute to teach their classes so they could surf all day. Peter laughs and denies this, saying Fred is stretching the truth again. He does admit to skipping a few afternoon meetings. When his department head asked him about his absences, Cole says he would calmly tell him, "I thought surfing was more important for my mental health than the mandatory meeting." Once when Fred took a day off from school to go surfing in Makaha, he came in from his morning session and accidentally walked right by his boss on the beach. Fred said the silver-haired administrator was sitting next to an attractive woman and was shocked to see Van Dyke. His boss was a hard-nosed administrator, and normally he would have fired Fred on the spot. But he was also a ladies' man, and the young lady lying next to him was not his wife. So Fred says they just looked at each other, nodded in tacit understanding and never said a word about the incident again. When they told stories about cutting school to go surfing, Eddie would just shake his head, laugh and slap his knee. He remembered cutting school himself and thought it was hysterical that these respectable teachers would do the same!

Roger Pfeffer was another transplanted California surfer who worked at Punahou School. He taught science and also wrote articles about surfing for the local newspapers. He published stories about Peter and Fred and would later write pieces about Eddie. Roger remembers how Peter and Fred seemed to be surrounded by an odd aura of fun, power and prestige. "They were competitive athletes in college, and they came here from the mainland already established as skilled surfers and great watermen. They fit right into the picture in Honolulu and could go to the best parties. They were well-groomed, educated and had standing in the community, and they were seen as up-and-coming young men." Both had come from prominent mainland families. In fact, Peter's great-grandfather had been a U.S. senator from California. But they had left behind the socially and politically divisive world of mainland America when they came to the Islands. In Hawai'i, they could mix with all kinds of people, including their wealthy friends at Punahou and the Aikau family just down the road at the graveyard.

Roger remembers how the Aikaus went out of their way to make Fred, Peter and himself feel at home in the Islands. "They represented the traditional Hawaiian family, values and lifestyle, and that was part of their allure for people like myself who came from the mainland. You could go over to the Aikau house after surfing and be guaranteed food and a cold beer, no questions asked. You were always welcome. There was always room for one more plate at the table; there was always something to eat and someone to talk to; there was always aloha. They truly represented what most of us thought of as the best of Hawai'i: strong family, good work ethic, laidback lifestyle, and open, warm aloha for everyone. This was what we had hoped to find in Hawai'i." Though they came from different worlds, the Aikaus and these men were linked together by their love of the ocean and big waves, not to mention their propensity for Primo beer and storytelling. More than anything, Eddie loved hearing stories about their epic surf sessions at Waimea Bay. He had surfed the Bay a few times but still hadn't ridden the really giant waves that come through maybe two or three times a year. He was eager to learn more about the place so he would be ready when a mammoth swell finally hit.

Fred would talk about how Waimea Bay was considered the deadliest of all the North Shore breaks and how one surfer had already lost his life there. For years, most surfers stayed away from the Bay, believing it was haunted by the Hawaiian *heiau* on the cliffs above and the bones of Dickie Cross in the water below. Surfing Sunset Beach as early as 1943, big-wave pioneer Woodie Brown and his friend Dickie had gotten caught in a rapidly building swell, when it suddenly became gigantic. Unable to come in through Sunset's huge waves, they paddled almost three miles down to Waimea Bay, hoping to get through the channel before nightfall. But as they were paddling for the shore, an enormous, 30 foot clean-up set rose up before them. The waves closed out the Bay in a thundering wall of whitewater, taking Dickie with it. When Woodie finally crawled to shore on his hands and knees and collapsed on the sand in the darkness, those on the beach said they had lost sight of Dickie—neither he nor his board was ever recovered. It would be more than a decade before anyone tried to tackle the Bay's mountainous waves again.

If the North Shore was the Himalayas of the surfing world, Waimea was its Mount Everest. Greg 'Da Bull' Noll was part of the first expedition to surf at Waimea and scale its massive peak. He loved to tell stories about that day and Eddie loved to listen. Like everyone else, Greg had been scared to death of the place. Intimidated by the *heiau* on top of the cliff and the church beneath it, Noll says he and "the local Hawaiians truly believed the place was haunted." Whenever the surf got really big there, the locals would line up in their cars to watch the huge waves come roaring through the Bay. "At that point, man, there was an evil cloud hanging over the place. If you went out there, it was going to eat you alive."

Then, on a sunny day in the winter of 1957, Greg and a group of his friends decided it was time to take their chances. Waiting for a lull in the massive sets of waves rolling across the Bay, they paddled out through the turbulent water and waited for the next set to come roaring through. When the first waves rose up on the horizon, the surfers would wipe out on their way down these moving mountains of whitewater. Their boards kept sliding out sideways because the faces of the waves were too steep. Still, they kept paddling back for more, like climbers hell-bent on reaching the summit. People gathered to watch, and the news spread fast. "The word had gotten back to Haleiwa that the crazy *haoles* were committing suicide at Waimea Bay," Greg chuckles. "I remember being in the water and looking at the area across the Bay. The cars were bumper to bumper with all the local Haleiwa guys watching and going, 'Heh, somebody's going to die today for sure.' But basically we just had a great day. The *kapu* was gone, and Waimea Bay was on the loose as one of the number one surf spots on the Island of O'ahu."

Whenever Eddie heard about those first sessions at Waimea, he would sit back, drink his beer and stare in wide-eyed amazement. He was still the 'new kid' at that point, surrounded by veteran big-wave riders. He was in awe of these guys, even though he had already surfed a few big swells at the Bay during the mid-60's. Once Eddie had a taste of its physical and spiritual power, though, he was hooked and wanted more. Surfing with experienced mentors like Peter, Fred and Greg, Eddie had learned all about the Bay's complex dynamics and was ready to move to the next level. He was part of a younger crew of surfers who had been waiting in the wings, eager to take center stage and make a name for themselves. These rising surf stars wanted to prove that they too could ride the massive waves at Waimea. In the winter of 1967, ten years after Greg and his gang first surfed Waimea, Eddie finally got his chance to take the stage. He was 21 and about to make his big wave debut in one of the largest swells of the decade. His performance that day would remain a vivid memory for those who witnessed it.

Due to a raging storm in the North Pacific, a large 'swell train' began traveling toward O'ahu at speeds of 35-40 knots per hour. The forerunners of the swell hit the coral reefs off the North Shore on Sunday afternoon, November 19. The deep-water waves suddenly jumped up to twice their size, reaching heights of 30-50 feet. They washed out roads and flooded scores of homes on the North and West shores. Two servicemen walking on the beach, one at Waimea and the other at Sunset, had been swept up in the deadly surf and washed out to sea, never to be seen again. The swells continued to grow throughout the night, thundering in the darkness and shaking the foundations of homes up and down the coast. An elite corps of surfers around the Island started calling each other to prepare for Monday's surf session. After working the morning shift at the Cannery, Eddie pushed the gas pedal to the floor and sped across the Island in his old VW Bug. With his big, red Hobie board strapped to the roof, he headed for Waimea Bay, the only place that could handle such huge waves. At the other surf spots, the waves looked like a boiling cauldron of water.

As he drove around the cliffs of Waimea, he could see lines of swells coming in off the point and exploding across the Bay. He stood on the beach where a crowd had gathered, studying the conditions. He watched where and how the waves broke, how many were in each set and how far apart they were. Every so often he could see someone dropping down the face of a huge wave, probably Peter Cole—only Peter would take off on waves that big. When other surfers on shore tried to paddle out, they kept getting pummeled by the shore break and thrown back on the beach. Broken boards littered the shoreline. Watching the ferocious waves slam on the sand, he thought about the two servicemen who had died the day before. If he had been there, he probably could have saved them—he had rescued many others from big waves. Despite the desperate need for lifeguards, there were still none on the North Shore. The Fire Department was in charge of ocean rescues, but they could only do so much.

Many experienced surfers stood on the beach, saying the waves were just too big. But Eddie knew they could be ridden. It was the challenge of a lifetime. To the astonishment of those around him, he grabbed his big red board, slung it under his arm and walked toward the wall of waves pounding the shore. Waiting for a brief pause in the shore break, he ran with his board and dove through the face of a wave and emerged out the back. He then paddled out into the Bay, which was seething with enormous surf. He'd been in big waves before but nothing like this. Inscrutable as ever, the quiet Hawaiian made his way through the roaring water, clawing his way up the face of each giant swell that threatened to devour him in its gigantic maw.

When Eddie finally made it to the outside, Peter smiled and welcomed him to the lineup. The other surfers just looked at him with fear in their eyes, wondering how to get back in. Waiting for the next set, Eddie looked and saw a hill on the horizon suddenly grow into a mountain of moving water. The other surfers scrambled to paddle over the top of the wave, but he turned toward the shore and calmly stroked to catch the rising swell. He paddled as hard as he could for the massive wave moving at about 30 mph. As it lifted him up in the air, he jumped to his feet in a tight crouch. Like a snowboarder taking off from the edge of a sheer cliff, Eddie could feel his board slipping down the face of the vertical wave. He managed to make the 40-foot drop. As he turned at the bottom, he could see a dark wall of water roaring above him. Using the speed from his take-off and the momentum from his bottom turn, Eddie would shoot down the line, racing just ahead of the vortex of churning water. With the wind rushing by him, he rode the wave across the width of the Bay until it collapsed. He had made it. And the smile on his face showed he was ready for more.

Rumors of the giant swell began buzzing around the Island. Eager to see his older brother in action, Clyde decided to cut school and go see the epic surf. He knew Eddie had been waiting to charge Waimea's huge waves for years, and he wanted to witness the moment. When he arrived at the Bay, he joined the small crowd of tourists, hippies, housewives and surfers gathered on the cliffs. The sun was out, and it seemed like a calm and peaceful day. But when he saw the next set come rolling in around the point, Clyde was blown away by the force and power of the waves. When they exploded against the rocks in geysers of spray, they looked like they would wash away the houses on the point. Walls of whitewater washed over the long stretch of beach and surfers had to save those tourists foolish enough to get caught in the deadly shore break.

An aspiring young surfer himself at the time, Clyde says he was a "sixteen year-old scaredy-cat," frightened to death of surfing waves that big. The ocean seemed angry to him, launching sets of killer waves to attack and destroy any surfers foolish enough to be in the Bay. The faces of the waves were larger than the giant movie screen at the Waikiki Shell, where they had seen their first surf movie. And there were cameras all along the beach filming the action for future generations. Clyde watched as Eddie paddled after the biggest waves of the day, trying to drop into the steepest and most vertical section. "I got out there just in time to see Eddie take off on a monster wave, and his whole board spun sideways as he free-fell 30 feet down the face of the wave. And all I could see were his red and white shorts falling down the wave with his red board." For a breathless minute, he anxiously waited to see if his brother had survived the horrendous wipeout. Scanning the churning whitewater for some sign of his brother, he finally saw Eddie paddling back out for more. On another ride, he saw him racing down a wave that looked like a football field turned on its side.

Fearing for Eddie's life, Clyde was thrilled to see him holding his own in such massive surf. Still in awe of his older brother after all these years, Clyde tends to speak in superlatives about him, and you can see the excitement in his eyes. "Eddie was definitely the master of Waimea Bay, surfing the biggest waves in the world. He made his mark in November, 1967. It's still the undisputed biggest day at Waimea Bay that's ever been surfed. I don't think Waimea Bay ever got as big as that day and still ride-able. That was the first time I ever saw Eddie ride big waves. It's incredible how one day can really change your life."

After watching his brother perform that day, Clyde himself would later become one of the better big-wave riders on the North Shore. After proving themselves in giant surf, Eddie and Clyde were welcomed into the inner circle of the big-wave brotherhood. "Guys like Peter Cole, Ricky Grigg, Jose Angel and Sammy Lee—they were all beautiful men who took Eddie and myself under their wings and made us feel comfortable surfing big Sunset and Waimea Bay. All of these guys were like gods to us. For us to be surfing with all of these god-like people was a real treat. They had a lot of class, a lot of class." While mainland society often looked down on surfers, stereotyping them as rebels or delinquents, these men were looked up to like demigods in Hawai'i.

During the swell of 1967, Clyde and the North Shore veterans were struck not only by Eddie's utter fearlessness but by his playfulness in the face of such potentially fatal waves. "Eddie's the only guy I know even today who will take off on a monster wave and still have a smile on his face," Clyde says, his eyes wide with wonder. "It wasn't just the idea of him paddling into it, it was a matter of him taking off on impossible waves that nobody could make, that nobody could dream of making, but somehow time after time, he would make the impossible waves. You talk to Peter Cole—he'll tell you."

Peter remembers the day vividly. "Eddie was just charging right off the bat, and he must have been pretty doggone young at that point. He really made a mark that day at Waimea. It was a really big day. He took off on as big a wave as anyone was taking off on. I'd say the bigger sets were 20-25 feet [35-50 foot faces], but it was so clean, so good and consistent. The sun was out. There were some good pictures that day." Indeed, there's a well-known shot of Eddie racing across a wave more than six times his height. He's riding his big red Hobie board and wearing his red and white trunks. With his arms spread out and his legs bent, he races across the dark face of the beast, just under its curling lip. The Aikau family still displays a blown-up version of the picture each year at the Bay during the Quiksilver in Memory of Eddie Aikau blessing. One photo of him became so famous that it was used on Bank of America checks for years, and other pictures appeared later in *Sports Illustrated* and a best-selling book called *The Hawaiians*.

On the wall of Peter's living room, there is a blown-up picture of him surfing a massive wave that day. Crouched at the bottom of the wave, Peter looks like a small waterbug about to be consumed by some monstrous creature of the deep. At six feet, three inches, he is an imposing figure, but his long, lanky body seems tiny compared to the massive wall of water that towers almost forty feet above him. Most men his age have retired to their gardens or the golf course but not Peter. After teaching at Punahou, he became a computer programmer for the military and chairman of the O'ahu chapter of the Surfrider Foundation, an environmental organization like S.O.S. At the age of 70, he actively fights for cleaner coastlines and also continues to surf big waves at Sunset Beach. (Fred still insists it's because he's half blind and can't see how big the swells are.) But the years just disappear when Peter talks about Eddie's rides that day at Waimea. He is sitting in his North Shore home where they used to gather three decades ago to drink beer and swap stories. Peter watches the windblown surf at Rocky Point with his one good eye as he conjures up images of Eddie at the Bay. "There was a crowd of guys out there who weren't really riding. But Eddie charged that day, and that's when he started getting a trademark for his Waimea surfing. He had a wide stance, and he stood straight up, kind of a Hawaiian style, and he was real fluid. He always seemed to be in the right spot and just kept charging on really steep takeoffs. He just had this uncanny judgement, this feel for the ocean, and he always managed to be in the right spot."

Fred Van Dyke agrees. "The thing that is fitted in my mind that will never leave is that no matter where Eddie took off, when he stood up, he was almost always in an impossible situation for a normal person to handle. But he would crouch down and hold a full angle, and he rarely wiped out." Passionate about both Hawai'i and surfing, Van Dyke has a tendency to wax poetic about Eddie. "He was a Hawaiian Adonis in that he had the Hawaiian surfing style which is nothing like the Californians or Australians, who are frenetic—they are attacking the wave and tearing it apart, trying to dominate it. Whereas the Hawaiians, especially Eddie, became totally part of the wave, and you could feel the vibrations of understanding, love and compassion Eddie had for every wave he rode." Fred says Eddie had an intimate relationship with the ocean, and together they formed a perfect union.

While Eddie was coming up in the world of surfing, older veterans like Greg Noll were on their way out. According to Greg, "Waimea Bay is like a beautiful woman, and I had my time with her. When I drive around that Bay, I see these guys pouring down the side of her waves. She's turned her favors, and she's caressing some other young guy. We get older, yet she stays the same. I just appreciate the times she smiled on me. Eddie had his time with her, and now some younger guys are having their time."

Ricky Grigg was another veteran of the big-wave brotherhood who shared Waimea's beautiful but deadly charms and witnessed Eddie's debut there. After surfing with him at the Bay that year, Ricky saw the young Hawaiian as a new member of the tribe. He says Eddie was a bold surfer but a very shy person. "He was quiet, didn't get in anybody's way; he was respectful, and he was accepted by all of us and liked by everybody. He soon became part of the line-up. As we were gradually fading out, he started fading in. But it was nice, not too competitive; it was natural." That same year, Eddie and Ricky would have to compete against each other in the most prestigious surf contest of the time, the Duke Classic.

CHAPTER 3

Eddie and the Duke

"Heroes die hard."
– Anon.

To understand Eddie Aikau, you have to understand his hero, Duke Paoa Kahanamoku. For kids Life is a long search for people to believe in and look up to, and real heroes are often hard to find. But Eddie found one in Duke. As different as their fates were—one's life was long and happy, while the other's was tragically cut short—they both embodied the timeless spirit of Hawai'i. But they also helped shape their different eras. Though Duke was an old man when Eddie first met him, the silver-haired surfer was still a god in the young man's eyes. And though their paths crossed only briefly at the Duke Contest, it had a lifelong effect on Eddie.

In 1957, when Eddie was just 11 and still living on Maui, Duke had appeared on the popular TV program "This Is Your Life," hosted by Ralph Edwards. During the show, they brought on fellow Olympic swimmers, Waikiki surfers and Hollywood actors to share their memories of the Duke and facets of his life. Like most boys who become obsessed with sports figures, Eddie was already in awe of the Duke. An international celebrity, he had helped put Hawai'i on the map, and to visitors and locals alike, he was known as the "king of Waikiki." Eddie knew all about his mind-boggling performances as an Olympic swimmer and water polo player and how his competitive career had lasted over two decades, from 1912-1932. Diving into the international scene in the 1912 Olympics in Stockholm, Duke made quite a splash when he won the gold medal in the 100-meter freestyle in swimming and set a new world record. The young Hawaiian won the major events in the water, while Native American runner Jim Thorpe won everything on land. After the games were cancelled in 1916 due to WWI, Duke went on to win the gold again in 1920 in Antwerp. Then, in the 1924 Olympics in Paris, he came in second place in the 100-meter freestyle, just ahead of his brother Samuel, who took the bronze. He had finally been beaten by the young Johnny Weissmuller, who would later win more national swimming titles than any other American. Like Duke, Weissmuller eventually landed in Hollywood and played the part of Tarzan in the movies. Duke later joked, "At least it took Tarzan to beat me."

En route to the Olympics and other swimming competitions around the globe, Duke had put on surfing exhibitions in America and Australia, immensely popular events that helped spawn surfing cults in both countries. When Duke visited Australia in 1914, he gave them a gift they would never forget. Using a long, wooden plank from a local lumberyard, he designed, cut and shaped his own board. Then, he put on a surfing demonstration at a local beach break in Sydney, where large crowds watched him perform in the rolling surf. They were spell-bound by the graceful way he glided across the waves. As Duke's biographer Sandra Kimberly Hall puts it, "He introduced one of the world's oldest sports, a sport that is at least a thousand years old, to one of the world's newest countries." The Aussies would soon adopt surfing as their most popular national pastime and erect monuments to Duke across the country. In fact, they preserved his hand-made surfboard and made it into a national shrine. The most valuable board in the world, it is now insured for over $1 million.

After the Olympics, Duke took up acting and did a 10-year stint in Hollywood. With his dark skin, sculpted physique and warm smile, Duke looked like Hawaiian royalty—and he was. Just as Eddie's family had descended from *kahunas*, Duke's family had been *ali'i* (ruling chiefs). But his royal Hawaiian ancestry didn't carry much weight on the mainland, which was still racially divided. Even though he was a famous athlete and surfer, Duke was often typecast as a 'noble savage' because of his dark skin color. After his good friend Johnny Weissmuller had snagged roles as Tarzan, Buster Crabbe, the newest Olympic champion from Hawai'i, became famous as Flash Gordon and Buck Rogers. Although Duke was stuck with minor roles as fierce Arab chiefs and Polynesian warriors, he was still a heroic figure to local boys like Eddie.

Tired of Hollywood and homesick for the Islands, Duke eventually returned to Hawai'i. He was later elected Sheriff of Honolulu, a position he would hold for twenty-six years. He became known as "the Sheriff who never fired a gun." When the sheriff's position was eliminated, Duke was appointed the Ambassador of Aloha for Hawai'i. He basically became a one-man tourism bureau. Whenever any celebrity or dignitary visited the Islands, Duke was there to greet them. He danced a hula with the Queen Mum, clowned around with Charlie Chaplin and taught Franklin D. Roosevelt's sons how to surf. When John F. Kennedy visited Hawai'i in 1961, he walked by other local dignitaries to shake the hand of Duke, his childhood hero. The press and the public loved Duke, and his photos appeared in newspapers, magazines and films across the globe. Like most young locals, Eddie had always been in awe of his athletic abilities and easy-going charm. Duke could mingle with English royalty like the Prince of Wales and American movie stars like John Wayne (the 'other Duke'). But he never lost the common touch and enjoyed hanging out with the local beach boys in Waikiki, where Eddie first started surfing and competing.

In 1965, Duke made the headlines once again. Eddie read in the papers about how he was the first inductee into the new International Swimming Hall of Fame, along with Johnny Weissmuller and Buster Crabbe. They were considered the greatest swimmers ever, and photos of the three friends standing arm in arm circulated around the globe. In his mid-seventies at the time, Duke was showing signs of old age. He had begun to slow down after undergoing brain surgery for a cerebral clot. Yet in the eyes of Eddie and most Hawaiians, he still looked regal with his thick mane of silver hair, warm smile and dignified manner. Duke's friend and business manager Kimo McVay says in the book *Memories of Duke* that the old man still carried the good looks of his youth, the glory of his Olympic fame and the glamour of his Hollywood days. "My mother said he was the most magnificent human male that God ever put on the Earth. When he was young, he was built like a bronzed Adonis…He put Hawai'i on the map; no one had ever heard of Hawai'i before…He was so colorful, such a hero, just exactly what everyone expected a gold medalist Olympic champion to look like. He was Hawai'i… He was on a first-name basis with celebrities all over the world."

A shrewd businessman and promoter, McVay went on to capitalize on Duke's fame by opening a night club in Waikiki called Duke's, one of the most popular bars and restaurants in Honolulu. McVay also promoted a line of clothing and surfboards with Duke's name attached, and these items were sold in major department stores like Sears and J.C. Penney's. He even created the Duke Kahanamoku Surf Team, a handsome crew of young surfers who were the top competitors of the day. The team consisted of Eddie's peers, including Fred Hemmings, Butch Van Artsdalen, Paul Strauch, Joey Cabell and later, Jeff Hakman. Kimo sponsored the surf team on trips to the mainland to promote his products and put on surfing exhibitions. On one trip to Malibu, they drove up in a Rolls Royce with their boards tied to the roof. When Duke and his team stepped out of the Rolls wearing their matching aloha shirts and RayBan Wayfarer sunglasses, they created quite a scene—perfect publicity. But the highlight for the team members was spending time with the Duke, who enjoyed being with the young surfers and watching them compete. He loved the spirit of healthy competition and wanted to bring that to the world of surfing.

Some purists say surfing is not a competitive sport but a soulful dance between man and ocean, rider and wave. Yet Duke knew that surf contests were part of his cultural heritage, dating back centuries to the Hawaiian chiefs who challenged each other to ride the longest and fastest waves to the beach. This healthy competitive spirit had been revived in 1954, with the advent of the International Surfing Championships at Makaha. Eddie's mentors Peter Cole and George Downing had won the contest in the early years. Though the event was a popular one, it lacked the glamour and prestige that some promoters wanted to attach to surfing's hip new image in the media. Based on the popularity of surfing on the big screen, the major television networks were eager to broadcast the sport, bringing Hawai'i's huge waves into every living room in America. For years Van Dyke had dreamed of putting on a world-class, Olympic-style event for surfing. In 1965, he got his chance when McVay launched the first annual Duke Kahanamoku Surfing Invitational. Kimo asked Fred to organize the event, and the 'Duke' soon eclipsed the Makaha International as the biggest, most respected contest in the world.

As a kid, Eddie had dreamed of becoming a great surfer like the Duke and bringing honor to his family and his people. He had participated in small, make-shift surf competitions which his father had helped organize on the South Shore. Former surf pro Randy Rarick remembers competing against Eddie and the Aikau boys as a teenager. As the Executive Director of the Triple Crown, Rarick now runs the largest series of surf contests in the world, and it makes him chuckle to recall how fiercely competitive those early events were. He competed against Eddie and Clyde and says they were a force to be reckoned with. "Clubs were a big deal in the mid-60's, and they were in the Diamond Head Surf Club, which was more for local Hawaiians. I was in this club called the Freedom Riders, and there was a big rivalry between us." Randy says Eddie wasn't a great competitor in the small-wave events. "Actually, Clyde was a better surfer in smaller waves. At that stage, Eddie began to focus more on surfing the North Shore." He liked the challenge of riding big waves more than competing against his friends.

Randy remembers seeing the family when he first started surfing the North Shore. "I would drive out here from town, and the Aikaus would be camped out. They'd slept there overnight. We'd roll up early in the morning, and there they'd be in this old telephone truck, which always amused me. It was one of those pick-up trucks with the tool boxes built into the sides but a bigger version of it. There would be a different family member sleeping in those compartments. In the early days, they had rather crude equipment, and they didn't really have a lot of support." While other top surfers received free surfboards and clothing from corporate sponsors like Hang Ten, Eddie and his brothers had no commercial backers. "They certainly weren't the glamour gang," Randy says, "but that combination of family support and drive to improve overcame lack of money and sponsored equipment. Maybe there were other flashier surfers, but they had the determination, and it showed." This determination would take Eddie and Clyde a long way in the competitive circuit.

Eager to compete in bigger waves against the best surfers, Eddie had been training so he could enter the growing network of surf contests. Like a dedicated student of oceanography, he had studied each surf spot, noting how and where the waves broke, how deep the reefs were, what direction the swells came in and how the weather affected them. Then, in 1965, Eddie and his family drove out to Sunset Beach to watch the First Annual Duke Classic. Though not invited to the contest, Eddie hoped he would get the chance to compete one day. Nineteen years old at the time, Eddie sat on the beach on the day of the first Duke, restlessly watching the event with his family and hundreds of other observers. He yearned to be out there in the waves, competing with fellow big-wave riders like Fred Hemmings. Cameramen stood on the beach snapping shots, and helicopters hovered above the surf filming each exciting ride. The competition was intense, full of exciting rides and wipeouts. When the final heat ended, Eddie was stunned by the results. A small, seventeen-year old named Jeff Hakman had won the contest! If this 5' 4", 125 pound kid could win the most prestigious event in surfing, Eddie thought he could too.

Eddie had surfed with Jeff and Fred at Waimea and Sunset before, and he knew they were great surfers. Yet he also knew that if he were invited to the next event, he could give them a good fight. Eddie had already competed against them in amateur events and held his own, but they had better equipment and more privileged connections. Although they respected each other's natural abilities in the water, they came from different worlds. Hakman and Hemmings received free boards, clothes and sponsorship from the Duke Kahanamoku Surf Team, and they belonged to exclusive social clubs like the Outrigger Canoe Club. Both alumni of prestigious Punahou School, Jeff and Fred had connections to the most influential people in the state and in the surfing world. In fact, their former teacher Fred Van Dyke had invited both of them to take part in the first contest. But Eddie knew that he could hold his own with them in the ocean, the great equalizer.

As Director of the Duke Classic, Fred Van Dyke was in charge of selecting twenty-four of the world's best surfers to compete in the contest. Eddie was a serious candidate, but he wasn't established enough on the mainland or in the surf mags to be considered one of the top 24 surfers in the world. Roger Pfeffer worked with Van Dyke at Punahou and had been watching Eddie surf for years. Roger had written in local papers that he was one of the most underrated surfers in Hawai'i. "Who'd ever heard of Eddie Aikau, for God's sake? I had been writing about him and Ben [Aipa] for years, telling everybody that these Hawaiian surfers were as good as any in the world and they should be invited to the Duke meet. I influenced Fred's judgement on this. I was tremendously impressed with the day-in and day-out performances of the Aikau brothers and Ben Aipa and a number of other local surfers who were ripping the waves and not getting any recognition in the magazines. They were only taking pictures of guys who were already well-known on the mainland. I was trying to balance that picture."

When the list of candidates was being drawn up, Roger talked to Fred about including Eddie and Ben, both of whom had been rising through the ranks. His comments must have paid off. In February of 1967, Eddie was invited to surf in the Third Annual Duke Kahanamoku Classic at Sunset Beach. The Aikau family was ecstatic. Although there was a lot of racism on the mainland and in the Islands during this time period, Van Dyke wanted to give local Hawaiian surfers a chance to compete. "This was a good chance to give the Hawaiians some deserved glory." After all, it was their land and they had pioneered the sport. For an aspiring young surfer, receiving an official Duke invitation in the mail was like a rookie being asked to play on a professional baseball team. Selected as one of the top surfers in the world, Eddie had finally made it to the big leagues. He was going to compete against young California hotdoggers like Mike Doyle and experienced legends like Ricky Grigg. But he had the homefield advantage and would get to surf on his old turf at Sunset, a spot he had studied well.

After Eddie was invited to the contest, Pops became Fred Van Dyke's right-hand man. "We got pretty deeply involved," Van Dyke says. Pops and his sons assisted with parking, building the judges' platform and setting up the sound system and time signals. "Pops wanted to help with everything. He wanted to make sure everything went smoothly. He was also protecting his kids from: poor judging, somebody cutting them out or any mishap. He was a great help in that. He never missed anything. He was a real colorful character, and I think he got more involved with the contests than anything else in his life. So their whole family was greatly influential in making sure everything went right and that there were no screw-ups." Always at the center of each contest, Pops would hobble around, barking out orders for the kids to follow. While working as a stevedore down at the docks years before, Pops had been in a bad accident and suffered a serious back injury which left him with a permanent limp and a limited disability payment. From then on, he devoted his life to being with his family and advancing Eddie and Clyde's budding surf careers. Limping across the beach, Pops stared through his binoculars, trying to watch every wave they caught.

For Eddie, the Duke Contest must have seemed like a dream come true. All the contestants were given rooms at the Royal Hawaiian, one of the oldest and nicest hotels in Waikiki. They stayed there and partied for a week, all expenses paid. The surfers were chauffeured around town in a white Rolls Royce and invited to join the Duke himself for dinner. They were wined and dined at Duke's famous night club, where singer Don Ho put on a show for them. McVay had also helped make Ho famous, and the young entertainer reveled in his newfound success. His deep voice and good looks drove the women crazy when he crooned his hit song "Tiny Bubbles" and other favorites. He had a reputation as a hard drinker, and some began to wonder if all those "Tiny Bubbles" had gone to his head. But he knew how to schmooze an audience, and the drunken crowds and paparazzi loved it. All the socializing and media attention were almost too much for a shy, local boy like Eddie. As he sat in the crowded club watching Ho sing songs that were so popular among tourists, Eddie felt out of his element. He preferred sitting around the graveyard with a group of family and friends, drinking and playing music.

In the publicity shots for the contest, he and Ben Aipa, the other local Hawaiian, stood out like two dark-skinned brothers in an all-white fraternity. Although he and Ben were stoked to be competing against the world's hottest surfers, they must have felt like outsiders in this group. But just as Duke and runner Jim Thorpe had become the first indigenous people to win gold in the 1912 Olympics, Eddie hoped that he and Ben could do the same at the contest. But whereas Duke had traveled all the way around the globe to bring fame to Hawai'i, Eddie wanted to win honor for himself and his people in his own back yard. He was 21 at the time, the same age as Duke when he won his first gold medal.

Eddie was friendly with the California crew, but he felt more at home with big-wave chargers like Ricky Grigg. Ricky had flown in from San Diego, where he was studying for his doctorate in oceanography at Scripp's Institute. Though he hadn't surfed in Hawai'i for a few years, he was still considered a leading contender and consistently ranked as one of the top five surfers in the world. Ricky seemed to have the Midas touch. Not only was he in the process of becoming one of the leading oceanographers in the world, but he was also a handsome surfing champion with blond hair, blue eyes and a winning grin. He had appeared in magazines across the country, including ads for Dewar's Scotch and Jantzen sportswear. Eddie had seen many pictures of him in the surf magazines, including one great shot on the cover of *Surfer*.

Ricky was a celebrity in the surfing world, but he was often misunderstood and not universally liked. "Some people saw him as arrogant and cocky and representative of mainland surfers," says Roger, who had studied with him in grad school at the University of Hawai'i and written about his surfing accomplishments in the local paper. "In reality, Ricky Grigg was as good as he thought he was, and people who really surfed with him, like Eddie, came to respect him for his great ability." In spite of the differences between them, Ricky and Eddie had formed a special bond over the years. The older *haole* scientist from California and the local boy from Hawai'i were both students of the sea. "They shared a common love of the ocean," Roger says. "They respected each other for their judgement, their courage and their ability. They always had something to discuss and talk about." While Ricky's observations were often grounded in scientific research, "Eddie's knowledge of the ocean was based on associative observations about the wind, wave heights and wave period. He had the traditional Hawaiian knowledge of waves and ocean, built on thousands of hours of personal observation and experience." When the moon was full or the wind shifted, Eddie could often predict how the waves would be affected. During the competition, he and Ricky would test their understanding of the waves and weather conditions to see who would catch the best rides.

When the day of the contest dawned, all the surfers boarded a private bus in Waikiki for the long drive to Sunset Beach. On the ride out, Van Dyke said Grigg was unusually nervous, asking him, "What's going to happen today? Who's going to win?" And that's when Van Dyke looked him straight in the eye and told him, "Ricky, I had a dream last night that you're going to win. It was in the dream, and I know you're going to win." Although Ricky didn't know whether he was fooling around or not, he liked hearing it. Van Dyke then stood up and explained the rules of the contest to all the surfers on the bus. He told them that each heat would last 45 minutes, except for the finals which would last an hour. Each surfer was judged on his best five waves in each heat, 20 points maximum per wave, 100 points total. As the bus climbed through the sugar cane fields and reached the peak overlooking the entire North Shore, all the contestants shouted when they saw the thick, white lines rolling across the blue water. Looking at the waves breaking at outside reefs like Avalanche, they knew the bigger swells would be hitting 20-30 feet in height. With its huge, pounding waves, Sunset would be "going off the Richter scale."

By the time the bus reached Sunset Beach, everyone was amped on adrenaline and nervous energy. Staring hypnotically at the huge waves rising up on the horizon, they jumped out of the bus and watched the surf. Strong, offshore winds feathered the lips of the outside swells into a fine mist as they pitched and crashed in an explosion of white water. It was going to be an epic day, and Eddie knew it. He felt the support of his whole family, who had driven out before dawn to help get things set up for the contest. Jerry, Sol and Clyde were putting the finishing touches on the judges' platform, while Pops acted as "da supervisor." Momma and Myra were helping to organize the heats and hand out colored jerseys for each surfer to wear in the water.

Waiting for their heats to get started, the surfers studied the conditions and tried to figure out their strategies. Each surf spot is unique, due to differences in the contour of the coral reef below the surface and the shape and angle of the shoreline. Although it's not as big as Waimea or hollow as Pipeline, Sunset Beach has some of the heaviest and longest waves in the world. But it is one of the trickiest spots on the North Shore because it has three different peaks where the waves break, and it often shifts between the East, North and West peaks. This means that huge, rogue waves can suddenly pop up on the horizon and break right on top of the surfers, throwing them into a violent whirlpool of whitewater and sometimes pressing them against the jagged coral reef below. Eddie knew the break at Sunset Beach so well that he had an instinctive understanding of where the next big wave would break. He would sometimes paddle out way beyond the lineup of surfers and just wait. The others would look at him and wonder what he was doing out there—until a huge outside wave would suddenly rise up right before him! As Eddie paddled into the wave, jumped to his feet and gracefully glided down the face of the wave, the other surfers would paddle furiously toward the horizon to avoid being steamrolled by the crushing swell. In moments like these, Eddie's intuition had earned him a lot of respect on the North Shore, and he hoped it would help him win.

When the contest horn sounded, the first heat hit the water at 9:00 am, and the contestants were amazed at how much bigger the waves were up close. Having never surfed Sunset or such big waves before, one surfer from California and another from Florida opted to paddle out past the lineup when their heats went out, too timid to catch the monster waves crashing around them. Standing on the beach, Eddie studied the break and debated where he would surf in the next heat. He could see Ricky was already there at the West peak, catching some of the best rides. The crowds on the beach cheered with each great ride, and the cameramen tried to catch all the action on film. With their long, thick fiberglass boards, the surfers paddled into giant waves with steep drops, trying to get as deep as they could, without being pummeled by the falling lip. During take-off, some competitors freefell almost twenty feet down the faces of the waves, hitting the water so hard they bounced several times before being sucked over the falls. One contestant named Rusty Miller broke his leg during a horrendous wipeout and had to be driven to a local hospital.

Ricky surfed well on the West peak, but Eddie decided to try the East peak during his heat. It was considered more dangerous and unstable, but also bigger and less crowded. Nervous on land, Eddie found his stride in the water. He took off deeper in the pit of the wave than most of the surfers and caught some of the hairiest rides of the day. Beating former champion Jeff Hakman in the prelims, Eddie moved on to the semi-finals. He didn't do a lot of hotdogging like Mike Doyle and some of the other Californians, but he did take off on some of the bigger waves and surfed through the most critical sections. Wearing his red and white shorts and riding his big red Hobie board, Eddie could be seen taking off on immense waves with his signature wide stance and outstretched arms.

When they announced the finals over the PA system, Eddie heard his name called. He had made it, and the local crowd cheered for him. He and Ben Aipa were being pitted against veterans like Greg Noll and Ricky Grigg, who already had the lead. When the horn sounded for the final heat of the day, the surfers ran to the water, got onto their knees and paddled their long boards out into the surf. In the distance, the huge waves looked like wild horses charging across the blue water, their white manes waving in the wind. The conditions were perfect: blue skies, offshore winds and a strong swell. Helicopters hovered above the waves like dragonflies, and the surfers looked like water bugs flying across the giant waves.

The contestants pushed each other to take more chances, taking off on mountainous waves at the last second and trying to get deeper in the 'tube,' the hollow section inside the breaking wave, than they had ever been before. After several, heavy wipeouts, Noll and others lost their boards and had to swim all the way in to get them, losing precious time and energy. While most of the finalists clustered around the central peak, Ricky stuck to the West peak like before and caught some unforgettable rides. During one epic wave in the finals, he took off on a fast and hollow wave and ended up getting tubed three times on one ride! He received a perfect score from all three judges on that wave and another later in the heat. By the time the final horn sounded, everyone knew that Ricky had won the Duke, just as Fred had predicted.

Eddie didn't do as well as he wanted in the final heat, but he did better than anyone had expected. From the informal podium on the platform, they announced the winners: in first place, Ricky Grigg, followed by Mike Doyle and Fred Hemmings; and in sixth place, Eddie Aikau, right in front of Ben Aipa. Both of these local boys were hailed as hot new Hawaiian surfers. From that day forward, Eddie would become one of the leading contenders in almost every Duke contest over the next ten years.

At the Awards Banquet later that night in Waikiki, Duke congratulated each of the contestants and gave them their highly coveted Duke trophies. The sleek, golden statuettes resembled the Oscar Awards, which were made by the same company, and the surfers were treated like celebrities at the glamorous party. On the stage, Duke told the beaming, blond-haired winner, "Ricky, you really understand the ocean." At that moment, Ricky felt his love of the ocean as a surfer and a scientist had finally come together. But he also sensed that he had reached the pinnacle of his competitive surfing career, as young surfers like Fred Hemmings and Eddie continued to rise through the ranks.

When Eddie went up to receive his trophy from the Duke, it was a transitional moment in both their lives. Surrounded by tiki-style decorations, they came together on the brightly lit stage, one's career just beginning, while the other's was coming to a close. Duke shook hands with the young man, looked into his eyes and smiled, and then he put his arm around Eddie's shoulders, embracing him like a son. Two proud Hawaiians, bridging different generations. Duke represented the glory of their past and Eddie the hope of their future. As they stood together on stage, cameras flashed like exclamation points, as the drunken crowd clapped and cheered. Fred Van Dyke smiled as he looked at the two of them, knowing that this was a brief yet timeless moment in Hawaiian history, like the passing of a torch from one generation to the next.

Dressed in their best aloha shirts and wearing their ti-leaf leis, the contestants reveled in the attention. It was a first-class affair, and the surfers ate and drank more than their share, gloating on their newfound celebrity status. Eddie was secretly thrilled to be recognized by the Duke and finally receive attention for his surfing abilities, and it validated his decision to dedicate his life to surfing. At one point, Ricky wandered over to his table to congratulate him: "I remember Eddie and Ben Aipa were the up-and-comers at the awards dinner. I went over and put my arms around both of them and said, 'You know, you two are the wave of the future. You guys are really going to make your mark for the next generation and for Hawai'i.' That turned out to be fairly prophetic," Ricky recalls, "because Eddie became one of the best big-wave riders of the 70's and Ben Aipa is still going strong."

Eddie didn't realize his dream of winning the Duke while his hero was still alive, but he did get to know the man and experience his *mana*. Despite the ravages of old age during that last year, Duke's spirit remained young and strong. Until the end, he was a proud Hawaiian with a childlike innocence and integrity. He lived by a simple yet profound creed that he printed on the back of his business card: "In Hawai'i we greet friends, loved ones and strangers with aloha, which means with love. Aloha is the key word to the universal spirit of real hospitality, which makes Hawai'i renowned as the world's center of understanding and fellowship."

Shortly before he passed away, Duke and his wife Nadine visited the newspaper columnist Eddie Sherman at his home during Christmas. Sherman remembers Duke greeting them with warm expressions of "Aloha" and "*Mele Kalikimaka!*" (Merry Christmas) Then, he walked over to where Sherman's adopted Hawaiian son was playing with his new train set. "For the next two hours, Duke sat fascinated, absorbed with my son in the mechanical wonder of the train…They played, laughed and communicated." As he watched them, Sherman says, "The beautiful simplicity of the man shone—as always—like a beacon…In this day of pseudo ultra-sophistication, this unaffected quality was a joy to behold…It was honest. It was true. It was majestic. It was *ali'i*."

Duke died a month later at the age of 77. Having been an active part of Hawai'i's many transformations, from royal monarchy to republic to territory and finally to statehood, his death marked the end of an era. At his funeral service in Waikiki, Eddie joined the thousands gathered there to say aloha to Hawai'i's most popular hero. Duke's friend Arthur Godfrey, who was a popular radio and TV personality, gave a moving eulogy and described him as "the soul of dignity…and a mischievous, delightful boy at heart…He was unassuming, reticent, almost shy…It was the wonderful world of water that gave Duke his relaxed peace of mind." With Diamond Head in the distance, they carried his urn out to his favorite surf break in a solemn procession of outrigger canoes and spread his ashes in the water. According to Hawaiian belief, it always rains at the funerals of *ali'i*. That morning, a light rain touched the faces of those gathered on the beach and in the water. "Just as Diamond Head symbolized the geography of Hawai'i, Duke symbolized the people of Hawai'i," Representative Spark Matsunaga later remarked in his tribute before the U.S. Congress.

Some say Eddie Aikau shared Duke's generosity, humility and proud

Hawaiian spirit. Van Dyke goes even further: "I described Eddie once at one of the meets as the re-creation of Duke Kahanamoku because Duke liked him a lot too. They were the greatest of athletes. He had the same kind of chest and arms. He had the Hawaiian strength which is almost foreboding. Duke was more of a simple man, and I think Eddie was a simple person in his life. He didn't want complications. He got them, but he didn't want them." Eddie sought to simplify his life, focusing on family, friends, music and surfing. But as Bob Dylan sang on the radio, "The times they are a-changing." There was no avoiding the complications of race, politics and war.

Just as Duke and his brother Sam competed with each other in the Olympics and won fame for their swimming feats, Eddie and his brother Clyde would eventually do the same as big-wave surfers. Duke and Eddie both worked as lifeguards and often risked their lives to save those in danger. Once while surfing in California in 1925, Duke saw a fishing yacht capsize in the big waves off of Newport Beach. He immediately paddled out to help the survivors back to shore. He made three trips through the pounding waves and saved seven men before the boat went down. Thirty-two years later, three of these men appeared on the "This Is Your Life" TV show to thank Duke personally for saving their lives. As a surfer, Eddie had already rescued many people on the North Shore, but his biggest challenge would come as a lifeguard at Waimea Bay. He would eventually rescue hundreds of people at the Bay, but most never got around to thanking him.

CHAPTER 4

Lifeguards and Guardian Angels

"Never turn your back on the ocean."
— *Hawaiian saying*

On the beach at Waikiki just down from where Clyde runs his beach concession, a bronzed statue of Duke Kahanamoku stands with his arms open wide and his back to the ocean. Larger than life, his bronzed form is usually draped with fresh leis that tourists and locals put around his neck and arms every day. But some watermen believe the statue is facing the wrong direction. City officials and the Kahanamoku family placed it facing the street so tourists could take pictures of the Duke with the blue ocean in the background. But as Clyde and most lifeguards know, you should never turn your back to the sea. This is not only out of respect for the god of the ocean, who can be fickle and dangerous, but it is also a practical precaution. Like any experienced waterman, Duke knew what could happen when you took your eye off the sea or underestimated its power.

"I will never understand the stupidity of people who turn their backs on the ocean," Eddie once complained to a newspaper columnist. "People who have no knowledge of the danger the ocean threatens will walk right into it backwards while snapping pictures of the family. One wave and—ZAP—they are grabbed and sucked out in seconds. And worse, still, is the guy who won't let go of his camera, but keeps it high over his head while he is drowning."

During the famous November swell of 1967, when Eddie made his mark as a big-wave rider at Waimea, his personal triumph had been overshadowed by the deaths of the two servicemen. Not paying attention to the ocean, one man had been walking along the beach when a big shore break suddenly grabbed him and swept him out to sea. The other man had been sitting on a rock wall near Sunset Beach when a rogue wave ambushed him and sucked him into the raging surf. Unfortunately, no one was there to save them. In spite of these fatalities, people still flocked to the beach, carelessly following the surfers into the water as if they were Pied Pipers. The Fire Department's Rescue Squad members were trying their best to look after these people, but they clearly didn't have the experience or expertise in big waves to save all of them. Because there was no lifeguard service on the North Shore at that time, firemen depended on surfers to act as makeshift guards whenever they spotted someone in trouble. Whether surfing way out in the lineup or standing on the beach, Eddie and friends like Peter Cole and Fred Hemmings always kept an eye on those in the water and often had to make dramatic rescues. But the fatalities continued.

Smelling a good story, a reporter from *The Honolulu Advertiser* went to the beach to interview local surfers about the huge swell, recent drownings and lack of lifeguards. In the middle of the interview, Fred Hemmings spotted someone waving his hand for help in the angry shore break. Running and diving into the water, the former football player and big-wave rider swam toward the young man who had suddenly disappeared under the water. When he came back up, Fred grabbed the man and guided him through the large shore break which slammed them down like a line of angry linebackers. But before the young man could escape, another wave tackled him. Like a determined coach, Fred yelled at him to get up and keep moving. The swimmer crawled out of the water on his hands and knees and staggered up the beach where he collapsed in the sand.

"It was worse yesterday," Cole told the reporter. "The Rescue Squad must have pulled 15 people out of the water. Finally, I got so disgusted I went up on the beach and told the people to get back." Chief Chuck Freitas, head of the Fire Department's Rescue Squad, admitted that they were under-manned, overworked and not properly trained for this kind of work. He was also frustrated that people on the beach weren't heeding their warnings about staying out of the water. "On Sunday we practically provided a life-guard service. When you warn people to stay off the beach, they get mad. We're not worried so much about surfers as we are about servicemen. They don't seem to realize how dangerous the water is." Off base, young recruits didn't like to be told what to do. Many were headed for Vietnam. Facing the prospect of dying in a foreign country, many soldiers wanted to prove how tough they were. But these macho servicemen would often end up being caught in a deadly rip tide or thrown around in explosions of whitewater. Then, the Rescue Squad or some surfer would have to save them.

Meanwhile, out in the lineup, a handful of the Island's best big-wave riders were trying to ride the moving mountains of water. The surfers looked like tiny climbers scaling up the giant waves and being thrown back down. Fragments of their boards would later wash up on the beach. As Eddie and Peter paddled into the precipice of these 50-foot cliffs of water, they would build until suddenly collapsing in an avalanche of whitewater. If the surfers made the vertical drop, they experienced the ride of their lives—if they didn't, they would free-fall and bounce down the face of the wave until it consumed them and buried them underwater. Most of the riders looked out for each other and could handle these vicious spills. But tourists and servicemen had no idea what to do when they were swept out to sea. So surfers like Eddie would have to save them. Although a bad wipeout in waves this size could throw someone twenty feet to the bottom and hold him there, Eddie had trained for these waves and knew the risks. Why would these big-wave riders risk their lives for a few moments of glory? "This is our life," Hemmings told the reporter. "We live for two or three days like this out of the year."

By 1967, it had become increasingly obvious that lifeguards were desperately needed on the North Shore. But the question remained: who was capable and willing to work in such treacherous conditions? As one exasperated fireman put it, "Yes, we need lifeguards at Waimea Bay during the winter, but you'd have to find a crazy man to take the job. That's a wild place." He went on to say, "What I think we ought to do is put up a nice, impressive monument right on the beach. Everytime somebody drowned in Waimea Bay, we could add his name and the date. That might sober up some of these swimmers."

Under pressure from the public, City officials decided to hire lifeguards for the North Shore and looked for candidates who were skilled and committed enough to risk their lives in the huge surf. As the Director of Water Safety for the City and County of Honolulu, former Olympic swimmer Bill Smith was in charge of hiring the new guards. As he began his search, Smith logically turned to a 'crazy' yet qualified group of candidates: the big-wave surfers who intimately knew dangerous breaks like Waimea, Pipeline and Sunset. Their first choices were Butch Van Artsdalen, known as "Mr. Pipeline," and Eddie, the rising star at Waimea Bay. "Since Waimea was one of the popular areas, we were looking for someone who had the experience and expertise to handle the big surf on the North Shore so Eddie was the logical choice," Smith says. "There weren't many people who could handle it. He had the knowledge and skills to get to the big surf and effect any rescues that needed to be done. He was definitely the man for the job."

"He would be what I call a waterman," Peter adds, "somebody you can depend upon, somebody who knows the ocean and has a feel for it." Eddie was certainly qualified, but he had one problem: he didn't have a high school degree, one of the job requirements. During his interview with City and County officials, Eddie asked, "How will knowing about George Washington and Abraham Lincoln help me get people out of the water at Waimea?" Still defensive about dropping out of school, Eddie managed to convince the city officials that though he didn't have a high school diploma, he was in a class by himself when it came to knowledge of the ocean. Eddie was more than ready to leave the dark, industrial confines of Dole Cannery for the natural beauty of Waimea Bay. In 1968, the City and County of Honolulu hired Eddie and Butch as the first lifeguards on the North Shore. A close friend and fellow surfer acknowledged that while Eddie wasn't well educated, he understood the sea brilliantly.

For the first couple of years, Eddie and Butch became roving life-guards. Their daunting duty was to patrol the entire 7-mile strip of the North Shore and beyond. They were each given a truck, a lifesaving board and a radio. They would cruise up and down the beaches from Haleʻiwa to Sunset Beach, looking for accidents and waiting for the radio to crackle with sudden calls for help. In his first two years, Eddie logged in thousands of miles, driving up and down the coast. When the surf was building and the currents swirling, he would often have to make numerous rescues during the day. But it's not clear exactly how many because he hardly ever filled out official reports. As a Hawaiian, he believed in the practice of haʻahaʻa, which means being humble and downplaying your accomplishments.

Eddie's younger brother Sol also became a lifeguard and admired the way his older brother dedicated himself to his work. "His job was just every-thing. He took it very seriously, and he was very good at it. You could actually say he was married to his job. What stands out for me is that Eddie could get in and out of the water, no matter how big the shore break was, quicker than any other person. His talent for getting through the shore break was phenomenal. Or if it was too big, he would take you out [past the huge waves] and call for a helicopter, and they would lift you and bring you back to shore." Helicopter rescues took place only when the surf got too big and a surfer or swimmer couldn't get in through the deadly breakers. During these dramatic rescues, Sol remembers seeing Eddie charge through the powerful shore break and swim out to the victim when no one else would go. The rescue copter would fly overhead, dangling a wire cage in the water. After swimming almost a half mile out, Eddie would try to keep the frantic victim calm and help him inside the cage. Once inside, he would be lifted above the giant waves by the helicopter and flown to shore. After assisting with these rescues, Eddie would somehow swim through the huge surf all the way back to shore. When he emerged from the shore break, his co-workers and the crowd would watch in astonishment. Captain Aloha Kaeo, his supervisor, said, "Sometimes, I think I should put a leash on him to keep him on shore. He goes out when every other lifeguard would stay in."

As much as he looked up to his older brother, Sol was more like the black sheep of the family and very different. Because Eddie was shy and quiet, he enjoyed working in the "country," as the laidback North Shore was called. But Sol was a social animal, and he liked working in the city. He had secured a job as a lifeguard at Waikiki, watching over thousands of people each day, including some of the most beautiful women in the world. Whereas Eddie was "married" to his work and surfing career, Sol was some-what of a Don Juan. At the age of 14, he had already gotten his older girlfriend *hapai* (pregnant). By 18, he was a husband and the father of three children. When that marriage came to an end, he married another woman and had four more children. As different as they were, the brothers both enjoyed helping people. But like Eddie, Sol hated doing paperwork. "We got scoldings because we never filled out the reports for saving someone. We never did it. We saved you, got you out of the water and sent you home." While most victims were too stunned or embarrassed to thank them, Sol says others always remembered how they had been pulled from the jaws of death and brought back to life by the local lifeguards. "Every Christmas this priest would send us a postcard. This was one of the guys that Eddie saved, and the guy never forgot him."

The North Shore became Eddie's playground, office and home. He would usually surf before and after work, the first one in the water and the last to leave. He and Clyde had moved into an apartment together outside the sleepy town of Hale'iwa, the surfing capital of the North Shore, so they could be closer to the surf. Clyde was attending the University of Hawai'i and working part-time with Eddie as a lifeguard. Following Eddie's lead, almost all the Aikau brothers would eventually take up jobs as lifeguards on different parts of the Island. As different as they were, their supervisor Bill Smith realized they had the "right stuff" when it came to guarding people's lives in the ocean. "We hired Sol, and then we hired Clyde," he says, "because they were all good watermen." Working, surfing and partying together, the Aikaus established themselves as a local dynasty, a force to be reckoned with on land and in the ocean.

By the early 70's, orange lifeguard towers had been set up at the two most popular beaches on the North Shore. Eddie was stationed at Waimea Bay, and his friend Butch took up residence at Pipeline. Butch was a big influence on Eddie, and he had established himself as a legendary surfer during the 60's, especially at Pipeline. He was not the first surfer to ride Pipeline's dangerous waves, but he was the best. No other break on the North Shore had such powerful and hollow waves. After traveling a thousand miles across the North Pacific, these swells would suddenly jump up to twice their height when they hit the shallow coral shelf just off the coast. Then, they would slam down on a sharp jagged reef, forming perfect tubes that were as hollow as a "pipeline." The waves would then reel down the line like a locomotive, smoking all the way. The trick for a surfer was to crouch down inside the tunnel of the wave and try to get out just before it collapsed. The best tube-riders stayed inside the watery tunnel until they were spit out at the last minute in a huge gust of spray just as the wave exploded.

No one had even dared to ride Pipeline until 1962 because it was considered too shallow and dangerous. The next winter, Butch had decided to take on Pipeline, then considered the "ultimate challenge" of the surfing world. While other surfers like Mike Doyle were just trying to drop in the waves without getting killed, Butch boggled minds with his bold take-offs and deep tube-rides. Like Eddie's debut at Waimea, he stunned the crowd on the beach when he took off on a big wave at Pipeline and disappeared behind its silver curtain like a magician for what seemed like an eternity. Surf journalist Steve Pezman was there, watching in awe as the wave rolled on, thinking there was no way Van Artsdalen could make it out of that tube. "Then Butch did come flying out. We gasped in disbelief. Doyle fell to the sand face down, rolling over and over while muttering, 'Nobody does that!

Nobody does that!'" But Butch did, and he became famous for disappearing acts at Pipeline. Pictures of him appeared in the surf magazines, and kids across the country put them on their bedroom walls.

Originally from San Diego and part of La Jolla's infamous WindanSea gang, Butch Van Artsdalen had been a phenomenal athlete in high school. He had lettered in two sports and was offered a job playing professional baseball for the San Diego Padres right after graduation. But once he discovered surfing, everything else seemed like the minor leagues; so he took his signing bonus and bought a plane ticket to Hawai'i. Already known for his hard drinking and brawling in bars from Southern California to Northern Mexico, his wild reputation grew in the Islands. Butch wasn't afraid to get into a brawl over waves, women or whatever he felt the urge to fight about; but after it was over, he would laugh it off and buy everyone a round of beers.

Butch was considered one of the boldest, most talented surfers of his day. He could switch his stance while taking off on huge waves so that he was always facing the wave, whether he went left or right. Naturally a "goofy foot," he surfed with his right foot forward and faced the wave when he took off to the left, and this worked perfectly at breaks like Pipeline. But for big right breaks like Waimea, he had the ability to change his stance, with his left foot forward, so he faced the wave going right. This was almost unheard of at the time—the rough equivalent of being a world-class switch-hitter. Friends and fans started calling him "Mr. Pipeline." Fearless in big surf like Eddie, he seemed to push himself beyond all limits, as if he had a death wish. With his dark moods and drunken binges, he came to be known as "Black Butch" by those who loved, feared and knew him best.

As a member of the Duke Kahanamoku Surf Team, he was the controversial figure of the group. He looked like an All-American athlete with his conservative good looks and neatly trimmed black hair, but he had earned a reputation as a wild and sometimes sloppy drinker. Yet people got a kick out of his wild pranks and drunken antics. On one drinking spree, Butch stole a rickshaw in Waikiki and took the unsuspecting tourists on the ride of their lives. During another binge, he snuck backstage at Duke's nightclub and then appeared on stage, singing a drunken duet with Don Ho. When he was in good spirits, he left people laughing; but when he got mad, his victims often ended up bleeding on the floor. Despite his inebriated pranks and occasional hostility, Butch loved living in the Islands and had a tender spot for Hawaiians. He had known Eddie as a surfer and fellow competitor in the Duke Contests, and they became good friends after working together as lifeguards. After work, he would sit around drinking and talking story with Eddie, his brothers and their friends on the North Shore. Eventually, Butch was warmly accepted by the locals who got a kick out of his wild antics and liked the fact that he wasn't afraid to 'beef' with them. Having come from a culture that honored its warriors, they valued his physical strength and willingness to fight. Though Butch could be brash and violent, he proved to be a loyal friend and dedicated lifeguard. So the Aikau boys embraced him as one of their own. But while Eddie and Clyde were emerging as professional surfers, Black Butch had already seen his glory days begin to fade.

Surfing changed dramatically with the advent of the social revolution of the late '60's. Reflecting the war in Vietnam and the political changes taking place on the mainland, the sport became more radical and aggressive. Surfers' boards got shorter, and their hair got longer. Instead of simply cruising down the wave on a longboard, competitive surfers were now carving tracks across the wave's face and making as many turns as possible. Those who embraced the change excelled, and those who resisted it were left behind like yesteryear's crewcuts. Butch couldn't seem to make the transition, and his drinking became a way of coping with the changes taking place in surfing and the general culture. The more he drank, the less he surfed. But he still clung to his reputation as Mr. Pipeline, despite the fact that hot, young surfers like Gerry Lopez and Jock Sutherland were actively working to take the title away from him.

Despite their drinking binges, Eddie and Butch were very conscientious lifeguards and took their jobs seriously. Fred Van Dyke lived on the North Shore then and remembers seeing both lifeguards perform amazing rescues. "I saw Eddie save people a number of times at Waimea Bay, when he would be off-duty. I've seen Eddie, just before it was getting dark, swim out or paddle his board and make a rescue—sometimes a service person, sometimes a surfer. These kids from Schofield Barracks just didn't know what they were doing. They'd get drunk on their day off and get swept out to sea. Whenever he was there, whether he was on duty or not, he was out there first to make the rescue. He knew what he was doing; he knew the resuscitation process perfectly." Fred saw Eddie bring a number of drowning victims back to life on the beach. He would pump their chests with the palms of his hands and breathe air back into their clogged lungs until their heartbeat and breath returned.

Van Dyke also witnessed Butch in action and once saw him jump down from his tower, grab his rescue board and paddle out to the lineup. Some surfers were yelling about how they had discovered a body on the ocean floor. They didn't know who he was or how long he had been down there. A black soldier, probably from Schofield. Butch grabbed the lifeless young man and brought him to shore where he performed CPR on him. No pulse, no breath, nothing. His face was blue, and his eyes were white, rolled up into his head as if he'd already given up the ghost. But Butch went to work on the kid and ordered Van Dyke and others to massage his arms and legs. Although it seemed hopeless, Van Artsdalen didn't give up. Fred can still recall the gruesome scene. "Minutes passed, Butch yelling, 'Damn it, come back, come back,' in between breaths. Butch's face flushed, like any time a blood vessel would burst, but he didn't let up. Ten, fifteen minutes passed. He screamed at us to massage harder, help him with the heart massage. Butch appeared to be the master surgeon, the man so involved that when, suddenly, the kid threw up into Butch's mouth, he only turned sideways for a moment, spit and went back to mouth-to-mouth." The boy came back to life, coughing up water and bile and convulsing with each breath entering into his water-logged lungs. When the kid was taken away in an ambulance, Butch asked Fred to watch his stand for a while so he could take a break. He sat under a palm tree, cracked a Primo beer and smoked a cigarette, while looking out to sea.

While Butch's reputation slowly petered out, Eddie and Clyde's rising fame as big-wave riders and lifesavers made them into local heroes. They became mentors for younger surfers and aspiring lifeguards like Jim Howe, the current Chief of Lifeguard Operations for Oʻahu. During his first outing to the North Shore in 1970, Jim remembers seeing Eddie and Clyde and other pro surfers at Sunset Beach during a classic 10-foot swell. He was a kid, only 13, but after gathering up his courage on the beach, he decided to go and join the big boys out in the giant surf. "So I paddled out, and every major surfer in the world was out there. I'll never forget that day. And that was when I first saw Eddie and Clyde. It was my first experience seeing that whole cadre out there, and they were like kings…I was sitting there watching those guys get some unreal rides. Then I took off on my [small board with its] little 3-inch fins on a straight vertical drop. I just got slammed. It took me 10 years to go back out there. I was that petrified. Seeing those guys and how well they surfed was pretty amazing for a 13-year-old."

Jim Howe was humbled by his first session in big surf, but it made him a wiser man in the water. Years later, he ended up working at Waimea Bay on the weekends. During training, he remembers learning the Eddie Aikau Method of Lifeguarding, which consisted of scaring the bejesus out of those who were careless or clueless in the surf. During his first day on the job, the ocean was relatively calm, except for the large sets of 6-8 foot waves that would come thundering through the shore break every twenty minutes. There were about 300-500 people on the beach, and there was no way of keeping them out of the water on such a warm, sunny day. So as soon as they saw the sets begin to come in and 'indicate' out at the Point, which was about 100 yards outside, the lifeguards would tell everyone to get out of the water as quickly as possible. "Later in the afternoon," Howe recalls, "there were some military guys who wouldn't come in when we told them. Some guys got in trouble. Being the younger guard, I went out to get him and waited out the set and then we just came in. And the guys all said, 'That's not how you do it, man. He'll be right back out there—he didn't learn his lesson.' So the theory was, and this is the Eddie Aikau method, if somebody gets out there, you've got to make sure they get the fear of God put into them. So you bring them in during the set and make sure they see those giant waves breaking…We always made sure if you had to go and rescue somebody, they got the full experience. We didn't put them in jeopardy, but we made sure they came out of it with a very healthy respect for the ocean."

The City began to hire more young lifeguards for the North Shore, and Eddie would train many of them. Mark Dombroski was also just a young kid when he first met Eddie and started hanging out at Waimea Bay. Because his father was in the military and the family had moved around a lot, Mark didn't have a lot of friends. He started playing volleyball with the Aikau brothers at the beach, and he was stoked when they took him in and taught him how to be a lifeguard. "I hung out there with Eddie and Clyde, and after I graduated from high school, I ended up back at the beach. In some ways, Eddie treated me like a younger brother. He was a lifeguard but he was a friend also. After applying to be accepted as a lifeguard, I just kind of slid in there on his word." As one of the most respected lifeguards in Hawai'i, Eddie's word carried a lot of weight with the City.

Mark began working at Waimea with Eddie, who taught him everything he knew about the Bay, the North Shore and the ocean in general. He showed him how to charge through the shore break and dive under the huge waves when swimming out to help someone. Having watched Eddie risk his life to rescue so many people, most of whom were strangers, Mark was blown away by his laidback attitude. No matter how dangerous the situation was, Eddie always acted like it was no big deal. Just another day at work. Mark liked Eddie's humility and quirky sense of humor. Whenever people asked Eddie if he was the famous big-wave surfer, Mark remembers him saying, "'No, I'm a golfer.' He'd say he never surfed big waves…I'm sure he never picked up a golf club in his life." For surfers at that time, golfing held about as much excitement and appeal as a rousing match of croquet, both games for old farts and Englishmen. They would be stunned to see how many young surf stars now play golf regularly when they're not jet-setting off to some exotic surf spot.

Darrick Doerner was an up-and-coming young surfer when he was stationed at Waimea Bay and became a lifeguard under Eddie's watch. "Eddie was the main guy at Waimea Bay." While Eddie sat inside the orange life-guard stand playing his guitar, Darrick says, "I would stay outside the tower because the tower was real small. He didn't say very much, but he sang a lot." When he wasn't singing and watching the water, Eddie would be out in the surf. Darrick remembers him showing up each day with about five or six big-wave guns tied to the roof of his VW Bug, the most common surf car in Hawai'i. Then, he would either stay in the tower or paddle out into the waves. "He would go out surfing, and he would surf all day, and he wouldn't come in for food or water. But as soon as he saw us doing rescues, he would paddle in and guide us through it which taught us the right way. He had a real quiet way of teaching things." Though some might look at lifeguards as surf bums and laidback beach boys, Darrick says Eddie and his guards were dedicated lifesavers. "I swear they're guardian angels. They don't fly in with wings—they come in with fins and rescue tubes, and they will save your life."

A young Hawaiian named Terry Ahue learned to be a lifeguard by watching Eddie perform rescues that boggled his mind. Terry is a muscular man with dark skin and black hair, now peppered with gray. He grew up in the ocean, surfing, fishing and diving. After graduating from high school, he joined the Army and did a tour in Vietnam. "I was more like a grease mon-key than anything else," he says with a laugh. "I worked in the motor pool so I didn't really see much action." After his tour was over, Terry saw a lot of action working with Eddie as a lifeguard at one of the most dangerous surf breaks in the world. He wouldn't trade that time for anything. "It was really a humbling experience seeing a great waterman like that…He was like an ambassador for Waimea Bay at the time. He was a really fun guy to be with, and I learned a lot from him, working with him over the years. He taught me a lot of stuff about the Bay, especially when it's big—the areas to come in, where to be, where not to be, the safe zones. I was just picking his brain everyday I worked with him. When I first came, he taught me all about the river. When the river breaks open, all hell breaks loose."

The river that flows through Waimea Valley usually dead-ends into a big gully, separated from the ocean by large strip of beach. Normally, the river is very calm and only flows across the beach when the waves are really big or there are heavy rains. But if these conditions combine, it becomes like a raging river, sucking people into the ocean's mountainous waves. "The first couple of times that happened, I was kind of shocked because people used to jump in it and get flushed out to sea. When it's calm and flat, it's not too bad. But when it's 8-10 feet and the shore break's breaking and people are jumping in and getting flushed out to sea, we would end up making a lot of rescues.

"One day when the river broke, I went out on the surfboard to get a couple of people that were stuck in the undertow caused by the river flow. Then, a little girl got sucked out by the river and was pushed way out to the point, and the waves were like 10-15 feet [with faces of 20-30 feet] that day." Seeing people playing near the river, the small, 14-year-old girl from California had jumped in and been swept out to sea. "She was screaming and yelling, and I was over here going for the other two kids," Terry says breathlessly. Then, out of nowhere, Eddie came charging across the beach. "He suddenly ended up in front of me. He had grabbed somebody's board off the beach and just jumped into the river, using the force of the river to blast him out there. He picked up this girl and got caught on the inside for a little while." Holding and protecting her small body, he charged through the crashing shore break and brought her to shore. He returned the little girl to her near hysterical parents who thanked him for saving their daughter. They looked at him like some kind of guardian angel. But Eddie just nodded, flashed them the shaka sign and walked away.

After working with Eddie, Terry went on to become one of O'ahu's most famous and innovative lifeguards. During the early 90's, he and Brian Keaulana helped pioneer the use of jet skis or personal watercraft (PWC) for rough ocean rescues, a practice they have helped spread around the world. Both worked with the TV show "Baywatch—Hawai'i," but unlike the contrived rescues and melodrama of that show, the action they saw was real and dangerous. During huge swells on the North Shore, Terry and Brian could be seen gunning their jet skis through monster-sized waves to rescue surfers and swimmers in trouble. They also made headlines when they began tow-in surfing, using jet skis to tow surfers into the mammoth deep-sea waves that break almost a mile from shore. These swells would have been impossible to paddle into because they are so big and move so fast. Modern technology has changed surfing dramatically, but many miss the soulful element of the sport. Before the advent of jet skis, people had to catch their own waves. After all these years, Terry can still vividly recall seeing Eddie take off on some of the biggest waves at the Bay. Purists like to say, "Eddie wouldn't tow."

Surfers made the best lifeguards because they had experienced first-hand how powerful the ocean could be. They also knew the most about its many variables, including waves, wind conditions, currents, rip tides, channels and shore breaks. "The lifeguards here are unlike lifeguards anywhere else in the world," Howe says. "Here in Hawai'i, the lifeguard service really is the surfing community. We wanted to hire surfers because we need people who understand the ocean and are not afraid of it. That's the roots of our organization, and that's what sets it apart from any other ocean service anywhere." It was even common practice to let lifeguards surf while on duty, as long as there were guards on the beach. "We don't want all our lifeguards sitting up in the tower. We'd rather have them out in the surf where the action is. We have to make excuses to the Administration because they don't want to 'pay these people to surf.' But it's a heck of a lot easier to save somebody if you're out on a surfboard already in the water."

Working year round at the Bay, Eddie and the other guards saw the mood of the place change dramatically each season. For Howe and many others, Eddie embodied Waimea Bay. Generally calm for much of the year, the Bay rose up in all its glory and power each winter, and Eddie was there to meet the challenge. "It's the contrast between the summer and winter. In the summer, it's the most placid place on the face of the Earth. You swim, you fish, you dive and you can just bask in the serenity of it…But in my mind's eye, even on the most tranquil day, I can still feel the ground shaking because I have memories of being there and the challenge of going out in surf that literally made the Earth tremble.

"Surfing big waves is all about overcoming fear," Howe says. He remembers seeing swells so big his throat constricted and he could barely breathe. "Fear paralyzes and fear causes hesitation, and fear is something that we all have…So every year, if you're going to surf big waves, you have to go through a process of mentally and physically preparing yourself. The physical part is relatively simple—you have to be fit, you swim, you run. But the mental part is a lot more challenging because you have to revisit those old fears and you have to overcome them. If you look at a guy like Eddie, here's a guy who did that year in and year out. It takes a lot of courage to do that. Some people are real fearless because they use drugs. They block that out through drugs and alcohol. I think Butch Van Artsdalen was a good example of that. The guy was fearless because he was totally wacked all the time. Gerry Lopez conquered that fear through meditation and found that inner peace and grace to stand there in the eye of the hurricane." The eye of the hurricane was the inside of the tube, the still point of a spinning vortex of water. By the mid-70's, Gerry had mastered the art of tube-riding and soon took over Butch's title of "Mr. Pipeline." For Lopez, being inside the 'green room' behind a silver curtain of water was a better high than any drug or drink could ever create. He had quit drinking and just focused on his surfing. While Butch was spinning out of control, Gerry came to embody the pure and graceful spirit of soul surfing.

The final blow to Butch's pride came when he wasn't invited to the Golden Breed Expression Session in 1970. Sponsored by Golden Breed, a new surf clothing label modeled after the successful Hang Ten company, this invitational event allowed younger, more radical surfers like Gerry Lopez and Jeff Hakman to 'express' themselves in a non-contest format. Eddie hadn't been invited either, but it didn't bother him like it did Butch because he didn't surf much at Pipeline. After finding out they had been shunned, Eddie and Butch went on a drinking spree at the Seaview Inn that lasted all day and into the night. That evening, the Golden Breed sponsors had a get-together called the Good Karma Party at Jeff's house near Pipeline. Known as "Mr. Sunset" because he dominated that break, Hakman was their official poster boy and the one who had come up with the contest invitation list. Choosing who was invited to a contest was a thankless and dangerous job in the highly competitive world of pro surfing.

At the party, the sponsors and invitees were having a mellow time, when all of a sudden, a truck full of drunken locals pulled up. In his biography *Mr. Sunset: The Jeff Hakman Story*, Phil Jarrat describes the explosive scene from Hakman's perspective. "It was a big truck and it was holding big men. Locals. In the thick of it were the Aikaus, legends on the North Shore, as much a part of the Hawaiian tradition as the ukelele players at Nanakuli, or a jug of swipe at Thanksgiving. Clyde was in the lead, Eddie behind him with other brothers. Somewhere in back was Butch Van Artsdalen and a half-dozen other drinkin' bro's from Haleiwa's Seaview Inn. They were drunk and very unhappy. They had spent the previous six hours lamenting the fact that Mr. Pipeline had not received an invitation to the Expression Session. They might just as easily have lamented the fact that Eddie Aikau had not received an invitation either, but the subject of the beef was Butch. They lamented for a few hours in the Seaview, then they bought a few cases of Primo beer and sat over in the beach park and lamented some more…Then someone had the bright idea that they should all drive up to Pipeline and share their views."

The Aikau boys and the other locals barged into the house. After a heated exchange of words, their pent-up anger exploded into a brawl. Fists flew like fireworks, and the unsuspecting victims suddenly saw stars. Wanting to protect his corporate sponsor, Jeff had quickly hustled the older man outside and hid him under an overturned boat. Outside the house in the cool night air, Hakman could hear plates crashing, bottles breaking and bodies being slammed against the walls, as general pandemonium ensued. But then the fight ended as quickly as it began. A strange silence descended over the brawlers as they looked around at the broken glass and splattered food. Eddie and the boys felt bad about crashing the party and tried to come up with a coherent explanation of why they had been so angry.

Jarratt goes on to describe what happened later that night at the Good Karma Party. "At least two hours had passed. The boozy brethren inside were swaying to the sweet sound of the old songs, arm in arm. Clyde was sorry. Eddie was sorry. Butch was passed out somewhere. [Organizer] Dick Graham had broken ribs, but was putting a brave face on it. The problems of the world had been resolved. Butch was in the Expression Session. Shoot, Butch had always been in the Expression Session! Some prick just forgot to tell him." Or so the story went. Then, an hour later, Jeff remembered that the event's sponsor was still under the boat so they went outside and brought him in for a few cocktails. A little shaken, he stirred to life, and the party resumed. Yet the event had a sobering effect on Eddie and Clyde, who felt bad about their behavior and decided to cut back on their drinking. But it didn't seem to phase Butch, who continued consuming more and more of his beloved Primo beer while surfing less and less. When the Expression Session finally took place at Pipeline, he performed poorly, and this gave him even more cause to drown his sorrows.

After working as a lifeguard for three years and saving hundreds of lives, Eddie was finally recognized by the City for his accomplishments. As one of the first guards on the North Shore, he had basically trained and supervised a whole generation of younger recruits who had joined the swelling ranks of professional lifeguards. In spite of his shoddy paperwork, he was named Lifeguard of the Year in 1971, a title conferred by a vote of his peers. Soon after, he became the subject of a column called "Our Quiet Heroes" in *The Honolulu Advertiser*. The reporter came to Waimea and spoke to Eddie in his natural element. During the interview, the long-haired, quiet lifeguard was unusually talkative, sharing rare stories of his successes, failures and frustrations.

"During the summer this is a fantastic, clean, beautiful beach," Eddie said. "In winter the surf goes 30 to 35 feet. Man, there's power there. You can count on your fingers the men who can surf over 30 feet. The currents here are unbelievable. You can be swimming by the channel over there and I mean in seconds, not minutes, be way out to sea. When you are in the ocean, you have this giant mass of water around you…It just clamps around you, all that water, and you are helpless. The inexperienced swimmers, when the riptide grabs them, try to swim to shore. They are afraid, so they swim against the current and try to get to shore. They keep swimming until they get cramps. This is very common. The best thing is to go with the current and find a way out. You can inch your way out of the currents."

Eddie then described how he started working at Waimea at a time when most people had to swim at their own risk, and many people died each year. "Nobody wanted to come here to work. They knew there were the biggest waves here. You have to have the best knowledge and skill there is to work at Waimea. Not just better than average, or superior, but the best. This is the ultimate for people getting in danger. It's not like Waikiki." Referring to the military guys who wouldn't heed his warnings, Eddie shared his frustrations. "The service guys give us the most business. There's a whole bunch of guys. They want to prove a point. Some cannot even bodysurf that good, but they still go out. Pretty soon they are yelling, 'Help! Help! Help!' I bring them in and they always say the same thing: 'I didn't know the current was that strong.'"

There was never a single drowning at Waimea Bay while Eddie was on duty. He patrolled the beach even on his days off when the waves looked dangerous. One day while driving by the lookout above the Bay, the Aikau brothers saw a crowd of people taking pictures of the big surf. "One guy climbed down on the rocks," Eddie said. "He had his right hand up in the air trying to climb up on the rock. Sure as I'm sitting here, I knew that guy was going to get pulled in. It happened in just seconds—seconds and he was down, out to sea and I lost sight of him." He ran to his car, grabbed his flippers and went running into the water. Meanwhile, Clyde called a Fire Department rescue unit. Eddie swam toward where the man had gone under. "Luckily another wave brought him almost up to me. I grabbed him by the shirt and pulled him out. He was kind of drowned." The man was pale and limp so Eddie immediately began to give him CPR. He did compressions on his chest and blew air into his lungs, and the man suddenly came around, choking and coughing. "The Fire Department took him to the hospital," he said, shaking his head. "It was so quick it was unreal."

Eddie admitted that there were times when he wondered why he risked his life to save people who didn't heed his warnings or even thank him for his help. "A lot of times when I go out, I think, why am I sacrificing myself? Those people who are being saved are helpless. I trust myself. I think I can get out of the water. But they are helpless. I can't see a helpless person go down. I just can't stay here and do nothing." Like a fireman instinctively rushing into a burning building, Eddie would throw himself into waves that looked like collapsing glass towers.

Dealing with life and death situations in the North Shore's huge waves was part of being a lifeguard. It came naturally to Eddie because he was a "passionate person," Sol says. "He was always looking out for other people, and that's why he became a lifeguard. He was just a down-to-earth good guy." But the stress took its toll, and heavy drinking was often the release. Eddie and the Aikau brothers partied hard at times, but unlike Butch, they also knew when to stop. After getting into drunken fights or when preparing for big contests, the brothers would usually quit drinking for a while to get their acts together. "They did a lot of soul searching," Peter

Cole says. "Clyde and Eddie were always in control of their drinking. But Butchie was out of control." Some mornings, people would find him passed out on the beach after staying out all night. Slowly drinking himself into oblivion, Butch put on more weight and lost much of his strength. He didn't surf as much anymore; he seemed to turn his back on the ocean.

The son of alcoholic parents, Butch had been drinking, partying and fighting since he was a kid. He seemed to be at war with himself, shadow-boxing with demons from his past. For an intense, self-destructive man like Van Artsdalen, his frenetic lifestyle was a recipe for disaster. He continued working as a lifeguard, but he was the one drowning. Eddie still surfed and partied with Butch occasionally, but he could see that his friend had lost his touch, both in the ocean and on land. Like a surfer who takes off too late on a massive wave, Butch couldn't stop himself from going over the falls. He had rescued many others, but he couldn't save himself, as he drifted toward the rocks. Eddie felt helpless as he watched his friend slowly drown in alcohol, knowing there was nothing he could do to save him.

CHAPTER 5

Life in the Graveyard

"To everything there is a season, and a time to every
purpose under the heaven: A time to be born, and a time to die
… A time to kill, and a time to heal; A time to break down, and a
time to build up; A time to weep, and a time to laugh; A time to mourn,
and a time to dance…A time to love, and a time to hate; A time of war,
and a time of peace."
—*Ecclesiastes 3:1*

As Hawaiians, Eddie and his family came from a race of people who were once warriors. But they were also farmers and fishermen, canoe builders and healers. They understood there was a time for war, but they also knew there was a time for peace. While Eddie chose peace, his younger brother chose war. After graduating from Roosevelt High School in 1966, Gerald had wondered what to do with his life. He worked odd jobs as a lifeguard and as a mechanic, and then he signed up for military service. Following in the footsteps of his father, who had served in the Army in World War II, Gerald enlisted in the Air Force. A handsome and happy teenager who had sung in the high school choir, he looked sharp in his crisp uniform. But Eddie must have wondered if his brother understood what was awaiting him in Vietnam.

The family was proud of Gerald for choosing to serve his country, but they had doubts about the war and what the U.S. was fighting for. After basic training, he went to California's Edwards Air Force Base, where he learned to be a jet mechanic. He was shipped out to Vietnam in 1968. It was the first time an Aikau had moved away from Hawai'i or been separated from the family, and they worried about him constantly. But like many patriotic American families during the late '60's, they entrusted their son's fate to Uncle Sam. Though they knew little about Vietnam, they believed in the government's lofty mission to fight Communism and restore democracy in Southeast Asia. In the meantime (and a mean time it was), President Johnson's "nasty little war" lingered on, consuming more artillery, money and men than most Americans could have ever imagined. By 1970, more and more body bags were coming home from Vietnam each month, yet there seemed to be no end or purpose in sight. The newspapers ran pictures of the soldiers from Hawai'i who had been killed, and the pages looked like a high school yearbook.

While Gerald worked on the war machines in Vietnam, Eddie worked as a lifeguard at Waimea Bay. When it was slow at the beach, he would sit in his orange tower and play his guitar, singing popular lyrics about peace and brotherhood. Songs by the Beatles and the Byrds. With his brother so far from home, Eddie tried to fill the void by bringing new friends into the family and adopting those who had no home. In fact, his full Hawaiian name was Edward Ryan Makua Hanai Aikau, and the words "*makua hanai*" can be roughly translated into "adoptive or nurturing parent," a role Eddie played throughout his life. Not only were his family members his best friends, but his friends literally became part of his extended family.

Bill Pierce was one of those taken in by Eddie. One of the first black surfers in the Islands, he met Eddie and Clyde at the beach soon after he arrived in 1969. Known as "Big Bill" to most people on the North Shore, he stands 6' 7" and has tremendous hands and feet. Though he looks imposing with his tall frame, dark eyes and scowling mustache, he is transformed into a gentle giant when he smiles. Originally from Northern California, Bill moved to Hawai'i to pursue the "ultimate dream of coming to Mecca," he says. "Everybody from all over the world hoped to come to the North Shore to challenge the big waves. I was from the San Francisco Bay area. I surfed the freezing waters of Santa Cruz—that's where I started. Basically, I got my education out here in Hawai'i. My first time at Laniakea, it was only about four or five feet, but we didn't have leashes then, and I promptly lost my board. I got caught in the current and almost drowned." Seeing how he needed guidance, Eddie befriended Bill and showed him how to handle the local surf spots. "Eddie taught me about the various breaks and currents— you know, if you're caught in the current, what to do."

In awe of Eddie's surfing abilities and fearlessness in big waves, Bill became his sidekick and went with him everywhere. Along with their love of surfing, he shared Eddie's passion for music. At parties, he used to harmonize while Eddie sang and played his guitar. When they walked into a party or down the beach, they made quite a picture: Eddie looked more like a thick shortboard next to Bill, who towered over him like a thin longboard. Because Bill didn't know many people in Hawai'i, Eddie and the Aikaus took him in as a *hanai* (adopted) brother. He lived at their house at the graveyard off and on for years, which was like being a member of a prominent clan, with its own passport of acceptance. "The Aikau family took a lot of people in," he says. "They have had a lot of *hanai* sons and daughters through the years. I was just one of many. They've helped a lot of people." Coming from a broken family, he says, "I always wanted to be in a real family atmosphere, and this was more than I expected. It was fantastic. I learned so much about life and simplicity...People try to make it seem like life is so complicated. But that's one of the great things about the Hawaiian style of living—it's really simple, and it's genuine."

With all the people staying at the Aikau compound, the graveyard resembled a shelter for surfers, musicians and Hawaiians who needed a place to stay. But Pops didn't tolerate laziness, and everyone living on the compound had to pull their own weight. If he thought you were insincere or selfish, he would suggest that you "*hele* on down the road" or get lost. "That's the one thing about the Aikaus: they could tell if you are artificial or 'junk,'" Bill says. "But if you are giving of yourself and have a decent heart, they are going to take you in, and that's what happened with me and the others." Their *'ohana* (family) was based on love not blood.

Though Bill was considered part of the Aikau family, some locals still regarded blacks or *popolos* as outsiders. Sensitive to racial issues and his own dark skin color, Eddie decided to show everyone that he loved Bill like a brother. During one luau, he welcomed Bill into the family in a way that would have caused a major scene on the mainland at that time. "I remember one time we were at a big party—sure, we had a few beers," Bill says. "Anyone that you felt really good aloha for, you kissed them. And in front of everybody, that's what Eddie did to me. That's a Hawaiian tradition, and I really felt special—that was my bruddah." Touching their foreheads and noses together, Eddie showed Bill the true meaning of aloha. In Hawaiian, *alo* is face and *ha* is breath, and in Polynesian culture to touch faces and share a breath with someone was to share the essence of life—aloha. This sudden display of drunken affection and ancient tradition struck Bill as an essential part of Eddie's personality. It's what the Hawaiians call *lokomaika'i* or good-heartedness.

Bill enjoyed getting to know Eddie and Clyde, who were very close but unique in their own ways. "The two of them had different personalities," Bill says. "Eddie was more quiet and humble, and Clyde was more loud and brash. But even though they were different, they were two fantastic people. And of course, the love and aloha came from Mom and Pops Aikau because they were the hub of the wheel that made the whole family go round." And their lives seemed to revolve around having parties. When Gerald or one of their adopted sons was given leave to come home from Vietnam for a brief visit, the family would celebrate. Brother Sol never missed these parties. "Anytime, they had R&R, we would party down at the graveyard for a couple of weeks," Sol says. "And then, the next guy would come home, and we'd do it all over again." During these wild parties, the young soldiers would drink and sing, happy to be home and alive. But sometimes they would wonder what they were fighting for and talk story about how they had lost friends in 'Nam, adding a somber tone to the celebrations.

In contrast to the chaos Gerry faced in Vietnam, the other Aikau boys led a fairly peaceful existence back home, punctuated by frequent wild nights of partying. Subscribing to the popular credo "Make love not war," they threw big parties, played music, chased women and drank a great deal—probably in reaction against the war and the radical changes they saw happening all around them. Hawai'i didn't suffer from the racial division that was causing riots on the mainland, where major cities had literally been burning with racial tension. But a number of anti-war demonstrations and student protests began to erupt in Honolulu at the university. For Eddie and many young people at the time, going to parties and singing songs of peace felt like a form of protest, a way to celebrate life in the face of increasing violence at home and abroad. "Those were heavy, party times," Bill recalls. "You know, the whole counter-culture time."

For many surfers, smoking dope and experimenting with LSD became a hip way "to tune in and drop out." They rejected the conservative customs and rules they had grown up with and embraced the new era of free love and psychedelic drugs. But the surf world was divided, and some rejected the drug scene. On one end of the spectrum, there were surfers like Fred Hemmings, who took pride in his conservatism. "When mainstream surfing was in bloom with long hair, Nehru jackets, Cheech and Chong lingo, marijuana, acid and all the other psychedelic drugs, I was still in my Topsiders, jeans and T-shirt," Fred says. "I wasn't marching to the beat of the surfing drums at the time. The song should have been, 'Momma, don't let your sons grow up to be surfers." On the other end, surfers like Jeff Hakman dove into the drug scene and didn't emerge from it for decades. To avoid the draft, Jeff attended a local community college on Maui, where he partied and smoked copious amounts of dope. Later, he began dealing marijuana and smuggling hashish across the Mexican border in hollowed-out surfboards. He and his buddies started doing LSD and would wander around the beach for hours or trip at home listening to Hendrix. He then moved on to heroin and soon became hooked. He would wrestle with a chronic addiction for the next twenty years before finally coming clean.

Eddie's brother Sol also got sucked into the growing drug scene, smoking and dealing marijuana and other drugs. (Years later, he was arrested and sent to prison in California.) But the rest of the Aikau brothers weren't as conservative as Fred or as radical as Jeff. They drank heavily but didn't do drugs. In fact, they often clashed with those who did—like when they brawled with Jeff Hakman and the other 'psychedelic surfers' at the Good Karma Party. Eddie and his boys believed in the old school of 'wine, women and song,' whereas Jeff and his gang embraced the new creed of 'sex, drugs and rock 'n roll.'

As much as Eddie enjoyed the carefree life of a bachelor, he also wanted to settle down and find a wife. While Clyde and most other surfers in their twenties were actively avoiding marriage, Eddie was looking for stability in his life and hoping to start a family of his own. Handsome and strong, he had no trouble finding interested women. When he would play his guitar at luaus and sing romantic Hawaiian songs, the party girls would converge on the shy, quiet surfer. But Eddie had trouble finding the kind of woman he wanted, someone of substance. Then, one day in 1971, his friend Bill Kapuni asked Eddie if he wanted to meet two *haole* girls who were flying out from Seattle on vacation, one of whom was a distant cousin. Not knowing what to expect, Eddie decided to join Bill in welcoming his friends. As they walked out to the runway, Eddie saw Linda Crosswhite emerge from the plane, and something told him she was 'the one.' Just as many *haoles* found local and Asian women to be exotic, Eddie was instantly attracted to this smiling *haole* woman from the mainland.

A fun-loving, 20-year-old brunette who had grown up in Washington, Linda had been working at a credit bureau there when her roommate Kathy Rickenbacker invited her to come to Hawai'i to visit family. Restless and eager to escape Seattle's cold, rainy weather, she jumped at the chance.

"I actually met Eddie the day I arrived here," Linda remembers. "I can still remember getting off the plane and walking down the ramp and smelling the flowers. It was so beautiful. It was so unbelievable to get off in a place that was so totally different." They greeted the girls with leis, and Eddie and Linda immediately hit it off. "I don't know if it was love at first sight or lust at first sight," she says with a laugh, but there was definitely an attraction. The boys took the women to the graveyard and introduced them to the whole Aikau *ohana*. Being the suave bachelor, Clyde quickly stepped in to be Kathy's escort. Seeing how well the four of them got along, Willy just smiled and stepped aside as the Aikau boys turned on their charm.

Eddie drove Linda and Kathy around O'ahu, showing them the Island while Clyde pointed out natural landmarks such as: Diamond Head, which looked like a timeless sphinx watching over Waikiki; the whale-shaped ridge of Koko Head overlooking the ocean; the steep, jagged cliffs of the Ko'olau Mountains, where Kamehameha had driven thousands of natives to their deaths in his drive to conquer the Islands; the wet, green landscape of the Windward side and the dry, brown landscape of the Lee-ward side; the blue waters of Waimea Bay and the cascading waterfalls in the valley behind; the sacred birthing stones of Kukaniloko in the central valley's lush plateau where children of *ali'i* were born; and the long, arrow-shaped strip of desolate land called Ka'ena Point on the western frontier, where in Hawaiian lore souls departed from this world to the next. Inspired by Linda's wonder and excitement, Eddie began to see the Island through her eyes and rediscovered the mystery and diverse beauty of Hawai'i.

Seeing how smitten Eddie was, Pops offered to have a party in honor of Linda and Kathy. "We had a really fun time," Linda says. "It wasn't a typical vacation. They had a big luau and did the whole thing from scratch; you know, they dug the *imu* pit and buried the pig." Along with the barbe-cued pork, there was a strange variety of local foods like *poi* (pounded taro roots) and *poki* (raw fish with seaweed). The girls were also treated to the sweet sounds of Hawaiian music with its high-pitched ukuleles and uniquely tuned slack-key guitars. Linda and Kathy got to know the family and were impressed by the Aikau's generosity, especially considering their poor background. Kathy was surprised by everything she saw, from the huge cockroaches running around the houses and make-shift shacks at the compound to the endless stream of people coming through the graveyard for parties. "It was my first experience in another culture, and I would trip over the cultural differences," Kathy says. Instead of leaving her shoes at the door, she would wear them in the house. Or she would start to throw away leftover food that the family had planned on saving for their oldest brother Freddie, who often ate alone. Nothing was thrown away. "You became aware of the poverty the family grew up with."

Kathy and Linda were also struck by how popular the Aikaus were. Almost everyone they met either talked about their previous parties or the boys' recent surfing feats. "Parties were just an ongoing way of life there, people always over and singing. It was shocking and different for me," Kathy remembers. To get away from the crowds, Clyde and Eddie took the girls inside the main house to show off their surfing accomplishments. "I remember walking in, and on this side of the wall were all these trophies. That whole world of surfing was completely foreign to me. They explained to us that these were trophies from the Duke Kahanamoku Contest, which was like winning an Oscar in Hollywood. We were duly impressed." The Aikau brothers had become local celebrities. Pictures of them surfing big blue waves hung on the walls, and their big boards rested in the rafters above like museum pieces. The girls were impressed with Eddie and Clyde's passion for surfing, music and Hawaiian culture. They also enjoyed being objects of the boys' attention and affection. Each evening the couples would wander off by into the darkness and get to know each other better. By the end of the trip, Kathy admits, "Both Linda and I had crushes on the Aikau brothers."

When their two week vacation came to a close, Linda and Kathy reluctantly boarded the plane to go back home. Eddie promised to stay in touch, but Linda wondered when they would see each other again. Back in chilly Seattle, she found herself thinking about Eddie and Hawai'i, missing their warmth. But these romantic thoughts went against her practical nature and all her previous plans. "She had this whole life planned," Kathy says, "and that included marrying her childhood sweetheart and living in one of these little brick homes in Seattle's Seward Park Way. She was one of those people who had everything planned out. Before we left on that first trip, we had joked that *I* might be the one that ended up in a grass shack with a Hawaiian." But fate had a different plan. Kathy began talking about returning to Hawai'i to live. Having tasted the sweet, tropical lifestyle of the

Islands, Linda also longed to return. Her strong feelings for Eddie overcame her practical doubts about their cultural differences, but she sometimes wondered if she was falling in love with him or the prospect of living in Hawai'i.

After several months of intermittent phone calls and letters, Linda made a decision that would change her life: she was going to move to Hawai'i with Kathy. What did they have to lose? It was one of the most beautiful places in the world. After talking so much about the upcoming move, they also recruited two other girlfriends to join them. Linda broke up with her old boyfriend and put all her previous domestic plans on hold—it was time to try something exotic and new. "So we ended up selling everything we had and moving out to Hawai'i," Linda says. "Eddie picked us up, and we actually stayed with the Aikaus, and the boys later found us a place to stay in Mokule'ia [on the North Shore] by the airfields. We lived in a place called Owen's Field, and it was named after a cop who used to live there so it was safe. It was the neatest place." Nestled between the glassy, blue ocean in front and the serrated, green cliffs behind, the girls had the best of both worlds. "It looked like a mountain cabin, but it was near the water. It was like we were up in the mountains, but you could hear the ocean." Each girl had her own corner of the room, and they shared everything at first. But gradually, the other girls found local boyfriends, and they began spending more time apart. Kathy was usually with Clyde, and Linda was always with Eddie.

"Ryan and I just got closer and closer," Linda remembers. At this time, Eddie's family still called him by his middle name Ryan so that's what Linda called him too. But Pops insisted that the family start referring to him as Eddie because that's how the public knew him. To Linda, he seemed to have two sides to his personality: in public, he was Eddie, the famous big-wave rider and lifeguard who loved to sing and perform at parties; but in private, he was just Ryan, the introspective, local boy who didn't talk much unless he had a few beers. "Eddie was not someone who had an easy time communicating," Kathy remembers. "In retrospect, I think there was a depth to Eddie that wasn't immediately perceivable because he was so shy and quiet." But there was something in his dark, hooded eyes that conveyed a sense of mystery, power and tenderness. Those eyes won Linda's heart.

Linda was practically living with Eddie and the Aikaus at the graveyard and had become part of the family. Though many local aunties would have liked to pair him up with a girl from the Islands, they realized Eddie was hooked on this *haole* girl. But when Kathy and her roomates said they were leaving Hawai'i to return to the mainland, Linda was in a quandary about whether to stay with Eddie or go with her friends. Eddie knew what he had to do. "He said he didn't want me to go and he was ready to get married," Linda remembers. When he asked if she would marry him, "It kind of took me by surprise. I was only 21, and I didn't expect it." Flattered and flustered at the same time, she said Yes and was quickly swept up in wedding plans. "It was kind of a whirlwind. It was probably the most impulsive thing I've done in my whole life," Linda laughs. "It was a whirlwind for the family too because here I moved back over in September, and we're getting married the next May." Eddie was eager to tie the knot so they could settle down and start having children. "He was actually in the mood to get married. I don't know if he may have said that to his brothers or not. But now that I am older and wiser, I have come to realize that when men are ready to get married, they might not say anything about it, but their mind is made up...Eddie was still partying and going out, but deep down, I think he was ready. I think I just happened to be in the right place at the right time. It just seemed right."

When Eddie and Linda first began seeing each other, their relationship was overshadowed by the conflict in Vietnam. While one brother fell in love, the other was off fighting in a war that already seemed lost. After volunteering for another tour of duty, Gerald was still in 'Nam the first time Linda came to Hawai'i on vacation. "He re-upped so he could get out early because if he did another tour in Vietnam, then he would be able to get out of the Air Force early, and that's what he did," Linda explains. By the time she returned to Hawai'i later that year, he had just come back from the war. She had heard all about him from Eddie and looked forward to meeting him. But when they met, he seemed different than she had imagined, especially after a few drinks. He would be fine for most of the day, but as he started drinking at night, everything changed. "Gerry had a real upbeat personality, but he did have a real dark side after the war. Gerry shouldn't have drank at all because when he did, it all came up to the surface." Still struggling with what he had seen in the war, he needed someone to confide his troubles to, someone to share his burden. Someone like Kathy.

Soon after Gerald's return, he and Kathy became friends. When she learned that Clyde already had another girlfriend, she broke up with him.

"Talk about being a playboy, that was Clyde!" Linda laughs. That's when Kathy started dating Gerald. This sudden shift created quite a family scandal at first, but the brothers worked it out. Besides the fact that Clyde was dating someone else, he could see that Gerald had really fallen for Kathy. The two came to be pretty close in a short time. She was attracted to him because he was more intellectual and worldly than the other brothers. "He'd been away in the Air Force, and it gave him some exposure to the rest of the world," Kathy says. "I had a sense that he went away to the service because at the time he didn't know what else to do. He had left school, and he felt like he should be doing something. But then he went to war, and it was more than he bargained for. He didn't like to talk about it a lot. He didn't seem to come back proud of that experience. He definitely wanted to put it behind him…Gerry's being in the Air Force was a source of pride for the family, but it wasn't something he was proud of."

Though Linda came from a completely different culture, she was embraced by the Aikau clan. Just as Big Bill Pierce had been welcomed into their extended *ohana*, they took her in as one of their own. Yet she wondered if her family back in Seattle would be as accepting of her dark-skinned, Hawaiian fiance. After all, interracial marriages were taboo on the mainland. "My parents have always raised us to be fairly liberal in that respect, but when your family is actually faced with you marrying someone of a different race, you really find out how they feel." They sounded supportive on the phone, but she worried how they would get along with the Aikaus. After months of planning, Linda's parents finally flew in for the wedding. She says they were more shocked by where the Aikaus lived than what they looked like. When her father and his second wife Karen arrived at the compound, Linda recalls an awkward moment when they first saw all the tombstones in the yard. "I remember driving down into the graveyard, and my stepmother goes, 'This is where they live, in the graveyard?' And I said, 'Yeah, and this is where we're having our reception.' That was the last word I ever heard about the graveyard," Linda says with a chuckle. "I have to admit that my family handled it really well."

Linda's father Al Crosswhite was a short, stocky man who ran his own construction company in Washington State. He and Pops hit it off right away. Though they came from very different backgrounds, both were hardworking family men who liked drinking and swapping stories about their past. Momma Aikau got along well with Al's wife Karen, but she worried that Linda's mother Bernice would feel unwelcome. The Aikaus felt awkward having the two women there at the same time, but Linda assured them that there was no animosity between her mom and stepmother, who were neighbors in Washington. Besides, everyone was united in the common cause of getting the graveyard ready for the wedding reception. The Aikaus built a stage with a sound system and set up a long banquet table under a huge tent in the yard.

When the day finally arrived, Eddie and Linda were married at Blessed Sacrament around the corner. It was a big wedding, and the small Catholic Church was packed. Linda had asked Kathy to be the maid of honor, and she invited Myra to be one of three bridesmaids, along with her sister Connie and Clyde's girlfriend Susan. Eddie asked Clyde to be the best man, and Sol, Gerald and Freddie were the other groomsmen. Escorted by her father, Linda walked down the aisle, wearing a traditional, white wedding gown, with sheer sleeves and a long veil laced with flowers. Eddie waited nervously at the altar, dressed in Hawaiian style, wearing white pants, a white shirt, a red sash around his waist and a maile lei around his neck. After the vows and rings were exchanged, the local priest pronounced them man and wife. When the ceremony was over, the wedding party smiled patiently as they lined up at the altar for pictures. The bridesmaids wore white blouses with ankle-length, floral skirts and *pikake* flowers in their hair. The Aikau boys looked dapper in their formal white tuxedo jackets and black pants. In the photos, Freddie sports a mustache just like Pop's, and Clyde and Gerry both have long, wavy hair that was popular at the time. Eddie has on the watch Linda gave him, and she is wearing the necklace he had given her. On their fingers, they wear traditional Hawaiian wedding bands, carved gold rings with their names inscribed on the surface. In another photo, the smiling newlyweds are being driven back to the graveyard in a friend's white Chevy coupe sedan with surf racks on the top. The car had two boards on its racks, yet oddly one was broken.

Back at the graveyard, close friends helped prepare the giant luau that awaited them. Several pigs had been cooking in the underground *imu* (oven) since the night before, and Pops directed a crew of his sons and friends to dig it out. And when all the rocks, banana leaves and ashes had been removed, the crowd cheered at the sight of the perfectly cooked, succulent pigs. Hundreds of guests began pouring into the graveyard, wearing everything from business suits to bathing suits. Uncomfortable in their formal clothes, Pops, Freddie and Sol had changed into jeans and T-shirts as they helped lay out the food. The crowd began eating the sumptuous feast and consuming plenty of Primo beer, along with the lethal concoction of swipe going around. Pops joked that he made the swipe in the same crocks that were used for the bones in the temple, warning the crowd, "Don't drink from the bottom of the crock!"

Family members and friends made a series of toasts to the bride and groom who were seated at the center of the long banquet table, filled with food, drinks and flowers. They were young, happy and in love, and all those gathered around them that night knew it. Clyde went up to make a toast, his face glowing with sweat, alcohol and emotion. With tears in his eyes and a stutter in his voice, Clyde said that Eddie was not only his brother but his best friend. He then welcomed Linda as a sister and said that her family was now part of their own. Though she had come between him and his best friend, Clyde gave all of his aloha to the young couple. After a series of toasts, friends and family members began playing Hawaiian music. Local legends like Peter Moon of the popular group Sunday Manoa performed romantic songs as the drunken crowd swayed and sang along through the warm, humid night. Each of the Aikaus took turns singing on stage. Mom and Pops did a song together, and Myra played the ukulele. Gerald joined Eddie and Clyde for another song. Then, Eddie performed an old favorite for his new bride. As he sang to Linda and strummed his guitar, he seemed genuinely happy and at peace with the world.

Linda's parents never forgot their stay at the Aikau compound. "My stepmom doesn't drink much, but it was her first taste of swipe, and she was so happy!" Linda laughs. "They had such a good time, and the Aikaus made them feel right at home and part of the family. It was a real different experience for them. They never showed any signs to me that I was not making the right decision, which made me feel really good. I think they were real impressed with the family and how close they were, despite the fact that they were wild and crazy and partied a lot. They knew I was going to be well taken care of and that I was going to be safe. My dad was just so happy I was doing something different. He always wanted us to be adventurous and go places and do things. I guess he didn't really expect it from me. He was really happy when it all came together." Both families would become very close over the years, especially Pops and Linda's father. In fact, years later when

Momma Aikau passed on, Pops moved to Alaska and worked with Al Crosswhite doing construction. "My dad's an only child," Linda says, "and he told me that Pops was as close to a brother as he was ever going to get."

After a brief honeymoon in Waikiki, Eddie and Linda stayed at the graveyard for a few months, with the hopes of finding a place on the North Shore. Living with the Aikaus, she came to appreciate their gruff yet loving ways. "It was amazing and just a totally different lifestyle. They were such a great family, not that they didn't have their arguments and their fights. It was just so amazing to be with a family whose idea of a good time was to be together at home and sing and play music. The boys would love to hear their mother sing. You just didn't see that on the mainland, and I loved it. It was wonderful." Parties seemed to be a way of life for Eddie's family. "And yeah, they drank too much. That's kind of a local thing. I think over the years local families, just like everyone, have toned down their drinking a lot."

Needing a little space of their own and time away from the family's rowdy lifestyle, Eddie and Linda moved into an apartment near Waimea Bay to be closer to his work. The newlyweds tried to settle into the quiet harmony of married life, but Eddie didn't like living on that part of the North Shore because there were so many transient surfers and beach bums there. Eddie had planned to spend time alone with his new bride, but he soon found another apartment near Clyde's place outside of Hale'iwa, where he felt more at home. It might have seemed strange for them to live right next door to Eddie's brother, but Linda had grown accustomed to how close the family was. She knew Clyde was Eddie's best friend and tried not to come between them.

Linda was a long way from her family and friends in Seattle. "When you move to Hawai'i, you kind of have to give up your preconceived notions of how life should be," she says. Her life at this point centered around Eddie, his family and his love for the ocean. "I spent a lot of time at the beach with him. The water was a stress-release for him. It was soothing for him to be out there in the ocean, and it kept him on an even keel. There was always the stress of his job as a lifeguard. He was always trying to improve himself, like taking CPR classes. He was also trying to become a professional surfer." Needing independence and an extra income, Linda began working in Honolulu as an agent at the Pacific Insurance Company. Their careers were a study in contrasts. Her routine consisted of a driving to a 9 to 5 job in an office building downtown and processing insurance claims all day. Meanwhile, Eddie's days consisted of lifeguarding on the North Shore and working at one of the most unpredictable beaches in the world. As the fledgling pro circuit evolved, he also began competing in distant surfing events. These international contests would eventually take Eddie far away from his wife and home.

CHAPTER 6

Racial Pride and Prejudice

"It's been so long traveling on the road
Trying to find a place in the world. Now I know, now I see
My home is my heart.
I'll be home, I know now I'll never roam again
As long as I remember I am Hawaiian."
– from Sunday Manoa's song "I Am Hawaiian."

With surfing's growing popularity around the world and its sexy image in the media, large corporations began throwing money at the sport's organizers. The biggest international contributors were alcohol and cigarette companies, like Smirnoff and Gunston. These corporate giants would market their products at the surf contests, which often turned into huge beach parties. In 1971, in front of thousands of spectators at Sunset Beach, Eddie placed fourth in the prestigious new Smirnoff Pro-Am Contest. Standing on the stage, he watched as his friend Billy Hamilton accepted first prize and was showered in champagne. Three of the four finalists hailed from Hawai'i, including Billy, Jeff Hakman and Eddie. They all won free round-trip tickets to Durban, South Africa for the newly formed Gunston 500 Contest, sponsored by the international cigarette company. They were also given a free surf safari across the country, thanks to the South African Surfing Association, who organized the event. But not long after the invitations went out, racial problems arose for Eddie due to his dark skin color.

Because South Africa was still embroiled in apartheid, it was uncertain whether he would be able to stay in the same accommodations as Billy and Jeff or even compete at the whites-only beach. This came as a rude awakening for the Aikaus and many other Hawaiian surfers who were upset that one of their own would be treated so poorly. The anti-apartheid movement had just begun building momentum around the world, and many people thought the Hawaiian contingent should boycott the contest. But to young surfers consumed with wanderlust, a free trip to South Africa was just too good to miss. Apolitical animals by nature, Billy and Jeff knew about the government's racist policies, but they didn't think apartheid was their problem—like many young surfers, they just wanted to surf, travel and have a good time.

Jeff Hakman and Billy Hamilton were two of the hottest surfers of the time, and they had appeared in surf magazines and movies across the globe. They had sponsors who gave them all the surfboards and clothing they needed. As surfing celebrities, they were wined and dined and treated like rock stars everywhere they traveled. The two *haole* surfers didn't think much about Eddie's situation—he could fend for himself. Besides, after the Aikau boys and their band of locals had crashed Jeff's "Good Karma" party and trashed his house, they still weren't on the best terms at that point. All had been forgiven, but there was still tension between them. Jeff and Billy had fantasized about surfing at Jeffrey's Bay, which they had seen in Bruce Brown's epic surf film *Endless Summer*, and they couldn't wait to experience the legendary South African break. They flew over to Johannesburg and Capetown a week before Eddie, who was still trying to iron out his travel plans and make sure it was safe to travel there.

"So Billy and I went earlier," Jeff remembers, "and we flew into Joburg, and they picked us up and took us into Durban. Then, we went all around the country with these Gunston guys. It was first-class, and they paid for everything." As soon as the *haole* surfers arrived, representatives of the Gunston Cigarette Company and their co-sponsor Seven Seas Liquor took them on a surf safari that turned out to be more like an extended party. Sitting in the back of their chauffeured car, they drank, smoked and got high on "Durban poison," a potent strain of local weed, partying in each town they visited. A few of the country's young professional surfers joined them on their journey and took them on epic surf sessions at spots like Jeffrey's Bay. One skinny kid named Shaun Tomson, whose father Ernie promoted South African surfing and helped organize the tour, stood out as a real ripper in the cold, shark-infested waves. At the end of their whirlwind tour of South Africa, Jeff and Billy came back to Durban for the contest and stayed at the ritzy Malibu Hotel. They were given rooms overlooking the Bay of Plenty, with a view of the best surf spots and the whites-only beaches.

When Eddie flew in for the contest, he couldn't stay at the same hotel as his fellow surfers from Hawai'i. That's when things got ugly. In Jeff's version of the story, he blames the system of apartheid for coming between them. "So Billy and I are there [at the Malibu Hotel], and then two or three days later, Eddie came in. And we just went, 'Okay, I guess you're staying with us, just hop in the hotel.' But they wouldn't let him stay there. They basically went, 'You're black so you're not allowed to stay here.' And Eddie, being the *ali'i* deal in Hawai'i, couldn't believe it. This was something he had never experienced before…In hindsight, maybe we should have done something in protest, but we didn't really know what to do. But I know it really hurt Eddie. He tried hard to hold it in, but, boy, was he blown away. He was a local Hawaiian boy, and he had never been exposed to that kind of stuff."

It's not entirely clear whether Eddie was not allowed to stay at the Malibu Hotel, as Jeff contends, or if he just felt unwelcome there. "My impression was that he wasn't comfortable staying in the hotel where Jeff and Billy were staying," Shaun Tomson recalls. "So my dad invited him to come stay at the Eden Rock, where we were." Though he was grateful to the Tomsons for looking after him, Eddie still felt isolated. Traveling alone for the first time, the 26-year-old Hawaiian had just flown halfway around the world to a racist country where blacks were treated like second-class citizens. To make matters worse, contest officials had to make special arrangements for Eddie to compete at the whites-only beach where the contest was held. This created an embarrassing PR problem for the South African Surfing Association (SASA). In Jeff's biography *Mr. Sunset*, Phil Jarratt writes, "Eddie was an Aikau, for Christ's sake! In Hawai'i, the Aikaus were almost like royalty! Eddie kept his own counsel, but he nursed a deep and bitter hurt. The Durban press got hold of the story and raised the question: would this treatment of Aikau lead to a boycott of the Gunston by the Hawaiian team? On that score the organizers need not have worried." Jeff and Billy had come there to compete, and nothing was going to stop them.

When the local newspapers and media learned of Eddie's situation, they ran with the story. One liberal publication called the *Drum* interviewed him at length, and he was surprisingly candid about his feelings. When they informed him that local black surfers were not allowed to surf in the contest, he said, "Man, that's heavy, it's real heavy." He went on to admit, "You know, I fear to walk in the streets. I see people looking at me. Sometimes, they gossip about me being a surfer, and that makes me feel good. Then, there are those people who see me and sneer at me. I know some people think they are superior. I get scared, man, to think that someone is going to scream at me because I am walking on the wrong side of the street because it is for whites only. I am looking forward to going home. Not all the Whites have been like that. Amongst friends, I feel relaxed. But I can sense the racial discrimination. There is this color problem all over the world. But here in South Africa, man, it is really heavy."

Rattled by the racism and still jet-lagged from his 30-hour flight, Eddie didn't perform well in the contest and was beaten by Jeff on the first day. To rub salt into the wound, Hakman went on to win the event. Disappointed and bitter, Eddie wanted to fly home immediately to be with his wife and family, but his excursion fare required that he stay in the country for ten more days. He only knew two other people there, Jeff and Billy, and they had left him on his own. "My Hawaiian team mates abandoned me," Eddie would later tell a reporter when he returned to Hawai'i. In an angry interview with the *Honolulu Star-Bulletin*, he said, "I was all on my own there. During the day, nobody from home ever asked, 'Where are you going? Is somebody taking you around?' I was going against my own people. They forgot me, man."

Both Jeff and Billy were relatively clueless when it came to how serious the problem of apartheid was or what effect it would have on Eddie. In a *Surfer* article published later that year, Billy Hamilton wrote that the trip had been a success and that the racial tension in South Africa wasn't so bad. "Generally, the situation among the dark-skinned people is accepted; they are content with their working positions and the roles they play in the structure of society along with their European counterparts." Sounding like an old Southern or Hawaiian plantation owner, Hamilton's comments showed how unaware he and many other Americans were to divisive racial issues at the time. But he did acknowledge that "the chances of a black man reaching a higher state of equality in that country are highly remote." He also wrote that with his "dark brown Hawaiian tan and characteristic Island features," Eddie was the "target of a few tossed glances from the predominately white gathering...There were no unusual repercussions, but I imagine to be in Aikau's shoes was a trying experience, one that took a good deal of courage."

Thirty years later, Jeff still has mixed feelings about the whole episode. "I felt that it was unjust that he lobbed the blame on Billy and me. I don't know what we were supposed to do about it. We were little 21-year-old kids who were like, 'Wow, we get to see where Jeffrey's Bay is!' But I don't think he ever really got over it. I really wanted to sit down with Eddie and talk to him about it. I felt guilty about it, and I know he was carrying the resentment around with him. We probably should have sat down and had a few beers and talked about it." But the damage had already been done, and it remained a source of tension between them. In spite of his poor contest results and feelings of isolation, Eddie's luck changed dramatically when he met Lynne and Darryl Holmes, an Australian couple who basically adopted him as one of their own.

Living in Durban, the Holmes family operated one of the largest surfboard manufacturing companies in South Africa. When they read about Eddie's plight in the papers, they immediately contacted local contest officials to see what they could do to help. Sensitive to Australia's own strained racial relations with its Aboriginal people, Lynne had first seen Eddie at a local restaurant across from the beach. She observed how a crowd of local kids had gathered around him and were staring at him like an alien creature. "He was sitting at this table by himself. The kids were asking him questions, and he was answering them in pidgin. They were listening to this black person speak with such a different accent. And here he was intermingling with all these white people and competing against them in a contest. It just struck me as being so incredibly lonely," Lynne recalls. "So I spoke to Shaun Tomson's father Ernie and I said, 'There's something not right about this. Let's get together and have a party or a 'zoo.' We organized one there and then. We had hundreds of people at the barbecue, and I was only interested in seeing Eddie come walking through that door."

A talented surfer with tan skin and short, brown hair, Lynne is still surfing in her fifties. She has bright eyes and a spunky smile, and they light up when she speaks about Eddie. Having surfed with her father and then her husband, Lynne had always reserved a special place in her heart for Hawai'i and its people because surfing was their gift to the world. "I've had an interest in Hawai'i since I was a tiny tot," so when she met Eddie, she says it felt like destiny. When Eddie finally arrived at the party with his guitar, he and Lynne hit it off right away. She encouraged him to play his guitar, and that helped him relax and unwind. After performing, he started talking with

Lynne, and the two didn't stop for hours. "That night we just sat in the kitchen and talked all night long, talking about his whole family… Everybody started leaving around two or three a.m., and throughout the whole conversation, he covered his whole family. He could describe his family to you, and you knew exactly who they were." When it was time to go, they hugged and agreed to get together the next day.

Even after partying all night, Eddie still got up early to go surfing. With his dark skin color, he didn't know where he was allowed to go; so he would surf at dawn and dusk with Shaun Tomson. When the Holmes family went to pick him up at his hotel the next day, they found him passed out in his bed, still wearing his full wetsuit! The room was hot, and steam was rising from his wetsuit. Seeing how lonely he seemed at the hotel, they insisted he stay with them at their home. Darryl, Lynne and their two daughters, Tracey, 6, and Jodi, 2, quickly bonded with Eddie, drawn to his gentle spirit and easy-going personality. They also liked the fact that he could sing and play guitar. Knowing that Eddie had missed out on Jeff and Billy's surf safari around the country, Lynne made travel plans for Eddie and her family. "He came over to our place, and we quickly arranged a trip to Jeffrey's Bay. It's one helluva long way, about 600 miles. As we drove through the amazing African countryside, we'd stop at a certain place, and they would know who he was. They had seen him in the papers. He was blown away. He caused quite a bit of interest but none of it was malicious. We'd get maybe a couple of strange looks so we'd say, 'He's over here from Hawai'i. You probably read about him in the newspapers.' And that was it." The suspicious looks would soon turn to nods and smiles when they realized he was Hawaiian—the Islands had that kind of exotic appeal.

Driving down the long winding coastal roads to Jeffrey's Bay in their VW Kombi, the family had a lot of time to talk and get to know Eddie. He shared his frustrations about being left behind by Jeff and Billy. "They basically disowned him," Lynne says. "It was not the South Africans, it was not apartheid, it was his own people" who abandoned him. But the farther they drove away from Durban, the better he started to feel. When they finally reached their destination, it looked like they had arrived in a surfing Shangrila. Just like the climactic scene in the classic film *Endless Summer*, they stared out at a corduroy ocean lined with long, perfect swells all the way to the horizon. "We were very lucky: we scored great waves at Jeffrey's Bay." Watching Eddie suddenly come alive in the surf, Lynne was impressed by how different he seemed in the ocean. "I was amazed at how slow he was on land. And then seeing him in the water, he was like a totally different person. He had so much speed. It was such a contrast from this land person to this sea person."

"We surfed our guts out," Eddie would say later in the newspaper interview. He loved to talk about surfing and partying with the Holmes family, who had "saved" him during that trip. "People invited us to dinner. I took along a guitar—and it was a big success. I showed them slack key and played the kind of songs we sing here." *Ki ho'alu* (slack key) music literally means to "loosen the key" on the strings of a guitar so it has a distinct tuning and more mellow sound. One of Hawai'i's most popular musical innovations, along with the ukulele, slack key dates back to the *paniolos* (cowboys) who worked on Big Island ranches and pioneered their own form of Island country music. For generations, slack key music was passed from master to student like a rare art form. One bizarre ritual involved a teacher telling his student to bite the end of the guitar while he played the song so the music would flow into his soul. Eddie had learned slack key from some of the best musicians in the Islands, including Peter Moon and the Ka'apana brothers, Ledward and Nedward. Whenever he played his guitar, he played from the heart, and the music transported his listeners back to old Hawai'i. Driving in their van or camping under the stars, Lynne and her family loved listening to him play his guitar and sing Hawaiian songs.

During their road trip, Eddie was disturbed by the apartheid situation, but he didn't encounter much direct hostility. It was more like the South Africans were strangely intrigued by him because he was not quite black but certainly not white. "I tell you, I shook up whole towns." At the end of his interview with *Drum*, the reporter wrote, "Aikau said that he thought he would come back in 1974 because he was confident that there would be great changes and that surfers of all colours would be able to take part, without any fear. And like he said, he is going to be mighty pleased to be home—because there nobody worries about the colour of your skin." Eddie missed the diversity of Hawai'i, and though the Islands had their own racial tensions, he realized what a unique and special place it was. He also missed Linda and longed to return home. A world away from his wife, he was sad about missing their first wedding anniversary. Eddie sent Linda two cards, a funny one to make her laugh and a sweet one to make her cry.

At the end of his epic surf safari with the Holmes, Eddie had to fly back to Hawai'i. At the airport, he felt conflicting emotions. He was eager to see his wife and family, but he was sad to leave Lynne, Darryl and their two daughters behind. In less than two weeks, they had formed a friendship that would last a lifetime. Yet none of them knew if and when they would see each other again. After tearful goodbyes and long hugs at the boarding gate, the Holmes family stayed and watched Eddie's plane take off and fade into the distant sky. "When he left, we were absolutely devastated because we thought we'd probably never see him again. It was a devastating thing for us, especially Jodi, the youngest one. She was totally attached to him…She and Eddie were inseparable. She was so connected to him."

Only weeks after his departure, the Holmes started receiving gifts from Eddie and his family, along with invitations to visit. The Aikaus even managed to get a local politician to write up an official invitation. "We just kept getting presents from over there and they kept asking us to come to Hawai'i." Having always wanted to visit the land where surfing was born, Lynne started organizing a trip. She says the family wrote down the months of the year and put them in a hat for possible times to visit. Then, they started drawing months until they found the one they wanted. Within a year of Eddie's visit, the Holmes family boarded a plane in Johannesburg and flew around the world to Honolulu. Lynne and Darryl had decided to leave South Africa and start a new chapter of their lives in Hawai'i. Eddie and Clyde met them at the airport and took the excited yet jet-weary family back to the compound. "We went back to their house at the graveyard, and we stayed in a little grass shack, so to speak." The Aikaus had built a make-shift room, which was not the plushest or most comfortable place to stay, but it oozed aloha and local style. Though physically big and intimidating, the Aikaus embraced Darryl and Lynne's two young daughters and made them feel at home with stories, music and laughter.

Having heard all about each family member from Eddie, Lynne felt like she already knew each one individually: Momma Aikau was sweet and quiet like Eddie, both of whom loved to sing; Pops was stern yet outgoing like Clyde, and they both loved to tell stories; the only daughter in a wild brood of boys, Myra was thoughtful like her mother yet also stern like her father, making sure everyone was taken care of and carrying their load; though he was the oldest, Freddie tended to be the least assertive, deferring to Myra, and keeping his own counsel in his room; Gerald could be outgoing and fun like Clyde at times, but he could also be very quiet and solitary like

Freddie; as the comedian and black sheep of the family, Sol was the wildest, and he had a passel of kids from different women to prove it. And Big Bill was as tall and friendly as Eddie had said.

The two families bonded instantly. Lynne enjoyed getting to know Eddie's mom, Darryl and Pops hit it off, and their two girls played with Sol's small children. Like the Aikaus, Lynne says, "Surfing really is the mainstream of our life." Linda was probably a little jealous of the close relationship between Lynne and Eddie, who surfed together during the day and often had long, soulful conversations at night. Attractive and strong-willed, the two young women could have clashed, but instead they became friends. Linda understood that Eddie had found a "kindred spirit" in Lynne, and she respected their friendship. And Lynne could see that Eddie loved Linda, despite their different backgrounds and interests. Both women also shared an affection for Eddie's mom, Henrietta Aikau, the gentle matriarch of the family who treated these two *haole* women like her own daughters. "His mother really was one of those angels on earth. She was a very peaceful woman," Lynne says. "She was the sort of person who could walk up to you if you were feeling down and she would put her hand on your shoulder, and you would just get this energy from her." Both Linda and Lynne understood why Eddie loved his mom so much. And he was happy to see the three most important women in his life gathered together under the same roof: mother, wife and friend.

In classic Aikau style, the family started preparing a huge luau in honor of Lynne, Darryl, Tracey and Jodi. sounding like a sergeant in the military, Pops shouted out orders for everyone: the boys needed to mow the lawn and dig out the barbecue pit for the pig; the women needed to start preparing the countless dishes of fish lau lau, squid luau, lomilomi and poi. A mainstay of the Hawaiian diet, poi was made from pounded taro roots, and though it looked like purple glue, the Holmes family learned to like it. Pops would make the swipe and oversee the whole operation. Lynne enjoyed the process of preparing for the luau, almost as much as the party itself. "What was so fantastic was that we all took part in it. I was privileged enough to work with Pops and make the swipe, which is still a love of my life, though no one makes it like he did." He shared with her the secret ingredients and taught her how to make it: mix fresh pineapple juice and pulp, brown sugar, yeast and strawberry punch syrup in a wooden barrel and let it ferment for a while; then siphon it into a gallon jug, freeze it and serve chilled in a hollowed-out pineapple. The combination was potent, and many *haole* girls had fallen for the Aikau boys under its spell. Lynne fondly recalls the nasty job of cleaning and cooking the pig with Pops and the boys. "It was a huge job." Even though it was in their honor, Lynne loved that Pops put everyone to work. "That luau was a lot of giving from a lot of people." But she couldn't understand why they needed so much food and liquor—after all, how big could this party be?

On the day of the luau, Lynne was amazed by the steady flow of people into the graveyard all day long and into the late hours of the evening. News of the famous Aikau luaus would spread like a wild rumor over the Island, and hundreds of people would show up. And the characters! Local politicians like Mayor Frank Fasi knew that the Aikaus were one of the more popular and influential Hawaiian families on O'ahu so they would come by to mingle and schmooze with the local folks. Famous big-wave riders dropped in on the scene, including Peter Cole, Fred Van Dyke and Jose Angel, who were looked up to like movie stars in the surfing world. "Even Nadine, Duke Kahanamoku's widow, came along," Lynne says. "You know, she's part Australian. She was great." Nadine was also fond of 'dear little Eddie,' as she called him.

Everybody at the party drank a good deal. This sometimes led to heated emotions, arguments and misunderstandings, often involving race. Racism against Hawaiians had become a hot issue in the Islands, and resentment toward *haoles* was running high. When a few, drunken locals heard the Holmes were from South Africa, they questioned the guests of honor about the apartheid situation. They were still upset about Eddie's treatment over there. "We had a confrontation with people who thought we were South African," Lynne remembers. "So I looked and listened and said, 'I'm not South African. I did come from there, but I'm not from there.'" Once the locals understood that the Holmes were the ones who had helped Eddie, they apologized and gave them a drunken embrace. "Oh, sorry—no hard feelings, eh?" The locals liked the fact that they were well-known Aussie surfboard makers and international surf nomads. Their resentment now shifted toward Jeff Hakman and Billy Hamilton for abandoning Eddie. With anti-*haole* feelings still simmering beneath the surface, Jeff, Billy and other white surfers would leave the luaus early in case it boiled over. At other parties on the Island, they had seen peaceful gatherings suddenly erupt into violent arguments and fights over the smallest slight. But fights never broke out at the Aikau luaus because Pops forbade it, and his sons and their friends kept the peace. Despite the underlying racial tension, the graveyard was a safe place to be.

At the party, there seemed to be as many guests in the graveyard as stars in the sky. Hawai'i's most talented musicians stopped by to perform after finishing their gigs in Waikiki—the music would be playing all night long, and Eddie and Clyde would join in their jam sessions. Pops would be making the rounds, talking to people from every sector of society—like a politician, he had the common touch and knew how to use all of his connections. No matter how wild the parties got, the cops wouldn't shut them down because the mayor or one of their superiors might be there. Besides, they lived in a graveyard so who was going to complain? "That was a great place," family friend John Kruse remembers. "You could scream your head off, and only the dead guys were over there, and they didn't care." High on swipe, tipsy couples would sneak off into the darkness to make love on the grass between the tombstones.

With all the excessive drinking, many of the guests would pass out in the graveyard. This was a dangerous thing to do because the Aikau boys loved to play pranks on their friends, especially when they were dead drunk. Kruse remembers when a local boy named Brownie started drinking heavily at one of their parties and bragging about his girlfriend and his skiing ability. "This guy came back from Aspen, and he thought he was a hot-shot skier. He also thought he was hot-shot because his girlfriend was Jill St. John, the Playmate model. This guy gets all drunk so Eddie picks Brownie up and puts him in the wheelbarrow. The next thing, Eddie is putting him in the bone house with all them bones." Then, he and his brothers would put poi on his eyelids to seal them shut. When Brownie finally awoke and couldn't open his eyes, he panicked and thought he was dead. And when he finally managed to get his eyes open, all he could see were crocks of bones and skulls all around him. He was terrified. "About 1:00 or 2:00 in the morning, Brownie starts screaming. He realizes he's in there with all these dead bodies. Eddie is just cracking up." These pranks always brought howls of laughter from the drunken crowd.

The next morning, they would begin cleaning up the graveyard. The place looked like a battlefield with bodies passed out on the grass and inside cars. In order to soothe their raging hangovers, they would start drinking again, biting the dog that had bitten them the night before. All the lingering guests would help clean up and then start eating and drinking so the party would begin all over again for a second day. Lynne had been to some wild parties in her day, but none had this kind of aloha and intensity. "The Hawaiian spirit was never more prevalent than in that family."

Later that year when Eddie found out that Shaun Tomson and his cousin were in Hawai'i, he invited them to come to the graveyard for a party to thank him. Just as Shaun's father Ernie and the Holmes had thrown a party in South Africa for Eddie, the Aikaus were returning the favor. Like Lynne, Shaun was blown away by their hospitality. "Eddie and his family never forgot when someone did something nice for them." Shaun was only 16 at the time, and he remembers how everyone was having such a good time, drinking swipe, talking story and singing Hawaiian songs. At the end of the evening, Shaun says, "Eddie was driving us home and swerving all over the road, and then a cop pulled us over. The cop said, 'Give me your driver's license,' and I thought he was going to put us all in jail. But when he saw it was Eddie Aikau, he just said, 'Have a good night.'" Laughing about the incident, Shaun says that was the kind of clout Eddie and his family had in Hawai'i.

Even after they were over, the spirit of these luaus continued in their daily lives when the Aikaus and the Holmes would get together to eat and talk. "You'd just sit and talk story, and everything would come out," Lynne remembers. "We just covered so much stuff." Family, relationships, surfing contests, music groups, local politics, racism, war—whatever needed to be discussed. Lynne and Darryl loved the closeness of the Aikaus, along with their zest for good food, music and conversation. Tracey and Jodi enjoyed playing with Sol's kids and running around the graveyard. Although they had only planned on staying a few weeks, the Holmes lived at the graveyard for six months and became part of the family. "We stayed there from April to September, but it was like we were there for a lifetime." They wanted to make Hawai'i their permanent residence and set up a business making surfboards. Darryl was already making boards in the graveyard, but the family couldn't get visas and didn't want to stay there illegally. They eventually moved back to Australia, but life was never the same after their time in Hawai'i. Even thirty years later, after all the triumphs and tragic events that would change their lives, Lynne can still say, "That family is more my own family than my own flesh and blood."

CHAPTER 7

Triumph and Tragedy

"Show me a hero, and I will write you a tragedy."
— *F. Scott Fitzgerald*

While the war dragged on in Vietnam and friends came home in body bags, Eddie and Clyde continued working as lifeguards at Waimea Bay. With each big, winter swell, they often had to rescue servicemen from the turbulent waters, naïve young recruits who found themselves caught in a deadly undertow. Eddie would watch the waves detonate on the shallow reefs like bombs suddenly exploding and worry about Gerald. He wondered how well his brother was adjusting to life after the war. Meanwhile, Gerald was working as a lifeguard at the Kuilima Resort on the eastern end of the North Shore. He would sit in his tower all day and stare at the ocean, questioning why he had survived the war and other friends hadn't. Who determined who lived or died? At work, at home and even in his sleep, Gerald still seemed to be wrestling with his fate and fighting unseen enemies. Random incidents could trigger his memory and suddenly transport him back to Vietnam.

Like the war, Fate turned out to be equally capricious for the Aikaus when it came to matters of marriage and family. Some were blessed with enduring relationships and an abundance of children, but others' marriages would be cut short without even the consolation of kids to carry on their name. While Sol had fathered a new baby every year or so since he was 14, Eddie and Linda, on the other hand, still had no children after years of trying. Sol had already had two kids with his wife Elizabeth, known as 'Tweety,' when he met Frederika, or Ricky, a tall pretty, blonde-haired *haole* woman from the mainland. Charmed by his "happy-go-lucky ways and nice smile," Ricky fell in love with Sol and soon became pregnant. Meanwhile,

Tweety was also *hapai* with her third child at the time! To the Aikaus' chagrin, Sol became a father twice that year. After Tweety left him and moved in with her parents, Sol settled down with Ricky. They married in 1969 and eventually had two boys, Arcas and Zane. In September of '73, they had a baby girl named Pi'ilani. As they had done for all the children, the Aikaus began planning her first baby luau soon after she was born.

The baby luau is a festive local tradition with tragic origins. In the past, many Hawaiian children didn't survive their first year due to poor health and foreign diseases. When they did, it was a cause for celebration. Because Sol was a one-man tribe-maker, they were celebrating every year or so. For each child's first birthday, the Aikaus would throw a baby luau that would take months to save up for and weeks to plan. But these parties were bittersweet for Eddie and Linda, who would watch Sol's children and the neighborhood kids laughing and running around at the party, secretly wondering why they couldn't have kids of their own. "At that point, they didn't know what was wrong," Ricky says. "I don't know if they ever talked about adopting. I'm sure Eddie would have loved to have had kids. And, God, don't we wish he had because he was just wonderful with my kids."

The Aikau brothers led very different lives. The youngest, Clyde was an extrovert and enjoyed going out on the town and meeting as many women as possible. The oldest son Freddie led a solitary life at home with his parents, often remaining holed up in his room when he wasn't working at the Cannery. Gerald was always in transition, moving back and forth between staying with his new girlfriend out in Mokule'ia and coming back home to be with Mom, Pops, Freddie and Myra. Despite their different personalities and lifestyles, the brothers remained close—so close that they sometimes had trouble leaving home. The graveyard became the center of their world, and its gravitational force kept pulling them back. Like the banyon tree in their yard, the boys only branched out so far before setting down their own roots.

Of all the brothers, Eddie and Clyde were the tightest because of their passions for riding big waves on the North Shore and performing Hawaiian music at parties around the Island. More people knew about Eddie, but they were both rising through the ranks of professional surfing in the early '70's. The big contests were becoming increasingly commercial, and Eddie and Clyde often found themselves competing in the same heat.

Fate also played a role in these surf contests. Most of the time, skill and performance determined who won or lost. Yet on occasion, luck and intuition had a hand in deciding who would be in the right position to catch the best waves. Eddie competed in a number of contests, but none of them had as much prestige or sentimental value as the Duke. As a Hawaiian, he wanted to win this contest more than any other, partly in homage to his childhood hero. Yet no matter how hard he tried, Eddie couldn't place higher than third. At times, he must have wondered if Fate was working against him. He also had concerns about the way the contest was evolving. After Duke died in 1968, Eddie had seen the tone of the Duke Classic change. The major TV networks competed with each other to cover the event and surfers scrambled to get invited, especially when they first started offering cash prizes to the winners in 1968. What had once been more of a friendly contest suddenly seemed more aggressive.

"Prior to the Duke Classic, surfing was more for fun and enjoyment," Greg Noll says. "But this was the first serious contest. As soon as the magazine and TV guys showed up with their cameras and helicopters, there was all the bullshit that goes with it. And the end result was here's my best friend elbowing me out to catch a wave, instead of being stoked to be surfing with me. Of course, that's what contests and competition brought on." Noll and his generation had gradually bowed out of the contest scene to let younger, aspiring professional surfers take the stage. Randy Rarick was one of the young chargers, and he saw the contest scene change dramatically during the late 60's. "The winter of 1967 was the last year of the longboard," he says. "It marked the end of an era for dominance by the first North Shore surfers and signaled the beginning of the shortboard influence, a surfing counter-culture and a fledgling move toward professionalism." Like women's mini-skirts, the boards became shorter and shorter.

Though the Duke lost some of its glamour when its namesake died, it was the spirit of the man and these early contests that motivated Eddie to keep trying to win the title. He wanted his name inscribed on the towering Duke trophy (now on permanent display at the North Shore Surf Museum), along with some of the greatest names of the sport. He had placed third in 1969, just behind Duke Team members Joey Cabell and Paul Strauch, both of whom went on to become successful businessmen. Cabell was also a champion skier and founder of the Chart House Restaurants. Eddie was the only Hawaiian among the finalists and the only one who pursued a professional career in surfing. In 1970 and '71, Eddie had watched Jeff Hakman wiggle his way across the waves and into first place two years in a row! For the third time, Jeff's name was carved on the perpetual Duke trophy. Although the title still eluded him, Eddie had placed third in 1971, just ahead of his brother Clyde, who finished in fifth place. It was a good showing for the Aikau brothers, whose ratings and reputations continued to improve.

In 1972, a young local named James "Booby" Jones blazed his way to the finals of the Duke Contest and won in a dramatic display of power and style. Though they were competitors, Eddie liked James and treated him like a younger brother, showing him the ropes at Sunset and Waimea. Almost ten years younger than Eddie, James had grown up in awe of his big-wave abilities and admired his candor. "Eddie was a real straight-shooter, a real stand-up guy," he says. "There probably weren't many people as honest as he was then and even fewer now. We never really surfed *against* each other. Eddie was the kind of guy who would come up to you before a heat and say, 'Okay, brah, we go do this one for the brothers.' The guys in Hawai'i had a lot of pride and kind of wanted to defend the home court. I never really felt like I was surfing *against* them. I always felt like I was surfing *with* them."

James Jones had become one of the best surfers on the circuit during the 1970's, but he didn't enjoy the sport's growing competitiveness. Like Eddie, he was more of a 'soul surfer,' and the photogs loved him because he was lean, good-looking and committed to the spiritual ideals of the sport. "Surfing is not really a contest in its natural state. You go out surfing to ride the waves. It's kind of like a dance, a communication between yourself and the ocean. And the object is to achieve harmony with that manifestation of nature." Neither he nor Eddie liked being in big contests, but Jones says they were forced to learn. "I had the surfing talent, but you have to fit that into the competitive structure. You've got 45 minutes to catch the three best waves. There's a whole strategy going on. All that jazz. I never really enjoyed competing. But I loved to surf, and the only way I could see continuing to surf was to support myself in the sport."

James helped establish a new era of dominance by Hawaiian big-wave surfers, along with Reno Abellira, Barry Kanaiapuni and the Aikau brothers. James and Clyde were also full-time students at the University of Hawai'i, and they both struggled to keep up with their studies while launching their surf careers. Young, proud and eager to gain recognition for themselves and the Hawaiian people, these big-wave riders dominated the North Shore, which had become the epicenter of the surfing world. As giant waves erupted there each winter, photos and footage of epic surf sessions traveled like shock waves across the globe appearing in popular films and magazines. The shortboard revolution was in full swing, and a professional tour was beginning to emerge, thanks to increasing corporate sponsorship.

In an interview with *Surfer*, Jones talked about what it was like to be at the forefront of surfing at a time when the sport was just starting to take off. "I don't know if it was coincidence or fate, but I was really lucky to be a part of surfing then. Everyone who surfed really felt like they were doing something special, like they were carrying around this big secret," Jones said. "Our generation helped get the sport off the ground, but I look at the guys today and I can't help but think of the downside of our accomplishments. We never imagined it getting as commercialized as it is today. When I started surfing, we did it for the pure thrill of riding waves; it was like an escape from the world's commercialism. These days, though, you're smack in the middle of it all when you paddle out," he says, referring to the crowded conditions and hostile attitudes on the North Shore today. "It's sad—it's like our operation was a success, but the patient died." James can still remember pristine surf sessions in the "Country" with Eddie and Clyde when they would surf giant waves at Waimea Bay with no one else out. "We used to have to look for people to paddle out with. Not just at the Bay, but Pipe too. That's how the North Shore was then."

When the big swells started hitting the North Shore in the winter of '73, Eddie and Clyde waited anxiously to compete in the Duke Contest again. Although both brothers had been invited, Clyde was listed as an alternate, and his only chance to compete depended on whether or not anyone dropped out of the contest. Then, in late November, a sizable swell came in, and the news went out on the coconut wireless that the Duke was on! When one of the 24 contestants didn't show up, Clyde happily took his place. Once again, the brothers Aikau got a chance to compete against each other and some of the world's best surfers. Meanwhile, Pops, Myra and the boys watched from the beach, where they helped to coordinate the event.

As usual, the preliminaries were held at Sunset Beach. Both Eddie and Clyde advanced through the early rounds against heavy competitors from Australia, California and Hawai'i. But the weather turned windy, conditions worsened, and the swell died before they could finish the contest. It was postponed until the waves improved, as the surfers anxiously bided their time. Another huge swell came a week later, but the waves were so big and gnarly they closed out Sunset and almost every beach on the North Shore—except Waimea. No contest had ever been held at the Bay before because the waves were generally considered too heavy and dangerous for a contest—especially for surfers from the mainland who had never even seen waves that big, much less ridden them. But while other surf spots looked like the inside of a giant washing machine, the Bay was much cleaner and bigger. After much debate, contest officials decided to move the event to Waimea.

Waimea Bay, a natural amphitheater, provided the perfect setting for a major surfing event. The crowds swarmed the beach and lined the cliffs to watch the tiny-looking men do battle with the giant waves rolling across the Bay. The Finals were divided into two sessions, and the judges were looking at the best five waves of each session. Because Eddie and Clyde worked at the Bay and surfed it regularly, they had the home field advantage. They knew where to paddle for the biggest waves on the outside and what areas to avoid in the inside sections. But the day started badly for the Aikau brothers. Eddie wiped out early in the first session, and his board was smashed on the rocks. By the time he swam in and got another board, he had lost too much time in the heat. Clyde had taken out his 7' 6" board in order to do more hotdogging, but he discovered it was too short for the big, yet inconsistent 20-30 foot waves. Most of the riders stuck to the inside section of the Bay, but Clyde wanted to take off on the larger outside sets that came thundering through every so often. He caught enough waves to place in the finals, but neither of the Aikaus had performed to their potential. By the end of the semifinals, it looked like either Jones might win it again, or Jeff Hakman, who was looking to capture his fourth title.

When the event resumed that afternoon, some of the younger, hotdog surfers argued that the waves were too inconsistent. They complained that the outside sets weren't really connecting with the inside, except when the big waves or 'bombs' came exploding through the lineup periodically. But after the Duke officials met with the contestants and the ABC crew filming the event, they decided to go ahead and finish up the Finals that afternoon. During the second session, Clyde took out his 9' 6" gun, and this ended up making the difference for him. On one of his first rides, he took off on a big outside wave, and right as it started to close out, he ducked into the tube for a few moments, got totally covered and then burst through the wall of whitewater. As he was paddling back out, he spotted a bump on the horizon and decided to paddle way outside to check it out. Sure enough, his instincts paid off when he saw one of the biggest waves of the day charging toward him and his friend Reno Abellira. As the other surfers paddled in a panic to get over the beast, trying not to get caught on the inside, Clyde gracefully dropped down the face of this giant wave behind Reno. Since Clyde took off first on the inside of the wave, Reno risked receiving an interference from the judges so he kicked out of the wave as Clyde charged ahead. He cut a smooth line across the enormous face of the wave, staying in the critical zone just ahead of the beast's roaring maw. When he made it all the way to the shoulder of the wave and then cut out, the crowd on the beach cheered. Clyde felt his momentum building. He paddled back to the outside and waited for another giant wave.

While most of the other contestants went back inside where there were more waves, Clyde had counted the intervals between sets and knew from experience that another outside one would be rolling through soon. Based on what Eddie had taught him, he also knew where to sit, in the deepest take-off spot where the waves suddenly rose up like leviathans from the deep. When the set came, Clyde was ready. He took off on a large swell, dropping almost 30 feet down the face of the wave. He then rode it all the way across the Bay and into the inside section, to the amazement and frustration of the other competitors—except Eddie, who cheered for his brother and knew it was the wave of the day. The crowd on the beach and the surrounding cliffs went wild, yelling and whistling. Clyde later said, "That was the high point. Maybe it was just luck, but the wave held and I just slid into it." Reno also caught some giant outside waves, but Clyde had been the only one to milk them all the way to the inside section, where they gave out in a last gasp of foam. James hadn't been able to maintain his earlier performance. When the horn sounded the end of the finals, Clyde was confident he had won the heat. But he had no idea if he had won the contest, due to his poor performance earlier in the day.

The crowd and the surfers gathered anxiously around the judges' platform, as the ABC crew interviewed several of the contestants, trying to get some idea of who won the event. Tallying the scores took much longer than usual so everyone knew it was going to be close. Eddie and Pops told Clyde he had done well, and they assured him that if he didn't win it, at least it would be a Hawaiian surfer who did. Before the emcee announced the results, he said it had been a close tie between Clyde and Reno, and they had to go back and look at their last eleven rides. After calculating all of the points, the emcee shouted that Clyde Aikau had won the Ninth Annual Duke Kahanamoku Surfing Championship! Eddie and his mother hugged Clyde, who had tears in his eyes and could barely talk. Pops, Sol and Myra joined in the embrace, and at that moment, the Aikaus looked like they were the happiest family in the world. "My brother and I have been trying for so many years to win this," Clyde told the crowd. "I'm really happy for my family." A reporter asked Eddie what his feelings were and if he was jealous of his brother. Eddie just looked at him and said with a wistful smile, "It was his day, man. It was his day."

During the Awards Ceremony at Duke's club in Waikiki, contestants received their golden Duke statuettes. For Eddie, the whole evening went by in a blur of beers, speeches and applause. He had come in sixth place—and after eight years, he still hadn't won the contest. But now his youngest brother was becoming a fierce competitor, and Eddie must have wondered if Clyde had surpassed him. Clyde could surf smaller waves better, no doubt, and his more aggressive and radical style on the wave—carving more turns and cutbacks in the critical sections—was just what the judges were looking for. If not a better surfer, Clyde definitely had more of a competitive edge. "Eddie was more of a soul surfer. Competing for him wasn't a real big deal," Clyde says. "Except if it got big, then it was worth surfing. If it wasn't big, it wasn't a big deal."

At the Awards Banquet, Eddie remembered receiving his statuette from Duke himself six years earlier. Watching Clyde receive his first-place trophy and check for $2000, Eddie took pride in his brother's victory. It was exciting to be there with all the smiling fans, flashing cameras and endless drinks, but Eddie sensed that some surfers were still grumbling about the results, while others were angry they hadn't even been invited to compete. When Fred Van Dyke resigned as Director of the Duke the year before, he said the pressure from surfers and their sponsors to be included in the contest became too intense. Several surfers even threatened him. "I quit," Fred once joked, "because I wanted to stay alive."

Though the mood of the Duke Classic had changed over the years, Eddie was still stoked for his brother. It was not only Clyde's day but also his year. He was about to graduate from the University of Hawai'i with a bachelor's degree in sociology, the first in his family to earn a college diploma. On top of that, he had just won the biggest surf contest in the world. Swallowing any feelings of envy, Eddie smiled proudly as he looked around at Clyde and all their family and friends gathered together that evening. Little did he realize how soon it would all change, how one brother's triumph would turn into another's tragedy.

Following Clyde's victory in the Duke, Pops Aikau had planned to throw a big luau celebrating Clyde's graduation from U.H. In the meantime, Clyde invited his brothers to a grad party at a friend's place in Manoa. It was Saturday, December 8, and with Christmas just around the corner, everyone was in good spirits, enjoying the food and music. After eating, Eddie and Clyde picked up their guitars and started playing Hawaiian music. Wearing bandanas around their heads, they sat across from each other, strumming in unison and harmonizing together—they were so in sync it seemed they could read each other's minds. They sang popular songs like the Byrds' "Turn, Turn, Turn," whose lyrics from Ecclesiastes summed up the turbulent era of change: "To everything, turn, turn, turn, there is a season, turn, turn, turn, and a time to every purpose under heaven…a time to be born, and a time to die…" The other guests either sang along or sat back and enjoyed the show. By this time, the Aikau brothers had really established themselves in the local music scene. They were sometimes invited to sit in with Hawai'i's best musicians, including local legends like Gabby Pahinui and Peter Moon. They also performed with Momma and Myra at the Duke Classic parties.

Sitting at the party that night, surrounded by his brothers and friends under a beautiful, moonlit sky, Clyde felt like he was on top of the world. He enjoyed being in the limelight. Eddie, on the other hand, was self-conscious in front of crowds, but always felt more comfortable with a guitar in his hands. He would hold its neck and body like a forlorn lover and stroke its strings like a man in a trance. As shy and quiet as he was, Eddie could speak eloquently through his music. He touched people with the sincerity of his voice and words, especially Gerald, who would often sing along with him. Eddie played his favorite song "Waimanalo Blues," singing about how Hawai'i had been overrun with hotels and how he wanted to get away from it all. "Where I will go, the winds only know…get in my car, goin' too far, never comin' back again." His friend Liko Martin had written the song, which had become a popular hit in the Islands. But none of them singing and drinking that night knew how prophetic those lyrics would prove to be.

Gerald's ex-girlfriend Kathy was there that night at the graduation party. After moving back to Seattle and living on the Mainland for more than a year, Kathy had returned to Hawai'i with her new fiance for a vacation. Listening to the boys sing and perform, Kathy recalled the many luaus and fun get-togethers she had been to at the graveyard. "Parties were just an ongoing way of life there, people always over and singing…They were a very musical family. Eddie and Clyde would sing Beatles songs like 'Hey, Jude.'" She says Pops and all the boys would sing, and Myra would play the ukulele while her brothers played the guitar. "They all had their favorite songs." But the highlight of the evening would be when Momma Aikau performed. "Mom was next to a deity—those boys really worshipped their mother. When Mom sang, it was a treat. You considered yourself blessed if she got up to sing the old Hawaiian songs." Singing in a melodious language that was hardly spoken anymore, her soft voice would bring to life a peaceful vision of the Islands as they once were—and would never be again. Her sons would accompany her with tears in their eyes, and everyone at the party would grow quiet as the music settled over them like a soft mist, transporting them to the past. "It was life-altering having that experience," Kathy says quietly, lost in memories of that time.

Sitting behind the others at the party, drinking in the shadows, Gerald would join in the singing for a while and then retreat to his car to be alone. Lynne Holmes had noticed months before during her visit that Gerald had trouble adjusting when he returned from the war. "After all the things he had seen, how could he talk about it to anyone, even his family? We'd be sitting there singing and talking story, and Gerry would just turn off. He would go into his black VW Bug and listen to his Hawaiian music. 'Does anybody know what I've been through?' That's what I thought was going on his mind." Besides sudden mood shifts, Gerald started getting into arguments and fights when he drank too much. Even Clyde acknowledged his transformation. "When he went to Vietnam and came back, he was never the same guy. He was this vicious Hawaiian boy with a chip on his shoulder and a short fuse. I was really sad about how the war had changed my brother."

In high school, Gerald sang in the glee club and loved hanging out with his friends, but after the war, Gerald wore an angry scowl and preferred being alone. He often seemed ready to explode. "The war screwed up everybody," Sol says. "He had a tough-guy attitude. He was cool and stuff, but he wasn't the same guy. It just changed him. Before, you could play around with him, but when he came back, he had this no-nonsense attitude." But like Eddie, he was willing to risk his life to help others. The year before Eddie became Lifeguard of the Year, Gerald had won an Airman's medal for saving

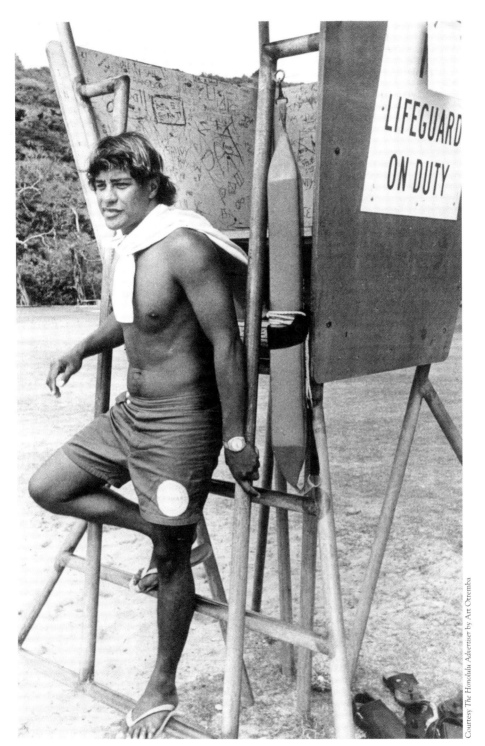

Eddie keeping watch at his lifeguard stand at Waimea Bay.

The Aikau family at the graveyard in 1976. Front Row: Eddie and Clyde. Back Row: Sol, Mom, Myra, Freddie and Pops.

Facing page top: The Aikaus pose as Eddie wins a Book of Knowledge on Maui in the 1950s. Back row: Pops, Myra, Mom and Freddie. Front row: Gerald, Clyde, Sol and Eddie.

Facing page bottom: The trophy case at the Aikau home. Gerald's flag holds a place of honor.

Linda Crosswhite and Eddie on their Wedding Day in 1972.

The Wedding Party—Freddie, Gerald, Sol, Clyde and Eddie; Linda, Kathy Rickenbacker, Myra Aikau, Susan Hughes and Connie Crosswhite.

The Aikaus—Clyde, Mom, Myra and Eddie—entertain at the Duke Banquet at he Kuilima Resort.

Clyde and Eddie singng at home in the graveyard.

Aussie Wayne "Rabbit" Bartholomew at the 2000 Pipeline Masters.

Three legendary wave riders, Peter Cole, John Kelly and Fred Van Dyke, at the opening of David Brown's documentary, Surfing for Life.

Right: Holding his favorite "elephant gun," Peter Cole scans the swells at Sunset Beach in 1989. He's still going out in 2002!

Below: Peter Cole (at left) and Fred Van Dyke catch the same swell on the North Shore.

Eddie speeding out of the tube on a picture-perfect North Shore wave.

Endless Summer Filmmaker Bruce Brown interviews Duke at the Awards Banquet for the 2nd Annual Duke Kahanamoku Contest in 1967. Ricky Grigg holds his First Place trophy, while Mike Doyle and Fred Hemmings watch from rear. Duke passed away at 77 a little over a year later in January 1968.

Eddie streaks across a Waimea giant in November 1967.

Promoter Kimo Wilder McVay created the Duke Kahanamoku Surf Team. Left-Right: Paul Strauch, Joey Cabell, Duke, Fred Hemmings and Butch Van Artsdalen.

In 2002, on the 112th anniversary of his birth, the U.S. Postal Service issued a Duke Kahanamoku commemorative stamp.

Jose Angel displays a shark he has just captured.

Photo by Stuart Coleman

Jodi Holmes Young, Lynne Holmes and Linda Crosswhite Ipsen reunited at Hale'iwa Beach Park in 2000.

Photo by LDan Merkel. Collection of Peter Townend.

Eddie taking off at Sunset.

Above: An ominous photo of Eddie paddling his board around Hokule'a prior to departure.

Facing page top: As seen through the HFD helicopter bubble Hokule'a returns to Honolulu Harbor after a 1975 training sail.

Facing page bottom:Eddie and Bernard Kuahulu on a training sail off O'ahu.

THE 1978 HAWAI'I-TAHITI CREW

Snake Ah Hee, Eddie Aikau, Charman Akina, Wedemeyer Au, Bruce Blankenfeld, Kilila Hugho, Sam Ka'ai, John Kruse, Dave Lyman, Marion Lyman, Buddy McGuire, Norman Pi'ianai'a, Leon Sterling, Curt Sumida, Tava Taupu, Nainoa Thompson.

Clyde at the Waikiki statue of Eddie's idol, Duke Kahanamoku.

his fellow servicemen in the Air Force. "He was in Vietnam, fixing jets," Sol says. "One of the jets he was working on caught fire, and he pulled everyone out of the airplane." As a jet mechanic, Gerald didn't see a lot of heavy combat. But Sol says he saw a lot of body bags and once had to kill a man. "I remember a story he told us one time. He was kind of bored being a mechanic so he volunteered to take these supplies to some place as the point guy." While moving through the jungle, he saw "this Vietnamese guy aiming a rifle at him, and he just turned around and shot him. That was his only kill, I think." But the memory stayed with Gerald, and he wondered if it was just Fate that he survived while the other guy died.

At the party, Gerald sat in his car brooding and drinking alone. Kathy says he was upset that she had brought her fiance. Everyone else continued drinking and talking story. As the night wore on, Gerald returned to the party moody and emotional. He wanted to talk to Kathy. His new girlfriend was there so Kathy had hoped that it wouldn't be awkward between them. But Gerald couldn't help saying how much he missed her. Not knowing how to react, Kathy told his girlfriend that he was just drunk. Then, she and her fiance said good night to everyone and quickly left.

The party died down after that incident. When it was time to go home, the Aikau brothers said their goodbyes and headed to the cars with their wives or girlfriends. Though they had all been drinking, they climbed into their VW Bugs and Vans and started the long drive back to the North Shore. "We were all in separate cars following each other," Linda remembers, "and Gerry and his friend were missing." They had planned to drive in a caravan to make sure they got home safely, but Gerald and his girlfriend's brother, Aaron Hagerfeldt, decided to go on their own. They drove to the windward side of the Island and stopped by an all-night drive-in in Kailua before heading home. After picking up some food, Gerald decided to let Aaron drive his Bug the rest of the way. After talking a while, he slowly drifted off to sleep, the evening's music still playing in his head: "Where I will go, the winds only know…getting in my car, goin' too far, never coming back again."

Driving on the Northeast side of the island at night was like taking a trip into Hawai'i's past. There were almost no streetlights, and the silent darkness had an almost hypnotic effect on the driver. Their headlights gently swept back and forth like a lighthouse beam moving across the road and the ocean beyond. Aaron could feel his eyes growing tired as his thoughts drifted into a kind of dreamworld. Then, suddenly, at a place called Pounders, Aaron fell asleep at the wheel and swerved off the road. Jolted awake, he slammed on the brakes. The sounds of screeching tires and a thunderous crash ripped through the night as the VW Bug careened into a telephone pole on the side of the road. The driver was thrown from the car and knocked unconscious, as he lay in a puddle of blood and broken glass. Sirens pierced the air as the police and ambulance workers arrived on the scene and approached the demolished car. Looking inside, they saw that the telephone pole had torn right through the passenger side of the Bug. The damage was so bad they couldn't even identify the victim at first. They knew the car was registered to the Aikaus, but they didn't know which son was in the car. The police called the family and asked them to contact all their sons to see if everyone was accounted for. When all but Gerald had been reached, the police told Mom and Pops that their son had been killed in a car crash.

The family was devastated. All the boys came home to the grave-yard, and the house was filled with tears and wailing. Everyone had been so happy the week before, celebrating Clyde's victory and upcoming graduation. But now everything had changed. Gerald Keliʻi Aikau's death would leave a hole in their lives for years to come. Voted Most Handsome at Roosevelt High School and decorated for heroism in Vietnam, he once seemed to have a bright future ahead of him. But the war had made him a bitter man. And that was the most painful part of all. He had survived two long and turbulent years in Vietnam, only to be killed in a senseless car accident, just when he was trying to make a new life for himself.

At the funeral parlor, they had dressed Gerald in his Air Force uniform, with his Airman's medal and Sergeant's stripes. The damage was so bad they had to put a veil over his face. Eddie and Clyde both put their Duke trophies in the casket with Gerald, crying as they looked at his face one last time. A Requiem Mass was held at Blessed Sacrament, where they had celebrated Eddie and Linda's marriage just two years before. The church was packed with extended family and friends, and the air was heavy with the sounds of sobbing, hymns and mournful prayers. Kathy remembers how hard the funeral was on everyone. "It was a horrible tragedy, with the jubilation of Clydie winning the week before. It was an awful emotional dichotomy that was just impossible to reconcile." She can still recall walking up to the coffin with her fiance and just staring down at her former boyfriend lying there. "It was an open casket which surprised me. It had been difficult to put him back together. Mom Aikau was leaning against the head of the casket, just sobbing and stroking the wood. The female members sat on one side and the male members sat on the other side. The whole congregation lined up to say their condolences. It was probably the most painful funeral I've ever been to. Just a couple of nights before, he had been crying over me. It was extremely awkward and sad, but I was sort of forced to deal with it. I faced it, head-on. But a pall hung over the rest of our trip."

In the reception area, the family had set up pictures of Gerry from different stages of his life, and cascades of brightly colored flowers—plumeria, torch ginger and bird of paradise—surrounded his image. As friends shared their favorite memories of him, he seemed to come alive for the moment, and then the reality of his sudden death would hit home all over again. Eddie and his mom seemed to take it the worst. They were inconsolable. At the end of the service, the family received emotional hugs and soft-spoken consolations from the large crowd. But the mantra going through everyone's mind was: Why?

The burial service was held at Punchbowl National Cemetery. Situated in an old volcanic crater in the middle of Honolulu, Punchbowl crater rises a few hundred yards above the Aikau's home in the graveyard. Once a violent volcano, it is now a quiet and solemn place where soldiers of previous wars rest in peace. The site overlooks the Ko'olau Mountains to the north and the Pacific Ocean to the South. Standing in the bright green grass, the family stared into the dark hole before them, trying to keep their composure. During the ceremony, Gerald was given full military honors. After the soldiers shot off three rounds of rifle fire, the bugler performed taps, and his mother received the folded American flag. His casket was interred in a beautiful plot near the National Memorial of the Pacific, a large, marble shrine at the head of the cemetery. From the Aikau's home below, the sun sets over Punchbowl during certain times of the year. And in Eddie's eyes, that's where part of him died.

After coming home from the burial, the family gathered at the compound to be together and console each other. Eddie couldn't stop crying and seemed to have come undone. As tough as he was in big waves, he couldn't handle the loss of his brother. Friends dropped by to pay their respects, bringing food and trying to console the family. By the end of the day, everyone was exhausted and ready for bed. No one had seen Eddie in a while, and they figured he had gone to sleep early. But the next morning, they discovered he hadn't slept in his bed. Remembering how upset he had been the night before, they suddenly became worried about him. Clyde, Sol and Freddie searched the entire compound looking for Eddie but found no sign of him. Then, it suddenly occurred to them where he might be. So the brothers jumped into the van and drove to Punchbowl Cemetery. They scaled the fence and ran across the cemetery to Gerald's grave. Lying there on a blanket of flowers was Eddie, still weeping and moaning, watering the freshly turned earth with his tears. His deep, wolf-like eyes were swollen and bloodshot. He looked like a wounded animal, frightened and alone.

Knowing how close the family was, Lifeguard Captain Aloha Kaeo gave Eddie, Clyde and Sol time off from their jobs to recover from the loss. The whole family stopped working and just focused on dealing with their grief and slowly rebuilding their lives. "Gerald's death was really hard on everybody," Linda recalls. "It was the first of many tragedies, but his death was the hardest…It was a very tough time, and it took a long time for the family to get over, and I don't think they ever really got over it." But life went on. The boys helped Pops take care of the graveyard and planted a torch ginger garden by the house in Gerald's memory. Eddie, Clyde and Sol went back and forth between their apartments on the North Shore and their home at the graveyard. But they eventually decided that the family shouldn't be living apart during this difficult time. In the course of one day, they packed up all of their belongings on the North Shore and moved back to the compound. Within months of Gerald's death, the Aikau brothers had all returned home and were living as one big family again. Eddie and Linda eventually decided to buy a small, three-bedroom house in town for about $10,000, and then they had it transported and replanted at the graveyard. They were there to stay.

Gerald's death had devastated the family, but it also brought them closer together. He had always wanted to take care of his mother and father, and the insurance settlement ended up providing them with needed financial support. They visited his grave often, and Myra still goes up to Punchbowl every two weeks to replace the flowers. When Sol and Ricky's last son was born in February of 1975, they named him Gerald in honor of his uncle's memory. Just before the baby's first luau, the entire family went up to visit Gerald's grave to pay their respects and introduce his young namesake. As the little boy crawled on the grass, the rest of the Aikaus shared stories, memories and tears with their departed brother.

CHAPTER 8

Wipeout

*"The worst wipeout I ever experienced was when Ricky
and I were surfing Waimea. I got a concussion from hitting
my board and I totally blacked out underwater…When I came
to, I was still underwater…all I felt was nausea and total
disorientation. I panicked and started clawing my way to the surface…
I broke the surface just as another wave hit and pounded me back
under the water. I gulped more water than air, and almost blacked out
again, waiting for the turbulence to release me…I had worked myself
up to the point where I could hold my breath for three minutes, but I'd
exceeded my limit this time. I felt doomed."*
— Greg Noll, Da Bull

All big-wave riders have experienced horrendous wipeouts that
made them wonder if they would survive, and Eddie and his friends were no
exception. Great rides tend to fade with time, but terrible wipeouts remain
vivid and horrifying memories. As the eyes of Waimea, Eddie kept watch
over all the other surfers at the Bay. He knew that a bad wipeout could be
fatal. The waves at Waimea were so powerful they could easily break a man's
board or his bones, as Titus Kinimaka discovered years later when a giant
Waimea wave snapped his femur in two. After losing his brother, Eddie
became increasingly vigilant in the water, determined not to lose one of his
friends. But he was not prepared for his own wipeout.

During one of the year's biggest swells at the Bay, Eddie took off on a
nasty wave that seemed determined to kill him. Sol can still picture what
happened the moment he almost lost his brother to the sea. "I remember
that day. He was on this wave, it was a big one, and he wiped out. It took

him right down to the bottom and rolled him across it." After the shock of falling through the air and being slammed into the water, Eddie felt his head hit the rocky bottom. He blacked out for a moment and awoke in an underwater netherworld. Being buried under tons of churning water during a bad wipeout can feel like dying. Cut off from the light and air, he looked around in a daze, wondering what happened, where he was and which way was up. Like Odysseus in the Underworld, he felt time suddenly slow down and darkness envelop everything. Boulders the size of VW Bugs rolled around in the underwater tornado. Caught in a dreamscape between the living and the dead, he tried to escape. But like a nightmare he could not yell for help or run away as he was thrown around like a rag doll. He tried not to panic but his lungs were screaming for air, his pulse was pounding, and the whitewater kept pushing him down. For a moment, he must have wondered if his time had come. But then the ocean let him go, and he swam toward the light.

"I remember him telling us that what saved him was just saying to himself, 'I'm going to push myself from the bottom to the surface,' and that's what he did. That was a close call for him," Sol says. Eddie made it to the surface, gasping for air and choking on sea foam, and then he managed to swim in without help. "He came into shore. He had split his head open, and I guess that was the time he lost his tooth. I remember seeing him on the shore, and everyone was talking to him. They bandaged his head up because he was all bloody." Eddie probably felt embarrassed and uncomfortable with this sudden role reversal—after all, he was the one who was supposed to help other hapless victims in the surf. But as any lifeguard knows, the ocean is the most unpredictable entity in the world and can catch even the most experienced watermen off-guard. It can kill without warning. Eddie knew this in his bones, and he had seen friends and fellow big-wave riders almost die right before his eyes. He thought about these things on the beach that day, his head throbbing and heart still pounding. Eddie then realized he had to return to the scene of the accident and face his fears. Including his fear of death.

"He sat on the beach, looked at the surf, and then went back out," Sol says with disbelief. "With the bandage around his head, he surfed for a few more hours. I mean, that was phenomenal. I guess he felt confident that he wasn't too badly hurt." Worse than any physical injury was the debilitating disease of fear. As a big-wave rider, Eddie knew that if he gave into his fears, he could easily die in such huge surf. If he hesitated for a moment during the take-off, the lip of the wave would catapult him into the air and slam him against the water. As a legendary surfer once put it, big waves were not measured in feet but in increments of fear. As Eddie dropped down the faces of these enormous waves, he understood that he had to overcome each increment of fear with a greater degree of courage or else it would overcome him. Surfing became a metaphor for his life: Eddie had to regain his balance and find the natural flow, or he was going to wipe out all over again. In this way, he rediscovered the danger and thrill of riding mountainous waves.

Almost a year after Gerry's death, Eddie and Clyde found themselves pitted against each other in a near replay of the '73 Duke. Once again, the contest was to be held at Waimea Bay with the same top contenders, including Reno Abellira, Jeff Hakman and James Jones. This time it was the '74 Smirnoff Pro-Am Surfing Classic, the richest contest on the circuit. But on the morning of the contest, the waves were too big, some reaching 50-60 feet high. It was Thanksgiving Day, and thousands of people planned to come watch the epic rides and potentially deadly wipeouts. Rather than sitting at home and watching the football games on TV, the fans began lining up along the cliffs of Waimea's natural arena to witness surfing's greatest matadors challenge the giant waves charging across the Bay.

The entire North Shore lay buried in a shroud of mist from the giant surf. Sounding like a huge offshore power plant, the megaton waves made a thundering crash as they closed out the Bay, creating a wall of whitewater two stories high. Fred Hemmings and the other contest officials wondered whether they could even put on the event because the road by Laniakea was washed out, creating a mile-long traffic jam. They also had to wrestle with the issue of safety. Struggling with the real possibility of being seriously injured or even killed, many of the surfers refused to go out in such deadly conditions. But Fred knew the contest would be a blockbuster event, the biggest ever, and the camera crews and sponsors were eager to televise what would be the most extreme surfing footage ever shown on TV. Peter Cole tried to warn him, saying, "Fred, don't send them out in those waves—they're going to die!"

Despite the warnings, "Dead Ahead Fred" wanted to go ahead with event. His dogged determination and media savvy had made him the biggest contest promoter of the time. (These same skills would later lead him into politics and seats in the Hawai'i State House and Senate.) Capitalizing on surfing's growing popularity in the media, Fred brought together vagabond surfers, conservative corporate sponsors and sophisticated TV producers to televise the sport. But surfers like Eddie resented the growing commercialism of the sport. Over the years he had witnessed Fred's transformation from a fellow surfer and competitor into a contest organizer, from 'one of us' to 'one of them.' During the first Smirnoff Contest years before, Gerry Lopez remembers how Fred and Eddie had come into conflict over the issue of contest entry fees. "Fred wanted everyone to pay a $75 entry fee, which was pretty big money in those days. We were shocked and decided to have a big meeting down at the Outrigger Canoe Club. Fred's quite a statesman, and he got up and gave his side of the story. He talked for about twenty minutes about why we needed to pay to be in the contest. And he sat down and said, 'What do you guys have to say?' So Eddie got up—this was the first time I had ever heard him speak in front of a group like that. It was really hard for him, but we were all hanging on his every word," Gerry recalls. "He said, 'Hey, we're just a bunch of poor surfers, and $75 is a lot of money to come up with.' He basically shamed Fred for even asking for a contest fee. He went on to say that if that was the way it was going to be, he wasn't going to surf. We all said, 'We're not either.' So Fred ended up backing down." But he was not going to back down this time, not with such an epic contest on the line.

In *The Surfer's Journal* documentary "Great Waves: Hawai'i," former world champion Mark Richards talks about being one of the contestants in the '74 Smirnoff. He says Fred pressured them into surfing in the giant waves—even when big-wave titans like Barry Kanaiaupuni were claiming it was too big. "A lot of the guys who had experience in Hawai'i were questioning the sanity of actually running the event," Richards says. "And Fred Hemmings basically said, 'Look, you guys are a bunch of wusses. I'll paddle out there and catch a wave and prove it can be ridden.' As soon as he said that, everyone knew it was going to be on because we knew Fred would actually do it." Hemmings later admitted how relieved he was that the surfers didn't call his bluff! After taking a poll of the contestants, the majority decided to go ahead with the contest. The surfers who couldn't handle the towering surf either stayed on the beach or paddled way beyond the lineup to wait out their heat. The early rounds went off in spectacularly big yet clean 40-50 foot surf. The crowds cheered when the surfers successfully dropped down the smooth faces of the huge waves and groaned each time they wiped out. Barry wiped out on one wave and ended up bouncing down its face before it devoured him and destroyed his board. After almost drowning on the way in, he got pounded in the shore break. There was still time in his heat to paddle back out and catch more waves. But after thinking about his wife and kids and what would happen to them if he were injured or paralyzed, Barry decided it wasn't worth it.

Though considered one of the best big-wave surfers at Waimea Bay, Eddie just missed making the finals. As a lifeguard, he was more preoccupied with the safety of other surfers, and this hurt his competitive edge. Constantly on the lookout for accidents and bad wipeouts, he had trouble concentrating on his own rides. After losing his brother Gerald in the car crash, Eddie wasn't going to let another life slip through his hands. He was also more of a team player and didn't like competing against his friends in such dangerous conditions. Along with Clyde, James Jones was in finals that fateful day, and Eddie was watching over them both. James shared Eddie's belief that safety and friendship were more important than competition, but he was young and proud, eager to win the event in front of thousands of fans. Like the other competitors, he had been seduced by the lure of public adulation, prize money and TV exposure. But up to this point, he had never competed in such deadly waves.

"It was really big, probably the biggest surf ever ridden in a competition," James says. "That was one of the first contests where they allowed what they called 'caddies'—you could have a guy in the channel with another board for you." Before the invention of leashes, cords which attach the board to the surfer's ankle, competitors had caddies with an extra board in case they lost or broke their own after a wipeout. Only the most loyal friends were willing to brave such big waves. "We were getting ready to paddle out for the final heat, and Eddie came out to caddy for Clyde," James remembers. "Eddie had on this thick leather belt slung over one shoulder and under the other arm, bandolero-style, and he paddled out with that. I couldn't figure out why he had that thing, maybe a new fashion or something. So we got out in the heat, and it was really big and closing out." Meanwhile, Pops was on the shore nervously pacing up and down the beach, stopping every few seconds to watch his boys through binoculars. Then, he saw the enormous shadow of a wave rise up out of the deep and swallow the whole horizon.

When the fateful wave suddenly appeared, the three titans spotted it first. "Peter Cole, Ricky Grigg and Jose Angel were not in the contest, but these guys were the most experienced big-wave riders of the day so they were out there surfing," Jones recalls. "Contest or not, you couldn't get them to go in. So when we were in the line-up, Peter Cole looked over at the competitors and said, 'Whoever catches this wave is going to win the contest!' And I thought, 'Well, that must be me.' I caught what was probably the biggest wave ever ridden at that time, and I didn't make it." The towering wave was more than seven times his height. Like a skier poised on a vertical cliff, the drop was just too steep. "I got half-way down the face, and I hit a big chop, and the board broke in half while I was standing on it. I got slammed. I fell face-first into the water. It would be like if you were a kick returner in football and some guy just chopped you in the knees and you fell on your face. The worst part of a wipeout on a big wave like that is when you hit the water; the impact kind of stuns you, if it doesn't knock you out. I came up, and I was numb on one side of my body. I couldn't use that arm or leg. I was semi-conscious, floating around in the impact zone, and there was another wave coming. There must have been 10,000 people on the beach, and I thought, 'Shit, here I am and I'm gonna drown in front of 10,000 people.'"

As Jones struggled to stay afloat and catch his breath, another huge wave was on its way, but so was his rescuer. "Eddie had been watching, and he was paddling over toward me. He pulled that leather strap from around his shoulders, and immediately I knew what it was. He paddled into the lineup and held the strap out to me, and I put the arm I could use into it. And the next wave came and broke on top of us and took his board, but he held onto the strap." As they went over the falls together and were thrown around underwater, Eddie wouldn't let go of his friend who was paralyzed and starting to panic. "We got blasted by the waves, but he held onto that strap. So he swam me in almost to the beach. I guess you could say Eddie Aikau saved my life."

When he was out of the impact zone, Peter Cole came paddling up and gave Jones his board to make it in through the shore break. But then his caddy came out with another board, shouting that there was still plenty of time to catch more waves. "I just wanted to go to the hospital," Jones says. "But everyone was watching. So I paddled back out, but I couldn't surf—I was out of it. I could barely paddle with one arm, but I did catch a wave in. I was bent out of shape after that. Something happened in my spine, and I had to go to a chiropractor for a long time. To this day," he says, "I have back problems."

Meanwhile, out in the heat, Clyde and Reno were going head to head, taking off on the biggest waves of the day. Reno caught some of the biggest waves and rode them more consistently. On one ride, though, Clyde caught a wave way outside the lineup of the other contestants and rode it all the way to the inside section, while the crowd on the beach stood up and cheered. But then Jeff took off on a wave and carved his S-turns down the face all the way to the end. On his next wave, he dropped down into the huge pocket, stalled for a moment and managed to get barreled on a 40-foot wave. These two exceptional rides suddenly catapulted Jeff into the running for first place at the end of the final heat. As the surfers waited restlessly on the beach for the results, the judges took a long time calculating the final scores. Finally, they announced that Reno had barely beaten his rivals Jeff Hakman, who came in second, and Clyde Aikau, who came in third. Though Eddie didn't place in the Smirnoff Contest, his performance that day remains a vivid memory for James Jones and all who witnessed his dramatic rescue.

Like the sirens' song, the roaring surf at Waimea Bay had an almost irresistible appeal to surfers eager to prove themselves in the world's largest waves. From the shore, the swells often looked beautiful and inviting, but out in the lineup, surfers discovered just how deadly and destructive they could be. Young daredevils and experienced big-wave riders alike would fall for Waimea's seductive charms. Then, in that moment of truth after a terrible wipeout, they would find themselves swimming for their lives to avoid being crushed on the rocks. Eddie had been there and knew how bad it could be. He cautioned younger surfers about the dangers of the Bay and shared his wave knowledge with them. But there were always the brash newcomers like Ken Bradshaw, who couldn't be stopped.

Originally from a wealthy family in Texas, Ken Bradshaw started surfing in the Gulf of Mexico, and once he got his first taste of its small, murky waves, he was hooked. Rejecting his father's offer to take over the family's lucrative business Ken moved to California to surf while still in his teens. As his appetite for bigger surf grew, he moved to Hawai'i in '72 with the express purpose of riding the largest waves on earth. What Ken lacked in style and experience, he made up for in sheer courage and bravado. Seeing him surf at Waimea, Eddie was impressed by his insatiable hunger for big waves. When they met on the North Shore, Eddie only heard the burly

Texan's last name. He thought his first name was Brad and his last name Shaw so he started calling him Brother Brad. One day while surfing at Waimea, Eddie told him, "'Hey, Bruddah Brad, you gotta sit over here, brah. Sit with me.' Eddie just took me in and said, 'Hey, you gotta do this, you gotta do that.'" Eddie taught Ken all about the Bay and helped him become one of the best big-wave riders of his generation.

During an enormous swell in the winter of '76, North Shore residents woke up to the sound of thunder coming from the ocean. Waimea was exploding with huge 40-60 foot waves that completely closed out the Bay and threatened to wash away nearby houses. The swells were so large they came crashing all the way across the wide beach and into the parking lot behind. Unlike the Smirnoff Contest, these waves were choppy, confused and even larger. Even for veteran big-wave riders, this kind of surf was off limits. Too big, too dangerous and too deadly. "It was so big that the houses were getting knocked off their foundations at the Point at Waimea," Bradshaw remembers. "It was crossing the road at the Foodland." This kind of flooding only happens once or twice a decade, and the cars were backed up in both directions waiting for the water to subside. The drivers stared out at the raging sea with fear and wonder in their eyes.

"We had been watching it all morning, and it was just one close-out after another," Ken says. "Eddie and Clyde pull up, and they say, 'Hey, Bruddah Brad, this is incredible, huh, brah?' And I said, 'Eddie, I think we can surf out there.' And he goes, 'No, Bruddah Brad, you can't go out when the whitewater is hitting the bathhouse.' And I said, 'No, I think you can. Look, I've got it timed. The close-out sets are 12-15 minutes apart, and it only takes us 10 minutes to get out.' And he said, 'No, Bruddah Brad, go home, relax, brah. Don't go out.' But I didn't take no for an answer." That afternoon, Ken and his friend Roger Erikson paddled out into some of the largest waves ever surfed at that time. They wanted to push the limits, even if it meant risking their lives. It's one thing to push the limits but quite another to ignore them all together.

Bradshaw says he was able to make it through the crushing 15-foot shore break and all the way to the outside lineup that day. "I even picked off a couple of waves. Then, I remember Eddie paddling out. He and Kimo came out. It was just the four of us." What changed Eddie's mind to make him go out in such deadly conditions? Not one to be outdone, Eddie must have thought that if Bruddah Brad could do it, so could he. Yet he was rarely reckless. Being the head lifeguard at the Bay, Eddie probably worried that if one of his friends got hurt, he should be out there to help them. Especially someone as young and brash as Bradshaw.

"I remember taking off on this one wave," Ken says, "and it was a complete close-out at the Bay so I straightened out and went all the way to the shore break and I finally let go. After all this tumbling and rolling, I feel the sand. When the thing backs off, I was sitting in the river. And I said, Wow, what a trip!" Ken laughs about it now, but he remembrs being tossed around like a piece of flotsam that day and carried more than thirty yards across the beach and into the river. He could have died, and one veteran wave-rider almost did. "That was the day Kimo got caught inside," Bradshaw says, suddenly serious. "I started paddling back out, and Eddie literally rode past me, yelling, 'Go in! Go in!' I basically took one pounding and got pushed back to shore." On the beach, Ken could see that Kimo was in real trouble.

Kimo Hollinger had been a mentor to Eddie, and they often surfed big Waimea waves together. A tall, dark man who now walks with a limp, Kimo worked as a fireman on the North Shore for thirty years and eventually became a captain. His friendship with Eddie began in the surf and almost ended there. He was generally considered a fearless man, but he got the fear of God pounded into him that day. He speaks of the occasion in a somber tone like a man who has been saved from dying. Kimo knew the waves were big, but due to his poor vision, he didn't realize how huge and deadly they were. "You're having a good time, and the next thing you know you are in trouble," he says. "The waves just got too big. The most important thing in surfing is your eyesight. And when I made 35, my eyes just went bad all of a sudden, and I couldn't see that well anymore. But Eddie could see [a massive wave] was coming, and he tried to yell at me. But because of the sound of the surf and the wind, I couldn't hear him. He and Roger made it out, but I didn't paddle quick enough. When I was paddling out and finally realized what was happening, the waves looked so goddamn big, bigger than I had ever faced. I tried to take off on the wave, not so much to get a thrilling ride or anything, but just to escape the ones in back."

Kimo attempted to catch the giant wall of water before it crushed him, but he took off too late. "I just got the shit beat out of me. It broke my shorts, it broke my wetsuit. It just kept me down. When the second wave came, it kept me down too. I wasn't able to come up so I stayed down for two waves." Imagine being held underwater and trying to hold your breath for more than a minute while the exploding whitewater delivers a thousand invisible blows to your body and throws you against the bottom. You become punch-drunk as you struggle not to pass out. "When I finally came up, the surface of the water was just all whirlpools and currents. I was tired and out of air, and there was so much foam on top of the water I couldn't breathe. I was crying and asking the Lord, 'Please, I will never do this again.' I swam the wrong way toward the rocks. I was crying—I had lost it already."

After being blasted in the impact zone, known as the "boneyard," he was helplessly drifting toward "coffin corner," where the waves threatened to slam him against the jagged rocks. He was caught in the vicious whirlpool between the huge shore break and the even bigger waves outside. "The shore break must have been about 15 feet, and I was getting pounded," Kimo remembers. At the same time, the lifeguards on the beach had spotted him and were frantically trying to rescue him. "Butch Van Artsdalen had seen what was happening to me so he came to help. He and the firemen and the other lifeguards formed a human chain and were trying to drag me in."

With huge waves exploding all around them, the group of men locked hands and arms on top of the 25-high rock and scaled down its slippery side, reaching into the raging surf to rescue their friend. If one slipped and fell, all the others would go with him. Straining to hold on, they managed to grab his hand and began pulling him onto the rock. With each man clinging to the one below him, it was like a tug-of-war with the sea; but slowly, they pulled Kimo out of the crashing surf and up the steep rock face. Despite Butch's trembling hands and drinking problems, he helped saved Kimo's life that day. "It was definitely a life and death situation," lifeguard Mark Dombroski recalls. As one of the men in the chain, Mark can safely say, "It was seconds away from being a disastrous situation."

Separated from Kimo in the massive waves, Eddie had done his best to get back in as fast as possible. "It was every man for himself out there," Mark says. Still, Eddie's instincts as a lifeguard urged him to scramble to shore and run over to the rock to help save his friend. By the time he got there, Kimo had already been pulled out of the surf. He was coughing up seawater and bile, trying to catch his breath. Eddie and the others did their best to comfort him, but he was too shaken up. He kept muttering to himself, "Never again." When Kimo finally recovered, he started to go home. On the way, he ran into Bradshaw, who didn't realize how close he had come to dying. "Kimo and I walked and talked for a while. I was 22 or 23 at the time, and I was so amped. And I was going to go back out, and Kimo's going, 'No, bruddah, don't go back out. I'm over it, I'm going home.' And I said, 'I'll see you when it drops tomorrow,' and he said, 'No, brother, I'm over it.' I didn't understand what he meant." Kimo gave away his boards and vowed never to go out at Waimea. "That was it. I never surfed big waves again," he says. "I figured you don't get a second chance. Something that can be so innocent and fun can just turn so deadly."

Later that day, Ken recalls, "Eddie came up to me and said, 'We're going home. And, Brad, please don't go back out.' So we called it a day. It was an amazing day, 35-40 foot sets, 60 foot faces. But what I've learned over the years is that Waimea after 25 feet just starts closing out and starts getting really dangerous. There's no way to get out of the Bay once you get stuck in there. It gets sick so quick."

Before going home that day, Eddie and Clyde stopped over at Kimo's place to see how he was doing. Eddie was probably feeling guilty that he hadn't been there to help him, and he knew how shaken up his friend had been. Barely escaping with his life, the veteran surfer and fireman struggled with all kinds of doubts, fears and depressing thoughts. So the Aikau brothers went over to his house to comfort him and boost his spirits. "Eddie brought his slack-key guitar," Kimo recalls, "and him and Clyde played music for me to help me feel a little better." Not wanting to talk about Kimo's near-death experience or relive it, Eddie and his brother filled the room with the soothing sounds of slack-key guitar and old Hawaiian melodies.

After that incident, Kimo had a new respect for Eddie, not only for his gentleness on land but for his fearlessness in the water. He says that many of the big-name riders who followed Eddie didn't possess his sense of humility and courage. "Of all the guys who go around talking about how famous they were and how they rode the biggest waves, hey, brah, I saw Eddie catch those waves, and it was something else," Kimo says. "None of those guys could hold a candle to Eddie." As the only one of his group who didn't graduate from high school, perhaps Eddie was trying to make his mark in the surfing world. "Maybe he wasn't educated...but when it came to surfing big waves, that guy was a genius."

After Kimo's accident Eddie noticed there was a gradual changing of the guard as older mentors like Fred Van Dyke began to retire from big-wave surfing. As a young man, Fred Van Dyke had loved the thrill of riding enormous swells, but as he grew older, he was forced to confront his growing fears. Like Kimo, he had experienced his share of deadly wipeouts, and they were beginning to take a heavy toll on his mind and body. At what point, he wondered, should he just walk away. Sitting in front of a picture of him surfing a giant Waimea swell thirty years before, Fred says in the documentary *Surfing for Life* that he can still recall dropping down the face of that enormous wave and feeling the thrill of a lifetime. "I can remember looking up at this 25 foot wave, and time stopped. It was like a still photograph. I was one with the wave, I was one with the water, with my surfboard, my body. The entire universe just melted together for that one second. And then the wave threw over, I wiped out, bounced off the bottom. Reality came. But that one second…," he sighs, lost in memory. "The wipeout is the ultimate in showing you what a fool you are, in showing you how vulnerable you are. The wipeout puts you on that edge where the most important thing is not the mortgage you have or the money you have or the cars or anything—it's getting one tiny little breath of air."

Fred says it was his friend Peter Cole who had originally pushed him to overcome his fears and ride the biggest waves. "You either attack fear or you retreat from it, and Peter attacks fear. It was his presence that stoked me to become a much better big-wave rider." As a young man, Fred enjoyed the rush, but as he got older, it became more of an obsession. "I used to be driven. I had to be out there every frickin' day. I had to be there when the cameras were on the beach. I was in *Life* magazine and *Sports Illustrated*. I had to be there…I lost a job over surfing. I blew so many relationships over surfing and hurt so many people," Fred admits.

As a husband, father and teacher, Van Dyke had responsibilities to other people. He began to wonder if riding big waves was worth the risk. He didn't recover from the terrible spills as quickly as he had in his younger, more carefree days. During his worst wipeout, Fred remembers being held underwater so long that he finally blacked out. The water turned bright green and then yellow before fading to black. Though scared, he said those final moments were actually quite peaceful. He says Navy Seals and other divers who have come close to drowning have also experienced this feeling of serene surrender. To this day, Fred can't remember how he made it back to the surface.

In his mid-forties, Fred began to lose his nerve in big waves. He recalls the day when it all came to an end. He was out at Sunset, and he was paddling for a wave more than three times his height. "Everyone was yelling, 'Go, Van Dyke, go, it's your wave!' I was in the perfect position, I went to go, I looked, and I didn't want to know anything about that wave. For the first time in my life, I had gotten in touch with fear, true, uncontrolled fear, and it had blown me away." Staring down the face of a huge wave about to break can be like staring into an abyss. With tears in his eyes, Fred says, "I'm supposed to be this macho, tough surfer guy, but I'm not—I'm really this total wuss on the inside." Fred stopped surfing big waves after that incident at Sunset, and he says, "From then on, as far as riding big waves, it was more or less downhill. I wasn't one of the gang anymore. I lost friends that way." Old friends like Peter Cole, Jose Angel and Eddie remained loyal to Fred, but they didn't share his view that big-wave surfing is about machismo. "When you ride a big wave, you're trying to prove something," Fred says. "Guys won't admit this, but that's the bottom line."

Peter totally disagrees. "I never thought of it as a life-threatening thing. It wasn't a really big macho thing. For me, it was fun, and if it wasn't fun, you should get out of there." He goes on to say that surfers like Eddie and Jose Angel actually liked being out in huge waves. "I think the thing I enjoyed the most about Eddie was that he just loved to surf big waves so much. The big macho wave-riding was a media thing and just a small part of the whole picture. I got the feeling that it was a natural thing for him to turn around and go on these big waves. If he had any fear, it didn't show."

Fred says he is still astounded by what seemed like Eddie's fearlessness in the face of such liquid giants. He recalls a time years later when Eddie was being interviewed by Howard Cosell for ABC's *Wide World of Sports* during one of the Duke Contests. It was a really big day at Sunset, and like most of the surfers, Eddie had taken an ugly spill on one of the waves. Cosell asked Eddie how he dealt with such horrible wipeouts? In front of the cameras, Eddie laughed and said in his pidgin accent, "Yeah, yeah, it was real bad out there today, so bad I like go surf Queens."

Referring to the gentle break at Queens Beach in Waikiki where he grew up surfing, Eddie had all the surfers laughing at that point. But the talkative Cosell and the ABC crew didn't get the joke. It would be like a professional skier saying he wanted to go back to the bunny slopes after taking a vicious spill on a vertical run. "I've felt like going to surf Queens many times," Fred laughs. "To hell with the North Shore—it's too heavy."

Fred, Kimo and others eventually backed down from riding such deadly waves but not Eddie. He never even considered giving up surfing his beloved waves at Waimea Bay, even when they came close to killing him. Nor did his older friend Jose Angel, who seemed hell-bent on pushing his limits as a big-wave rider and deep-sea diver—even if it meant flirting with death.

CHAPTER 9

Diving Deep

"If you gaze for long into an abyss,
the abyss gazes also into you."
— *Friedrich Nietzsche*

Eddie's life on the North Shore was a strange mix of calm and chaos. From April until October, it was mostly quiet in the Country, and the ocean often looked like a slate of blue-green glass. His days consisted of watching over Waimea, keeping an eye on the inexperienced swimmers and the kids jumping from the tall rocks at the end of the Bay. He also tended to tourists with severe sunburn or bad jellyfish stings. During his breaks, he played volleyball with the other lifeguards and local firemen. After work, he would often go free-diving for hours at a time. With his mask, snorkel, flippers and spear, he would explore the busy world under the water's serene surface in search of dinner. It was a tranquil life during these quiet months. But from November till March, when the waves rose up like leviathans from the sea and threatened to devour surfers and unsuspecting tourists, Eddie's job as a lifeguard went into high gear and so did his surfing. The ocean reflected both sides of his personality, the yin and yang of being a waterman. Like his wild friend Jose Angel, he was generally calm and contemplative, but he could also be intense and incredibly active when the conditions suddenly changed.

Working as a lifeguard with Eddie at Waimea, Clyde remembers how they could always find some activity to do in the ocean when they weren't on duty. For Clyde, being a waterman means always being "involved in the ocean and spending as much time as I can in the water, doing whatever is called for by the day." Looking out over the ocean on a sunny summer afternoon, he says, "If there's no surf, you do something else. If you've got high winds and no surf, you go sailing. If the waves are really tiny, you go longboarding. If the waves get big, you pull out your gun. If you're hungry, you go out diving and catch some fish. It excites me to do all these different activities in the ocean. It all depends on the wind and the waves." The biorhythms of island life. Depending on the wind and the ocean's fickle moods, the waves could vary from season to season, day to day and even hour to hour. Each swell had its own personality and musical rhythm. They could be gentle and flowing like Hawaiian songs, rough and fast like rock 'n roll, unpredictable and funky like jazz, or powerful and ominous like a classical symphony building to a thunderous crescendo.

When the new sport of windsurfing hit the Islands in the mid-70's, Eddie and Clyde jumped on this new form of sailing and surfing. Borrowing boards from friends and rigging up their sails, they would glide across the Bay, powered by the wind. As the equipment improved, Clyde would later become addicted to windsurfing because it combined the speed of sailing with the power of surfing big waves. Following in the wake of world champs like Robbie Naish, Clyde's talent soared as he flew across the waves. The new sport was a natural evolution of surfing, and it coincided with the boom in skateboarding at the time, which was a kind of street-surfing. Other boardsports like snowboarding, tow-in surfing and kite-surfing would later become offshoots of the surfing craze. Whether surfing across water, concrete or snow, the concept of riding boards was one of Hawai'i's great contributions to the world of sports. The Aikau brothers enjoyed windsurfing, but surfing was still their main passion.

Eddie and Clyde made the most of their carefree lifestyle during the summer. After working all week as lifeguards, they partied every weekend on the North Shore. "Here's how it went," says Clyde. "Saturdays was for partying and chasing girls. My job was to chase all the girls. Eddie's job was to dive into the water around 4:30 and by 5:30, he would come out with the biggest *uluas* [jack or pompano fish]. I would have the fire going and the beers ready, and we would party, brah. It broke da' mouth, brah." The Aikaus were legendary cooks, and they loved getting together with good friends on the beach, drinking beer and eating fresh-cooked fish. If the food was really *ono* (delicious), locals joked that it would 'break the mouth' because it was so good. More than eating good fish, Eddie loved catching them.

"My brother Eddie was one of the great skin-divers on the North

148

Shore," Clyde says, sounding like an awe-struck younger brother. "That's something a lot of people don't know. Eddie could free-dive 50 feet with no problem." He could also stay down for almost two minutes at a time. Wearing a mask, snorkel and fins, he would go as deep as many divers go with scuba gear. It was like a slower, more peaceful world down there, an underwater desert where exotic fish and sea turtles glided across the sky. Like a patient hunter, he would hold his breath and sit perfectly still at the bottom, waiting for an *ulua* to come by. Then, he would slowly point his spear-gun at the wide-eyed creature and Whoosh! The spear would pierce the fish, and he would return to the surface for air. After bagging it and resting a few minutes, he would go back down again for more. But there were times when the smell of blood and fresh kill attracted other hunters much bigger than Eddie. In fact, he sometimes ran into a big tiger shark out at Waimea, and once Clyde saw him come eye to eye with the 'landlord of the Bay.'

Clyde was there in the water with Eddie and saw the tiger approach his brother. "That shark would always follow him out there. One time I dove with him, and I saw the shark, like 20 feet long, coming toward him. All of a sudden, Eddie turns and sees it. I know that he's got everything covered, but I'm watching. That shark sees him and comes up to Eddie, and then stops and looks at Eddie, Eddie looks at him, and that shark just turned around. After I saw that, I told Eddie, '*Hele* on [let's go], brah, *hele* on, please!'" Clyde says the shark is the Aikau's '*aumakua*, ancestral spirits who take the form of natural guardians and watch over the family. But he is still afraid of sharks and has more of an affinity toward gentle sea turtles. Eddie, on the other hand, confronted sharks the same way he dealt with big waves—by facing them head on and not backing off in fear. In that way, he was in a special league, according to Fred Van Dyke.

Fred says Eddie used to take on the biggest waves in the most critical spot, a trait he shared with such seemingly fearless surfers as Greg Noll and Jose Angel. "Eddie was always so far over from where most of us took off at Waimea, and he was riding the Point [the most dangerous inside section, near the rocks], no matter how big it got. He was just phenomenal. Greg and Jose and Eddie were like three peas in a pod. The three of them were totally out of whatever realm all of us are in. They were doing things that were almost impossible. Like Jose doing a cannon ball or a back somersault off of his board right in the middle of the hook [curl] at Waimea. I'd never heard of that." Jose became infamous for taking off on huge, close-out waves and then doing a back-flip off of his board right before the wave came down on him. This was beyond daring—it was downright crazy. Eddie wasn't nearly as reckless, but he did take off on the steepest part of the wave, near the rocks. "No matter who took off, Eddie was on the inside. Like that saying, 'Eddie would go,' he did go, always. He was so good that people couldn't overlook him."

During the 60's, Greg Noll was known as the most daring big-wave rider of the time, but unlike Jose, he knew when to quit. In the mythic lore of surfing, Greg became famous for riding one of the largest waves ever ridden during the enormous swell of 1969. The wave supposedly towered above him like a glass skyscraper before imploding and almost annihilating him. After almost meeting his maker that day, Greg retired from big-wave surfing, moved back to California and became a deep-sea fisherman. But as big as his last wave was, even Greg admits that like some of his fishing stories, it seems to grow bigger and bigger with each telling! Some friends even joke that he has been riding that same wave for more than 30 years. In terms of sheer courage, Greg once remarked that Jose must have had "cast-iron balls." Clyde agrees, saying Jose was the "undisputed fearless one of all the big-wave riders. He was in such superb condition that getting a big wipeout was exhilarating for him. It was no fear. Eddie and Jose were like close buddies." Besides surfing Sunset and Waimea Bay together, they both loved diving. But Jose seemed to know no limits and kept going deeper.

Jose became a role model for Eddie because he was so brave in big waves and yet so humble and friendly. According to Peter Cole, "Eddie just worshipped Jose because he was a good waterman and he had a lot of guts—he would take off on anything. And he was such a nice guy and such an enjoyable person to be around. Everyone liked him. He was a leader in a sense. He was a principal in school. Eddie, Clyde and the whole Aikau family really liked Jose because of his personality and what he was." What he was was larger than life, a mythical figure whose life and mysterious death would have a profound effect on Eddie and help shape his future.

The only son of a Filipino cook named Jose and his Canadian wife Lilly, Jose, Jr. grew up in San Francisco. Sensitive to his racial mix, he threw himself into sports and eventually became a strong swimmer and water polo player. He started surfing in high school, and after he graduated, he took a trip to Hawai'i, where he surfed for three months in Waikiki. When he returned from his extended vacation in Hawai'i, he enrolled at San Francisco State College, where he studied to become a teacher. Blessed with good looks and an athletic body, Jose cut quite a romantic figure wherever he went. At that point, he was more into swimming and surfing than romancing. But one day at the beach, he spotted a pretty, blond-haired surfer named Mozelle, known as 'Mo' to her friends, who was also studying physical education. A spunky tom-boy from Tennessee, she was not only intelligent and athletic, but she could surf better than he could! They quickly fell in love and became what Mozelle calls "soul mates"—"We even had the same birthday. We were fated to be together."

Mozelle was in love but scared of settling down. So she moved to Hawai'i a couple of years later in search of adventure and better waves. Undaunted, Jose followed her, and they ended up living on a boat together in the Ala Wai Harbor for over a year. During this blissful period, they surfed, fished, dove and sailed to the neighbor islands together, practically living in the ocean. After graduating with a degree in physical education from the University of Hawai'i, Jose eventually became a principal at Hale'iwa Elementary School on the North Shore. He and Mozelle married, bought a house near Pipeline and settled down into the business of raising a family. They eventually had four kids, three girls and a boy. Jose surfed as often as possible, and he soon established himself as an intrepid surfer on the North Shore. At that point, he seemed to have everything: a beautiful wife, a healthy passel of kids, a good job, a house right on the beach and the best waves in the world. But there was a restlessness in his soul that made him take the most dangerous risks.

Ricky Grigg, who introduced Jose to coral diving, once wrote that big-wave riders and deep-sea divers were always aware of the possibility of dying. "Jose and I often talked about how close we were to the edge of death while surfing giant waves at Waimea Bay. We would train during the summers by skin diving 60 feet deep for green turtles off of the North Shore reefs." The thrills of being in the ocean and pushing themselves to the limit always seemed to surpass the risks. One summer when a group of them were competing to see who could dive the deepest and stay down the longest, Fred Van Dyke remembers how Jose swam down to the bottom to bring a 150-pound turtle back to the surface. "Jose makes a dive to go down to a turtle hole, and we see him coming up, and about 15 feet below the surface, all of a sudden, he arches back like a porpoise and starts sinking down to the bottom again. What he had done was hold his breath as long as he could and he was trying to get up for some air, but he never made it." Jose passed out. About three or four guys went down to get him, and when they brought him up on the surface, they gave him mouth to mouth resuscitation. When he revived, he was surprised and a little upset to see his friends kissing him! "Jose was pissed—Who's this guy giving him a French kiss?! He didn't even know he had passed out. Can you imagine this guy holding his breath so long going after a turtle and not making it? It's incredible."

A neighbor and fellow educator, Fred was a close friend of Jose's and admired his outlook on life. "He was a very positive person, and he was always stoked on living and diving and everything that was happening in his life. He had to be a damn good teacher to end up being principal—that's not an easy thing to do." By most accounts, Jose was a hard-working principal, but when the waves got really big and perfect, he was like Peter and Fred in that he couldn't resist the temptation to surf. During the epic swell of '67, when Eddie made his big-wave debut, Jose called in sick that day and joined Eddie and Peter in the huge waves. Mozelle says problems arose the next day when they saw Jose's picture on the front page of the newspaper! The principal had been caught cutting school to go surfing. "So his superintendent called him in," Mozelle laughs, and his boss told him, "You have to be a little more careful." For a big-wave hero like Jose, taking a day off from work once or twice a year was not unheard of. But as a principal, skipping school to go surfing and then getting his picture in the paper posed a problem. Of course, his students thought it was cool; and friends like Eddie thought it was funny.

Eddie enjoyed surfing and hanging around with educated men like Jose and Peter, who didn't seem to care that he never finished high school. They were older and wiser than most of the juvenile, transient surfers on the North Shore. As a married man himself, Eddie admired the way they could maintain a steady home life. While Jose, Peter and Eddie spent their afternoons surfing big waves, their wives would get together on the beach to take care of the kids, talk and commiserate. As fellow 'surf widows,' Mozelle, Sally and Linda enjoyed each other's company. They understood what it was like to be married to such hard-core watermen and would laugh about their husbands' love affair with the sea. Meanwhile, the men were still charging waves that made the younger kids cringe with fear on the beach. Handsome, muscular and slightly crazy, these surfers had appeared in magazines across the country, bold figures set against a backdrop of massive waves. Jose had been on the cover of the very first issue of *Surfer*, and years later, the magazine would call him the "Bravest Surfer of All Time."

Even though he was famous for his fearlessness in big waves, "Jose was always uncomfortable with recognition. I'm sure it pleased him, but he never asked for it, never bragged and never talked about himself. And, of course, everyone else was talking about how great they were," Mozelle says. Like Eddie, Jose was very humble and didn't like boastful people. Jose had a reputation of being fearless in the water and on land, but he was still a man of flesh, blood and nerves. He didn't seem to recognize that fear is an integral part of living, as Eddie would soon discover, and to deny it was to flirt with death.

Ricky Grigg has a slightly different take on the fear factor. "We all have some fear, and it's tough to admit to that. But the fear would be more a matter of cautious decision-making. There were some waves you wouldn't take off on, and those would be waves you knew were going to drill you to the bottom. It was the kind of fear that made you careful. But it wasn't the fear that Fred Van Dyke had, where he was just terrified paddling out, and he hated it. But he went out because he felt he had to. Some guys who get into the culture of big-wave riding aren't really doing it because they want to—it's more of a status thing. Though that would never occur to Jose. He couldn't care what people thought of him. He didn't have any self-doubt. He wasn't doing it to reassure himself, he was doing it because he liked to do it. Peter was the same way, and it was fun for him—he didn't do it for the cameras or the rest of that crap." Nor did Eddie, who surfed big waves for the simple thrill of it, even when no one else was around.

Roger Pfeffer surfed with Jose, Eddie and Peter and was in awe of their courage in big waves. "Their tremendous experience and confidence in their ability set them apart from other people. They could handle situations that would daunt other surfers, even the best." When huge sets would suddenly appear, Roger says, "I would be paddling for the sky and the horizon. I knew there was always a risk that you could get killed out there." The select group of surfers who dared to paddle out in such conditions would usually go into survival mode, instinctively worrying only about their own safety. But Eddie, Peter and Jose always watched out for others who might get into trouble. Like the guides leading climbers up Mount Everest, they wanted to make sure no one died trying to reach the summit.

Besides their extensive experience in large swells, Roger believes that it was their paddling ability and concern for others that made these men extraordinary. "Jose, Peter and Eddie were such strong paddlers that they could pick up a person on a 9 or 10-foot surfboard and paddle with two people on the board faster than you alone could paddle on the board. How do I know that? Because one time Eddie picked me up on his board after I got washed out toward the harbor at Haleiwa. I couldn't swim against the current, and he had caught a wave and come through and picked me up on the board and paddled against the current with the two of us on the board. I was dead-tired. I was in front, and he was behind. It was just amazing. I experienced the same thing once at Laniakea. I got swept out toward Himalayas, and Jose Angel paddled out and saved my life. He put me on the board, and he paddled that board with the both of us on it faster than I could have paddled it by myself—and against the rip! I couldn't believe it. And when he did that, I remembered the same experience with Eddie. They were really strong paddlers. He paddled us back to shore, and I just sat on the beach and got my breath for a while. And Jose went back out."

Though Eddie took incredible risks as a surfer and a lifeguard, he also knew his limits and was generally very cautious and careful. Jose was a different story. As he grew older, he went from taking dangerous risks to being completely reckless. Underneath his handsome, calm demeanor, Jose was wrestling with demons that made him do crazy things. Along with doing back-flips off of his board in huge waves, he would go on excessively deep dives. It was as if he enjoyed being thrown into the center of the abyss. He seemed to have a self-destructive streak, and his wife sensed it. "Ever since I've known him, I thought he was going to kill himself," Mozelle says. "I've always known that he wasn't going to live till old age. There was something in him that was erratic, unreasonable, but I admired that because I'm like that too. It's not like we ever tried to stop each other, but I had a foreboding all the time I knew him that he was not going to make it."

The crisis came when Jose found out his mother was dying of stomach cancer in San Francisco. By the time he arrived in San Francisco, she had already slipped into a coma and was being kept alive on life support. Her doctors said she had little chance of recovery, and Jose had to decide whether to keep her on life support indefinitely or let her die naturally. Financially unable to pay the exorbitant costs of an extended hospital stay or a medical transfer back to Hawai'i, he made the most painful decision of his life: he pulled the plug on her life support system. His mother died shortly after. With tears in her eyes, Mozelle says he felt incredibly guilty, as if he had murdered his mom. Though she wanted to come and comfort her husband, she had to stay home and take care of the kids.

During his time at the hospital, Jose had met a young Filipino woman named Katie, who was there for her daughter's surgery. "While he was taking care of his mom," Mozelle recalls in a shaky voice, "he meets a little brown girl from Hawai'i Kai, and he was unfaithful to me for the first time in our marriage." Distraught and guilty about his mom's death, Jose had an affair with Katie, who convinced him to leave his wife. When he came back home, he was extremely upset and told Mozelle that he couldn't stay with the family any longer. "He kept saying, 'I killed my mom.' He was more than shaken up. It was more like he was saying, 'I'm not worthy of my family, I've been unfaithful, I'm not worthy of being a father to the four kids I love more than anything.'" Almost as soon as he returned, Jose moved in with Katie and her kids. It was a whirlwind relationship, and his life changed dramatically. Jose's friends, like Eddie and Peter, were torn between their loyalty to Jose and their sympathy for Mozelle.

Because he was now trying to support two families, he started a small business of diving for black coral. Found deep on the ocean floor, the black coral trees were being harvested for burgeoning local businesses on Maui that fashioned them into expensive jewelry. Instead of diving for pleasure, he was now diving for treasure in the form of black coral. He could make between $500 and $1000 for each tree. With a single tank of air on his back, he would go down more than 200 feet where the coral trees grew on the sea floor. Jose had a huge weight on his shoulders, and he was descending into greater and greater depths, physically and emotionally. "He changed," Mo says. "The first thing he did was go get the bends and almost die." Known for always going deeper and longer than the limits allowed, he stayed down too long on one dive and ran out of air. He swam toward the light as fast as he could, trying not to black out. As he ascended, the last breath of air in his lungs continued expanding as the nitrogen in his blood began to bubble. When he finally surfaced and gasped for air, he didn't have time to decompress. By the time Jose got to the decompression chamber at the local hospital, he had already suffered the bends and his leg was partially paralyzed.

A lifelong athlete, his body was suddenly and irrevocably incapacitated. He became depressed. Katie kept him secluded in her home as she took care of him, not letting friends like Eddie or even his family know how he was doing. "He was crippled," Mozelle says, sitting out on her deck. She is holding a cigarette in her trembling hands and crying as she looks out over the ocean her husband loved. "Poor Jose almost died so she took over. It was the saddest, most horrible time." To make matters worse, Katie insisted on living on the North Shore, near where Jose worked. He asked for a divorce and as soon as it was finalized, he married Katie, who seemed intent on taking over Mozelle's place. At one point, she even enrolled her children in the same school that Mo's kids attended so they had to see each other every day. That was the final blow. Unable to handle the grief and humiliation of seeing her husband with another woman in their old neighborhood, Mozelle packed up the kids and moved back to her parents' home in Tennessee for a year. Eddie was sad to see Jose and his wife drifting apart, yet he could feel a similar distance creeping into his own marriage.

Eddie's life mirrored Jose's in mysterious ways. They both seemed content as dolphins in the waves, but each struggled with his own doubts on land. Jose's life had spiraled out of control after the death of his mother, and Eddie was still having a hard time moving on after the loss of his brother. But they dealt with their depression in very different ways. After the breakup of their marriage and Mozelle's move to Tennessee, Jose continued diving even deeper. He seemed to give into self-destructiveness and a morbid death wish. Meanwhile, Eddie was struggling to keep himself and his marriage afloat.

More than a year after Gerald's death, Eddie and Linda decided to take a trip to Australia to visit the Holmes family. Linda knew Eddie needed a change, anything to get out of the graveyard for a while. She figured that surfing with Lynne and Darrell and playing with Tracey and Jodi would probably take his mind off of his brother. Gerald's memory often was still as vivid as the photos of him on the walls. Their home had become a mausoleum to his brother's life, and seeing the pictures and the memorial torch ginger garden they had planted in his memory made him morose. Eddie tended to dwell on the past when he was sad, but Linda looked to the future. She hoped the trip to Australia would revitalize their relationship. She didn't want to end up like Jose and Mozelle.

Although they hadn't seen each other in two years, Eddie had kept in touch with Lynne and the Holmes family by mailing them letter-tapes.

Guitar in hand, he would hike up to his favorite waterfall in nearby Manoa Valley, find a rock to sit on and turn on the tape recorder. He would play music for them and then share whatever was on his mind. "Mostly, everything came down to family, Hawai'i, music and surfing: those were the cornerstones of the conversation," Lynne remembers. Speaking in his slow, languorous voice, Eddie would tell them about recent birthdays, family luaus and surf contests. Then, he would sing the latest Hawaiian songs he had learned and talk story about important local events. He told them about the recent building of a voyaging canoe that was being modeled after the original vessels that first brought the Polynesians to Hawai'i. His was a rambling monologue about life in the Islands, but Lynne noticed he had begun talking a lot about this canoe called the *Hokule'a*. She planned to ask him about it when he came to Australia. At the end of the tape, he would always say, "God bless you and your family. Aloha."

After months of planning and saving, Eddie and Linda boarded the plane for Australia, the island continent. During the twelve-hour flight, they talked, dozed and stared at the endless expanse of sea below them. When they finally arrived in Sydney, the Holmes greeted them at the airport with hugs and gifts. It was a warm reunion, and the conversation picked up right where Eddie left off on his last letter-tape. They drove twelve miles to Narrabeen and didn't take any long trips out of the city because they just wanted to stay at home, talk, surf and go for long walks. "It was just a matter of coming and seeing where we lived and what Australia was about," Lynne says. "They stayed for about three weeks. We didn't travel anywhere; we did everything local because the surf was at the end of the street. It was just a matter of seeing the animals, kangaroos and koalas, and just meeting local people." Eddie had met a number of top Aussie surfers who traveled to Hawai'i each winter and were beginning to dominate the contests. Though he generally enjoyed their rowdy way of talking, drinking and partying, he and many other Hawaiian surfers sometimes resented their cockiness in the surf and on land. But he had a good time surfing with Lynne and Darrell, while Linda was content to look after the kids on the golden sand beach.

With no children of his own, Eddie spent a lot of time playing with Tracey and Jodi. "He was good with my kids," Lynne says, moved by how much he cared for them and clearly wanted his own. "He used to laugh with them a lot." Like Duke Kahanamoku, Eddie had a gentle, child-like innocence about him. He enjoyed playing with kids and listening to their imaginative stories. As a young girl, Jodi used to follow Eddie around every-where and remembers staring into his eyes whenever he played his guitar and sang for her. "I love dark Hawaiian eyes," she says. "There's so much depth. It's like a connection that goes through years in history. You look in those kind of eyes and there's so much there. It's like you can see their ancestors in there. The embodiment of spirit. I think that's probably why I ended up with my husband who is a fair bit older than me and who actually used to play guitar down at the graveyard with Eddie. That was where we first met. That was my youth." Jodi would later become a professional surfer and surfing promoter in Hawai'i.

For Lynne and the girls, the highlight of Eddie's visit was when he went to Tracey and Jodi's school to perform and talk to the eager 'keiki,' as Hawaiians call young kids. "He sat in front of the whole school, a big assembly" she remembers, "and sang some songs and talked to the kids. He actually got them singing 'Tiny Kangaroo,' which he had practiced for months. Being an oceanfront school, they were all water-kids, and of course, they all wanted to know about the big waves in Hawai'i. That was an absolute highlight for anyone in Australia, let alone kids who were just getting into surfing." After Duke Kahanamoku introduced the sport of surfing to Australia in 1914, it had become one of the most popular sports in the country. Hawaiian surfers like Duke and Eddie were looked up to like demigods in the Land Down Under.

Toward the end of their visit, everyone would become quiet, not wanting to think about Eddie and Linda's departure. To fill the awkward silence, Eddie would play his guitar and sing popular tunes like "I'm leavin' on a jet plane, don't know when I'll be back again...." Though Eddie and Linda seemed to be in good spirits, Lynne could see in his eyes that there was something wrong—she and Eddie were like soul mates so it was hard to hide their innermost feelings. Ever since meeting in South Africa, they had become fast friends who could share anything with each other. While surfing or walking together, Eddie could talk to her about anything, from his sadness over Gerald's passing to his excitement over the Hokule'a. There was a natural attraction between them, but of course, they resisted the temptation to act on it or even acknowledge it. Their marriages were undergoing some strain, but both couples did their best not to show the sadness behind their smiles. After dropping them off at the airport, Lynne remembers coming home to a silent house and feeling Eddie's absence for a long time afterward.

After their long flight to Hawai'i, Eddie and Linda resumed their old routine. He would drive out to the North Shore before dawn to surf and work all day in the hot sun and then come home to relax. Meanwhile, she would work indoors all day at the insurance office downtown and then want to go out at night. He was content to grab a teriyaki burger or Spam fried rice at the Rainbow Drive-In, while she liked going out to Italian restaurants for dinner. But Eddie didn't like going to restaurants or clubs that were crowded with people he didn't know. Because one of his teeth had been knocked out in a surfing accident, he had to wear a plate with a false tooth, and Linda says this made him self-conscious about eating in public. Unless he was performing, he was introverted by nature and generally preferred to stay in with family or hang out with close friends. Linda, on the other hand, was a classic extrovert and loved to go out on the town and meet new people. The differences that once complemented each other slowly became obstacles between them.

Like most surfers, Eddie took his personal problems to the sea in hopes that the waves would wash them away. He would see Jose on occasion and couldn't help noticing how his health had declined. Without fully recuperating from the bends, Jose had pushed himself to keep diving and surfing. He refused to give up his passions. But in the eyes of friends like Eddie, Ricky and Fred, he had lost the old magic. As they watched him take off on big swells, his bad leg would buckle under the incredible pressure of the drop and bottom turn, and he would suffer humiliating wipeouts on waves he had once ridden with ease. "When you get to the bottom of a wave, there's tremendous G-forces on you, and he used to just crumble," Ricky recalls. "That was really heart-breaking." But Jose kept taking all the punishment the waves could give him, too proud to give up surfing big waves but too weak to make the drop.

"It was a tough time for him," Fred remembers, physically and emotionally. Jose missed his family and started to regret his hasty decision to leave his wife and kids when his new marriage developed its own problems. "He had that diving accident so he was semi-impotent at the time, and that was really bothering him. So we used to sit out in the ocean and talk about his problems." As his troubles mounted, he began diving more often, going deeper each time. Weightlessly moving through the water like an aquanaut, Jose didn't feel crippled underwater, so the deep sea became his escape where he felt strong and vital once again. He continued risking his life with each dive for black coral, going down to near-lethal depths of 200-250 feet. At that depth, the darkness and narcosis distort a man's thoughts and the nitrogen in his blood becomes poisonous. In one diving accident, Jose lost a diving partner who drowned. On other occasions, he suffered from increasingly debilitating cases of the bends.

What caused Jose to push himself so hard and put his life on the line for the simple thrill of riding the biggest waves or diving the deepest? "I think he was driven to do himself in," Mozelle says. "It becomes an emotional breakdown that men don't want anybody to know about so they handle it and take it out on themselves physically. He would take it all out on himself. He learned very early that physical exertion was what he needed to release this emotion which is healthy; and that would mean that the more emotional he would be, the more he needed to exert, and the more rash he would get. I imagine him sitting at Waimea Bay on a huge day and just thinking, 'I'll just see if I can take off...How much can I really take?' It was a competitiveness with his own body, and that's why he was so crushed when he was damaged by the bends."

After a year in Tennessee with her parents, Mozelle and the kids had returned to their home on the North Shore in June of '76. By this time, Jose had separated from Katie and was living in a small apartment not far from his family. He had written Mozelle letters full of regret and resignation, saying how much he missed them and wished he could undo what he had done. "I have a letter from him that he wrote to me in Tennessee, and he said, 'I am so tired. I wish I could sit under a tree and rest.' And I knew he was going through so much." Jose was trying to support two families, keep up with his duties as a principal and continue diving for extra income. Meanwhile, he was sinking deeper into the abyss. But he took some comfort in seeing Mo and the kids. He began coming over to the house for dinner, and the family enjoyed being together again. He spent more time at the house, and for a while it looked like they might be reunited as a family. But Jose was still struggling with the siren call of the sea, which seemed to be calling him home.

Only weeks after the family's homecoming, Jose went coral diving off Maui with a friend and was lost at sea. He had gone down to about 200 feet and didn't realize how much he had drifted with the current until it was time to come up. When he finally surfaced, Jose was a long way from the boat. His friend searched for hours but couldn't find him so he finally returned to Maui to report that Jose was missing. The Coast Guard searched the area for more than three hours and couldn't find him either. Stranded thirteen miles from Maui and drifting away from the island in the strong current, Jose hung on to his flotation bag for most of the day and watched the summit of Haleakala drift away from him. When he realized he wasn't going to be rescued and saw sharks circling around him, he started yelling at the dull-eyed predators to keep them away. Finally, he took off his scuba gear and tied it to the flotation device and began swimming with all his might toward the island of Moloka'i, more than five miles away. Sharks circled him again, but he just kept swimming and screaming at them underwater.

Jose eventually landed at Keawanui Beach on the southeast coast of Moloka'i, where he walked down the road in his wetsuit, found a phone and called home to let his family know he was okay. "He was lost at sea all day, from 9:00 am till dark. We thought he was dead then," Mo remembers. "He swam all the way and reached the shore and called us. Everybody was jubilant again." His disappearance had made front-page headlines, and so had his miraculous swim to safety. Eddie and his family were relieved to hear on the news he was alive. They hoped that after such a traumatic experience Jose would settle down. Then, three weeks later, he went back to the same place for one last dive.

Jose returned to the spot off of Maui with Ricky because he said there were all kinds of valuable coral trees on the ocean floor. "I ran into Jose down at the dock," Ricky recalls. "He told me he had been diving over at a place called Shark's Ridge. He asked me to go with him: 'Come on, for old time's sake, let's take a couple of deep ones.' And I said, 'Well, how deep are you going?' He said, 'Only 250.' I said, 'I'll tell you what, I'll go with you, but I don't know if I want to dive to 250 feet. Why don't I just hang out and when you come up, I'll take some pictures of you decompressing. And so that was our plan." Ricky would take his underwater camera and snap a few shots as he was coming up. Previously, he had taken some striking photographs of Jose ascending to the surface, his dark form silhouetted by the dim light of the sun. In one ominous photo taken the day before, he is carrying a huge coral tree in one hand and waving with the other, as if saying goodbye.

Before heading out to sea that morning, Jose kissed his daughters goodbye on the dock and showed them a beautiful rainbow stretching over the West Maui mountains behind Lahaina. He smiled at the young girls and said this was going to be his last dive and that he would be back by noon.

When the boat arrived at Shark's Ridge miles from shore, Jose suited up in his dark wetsuit, which covered his body head to toe, and put on his fins and scuba gear. He then grabbed a heavy rock to accelerate his descent and jumped over the side. Ricky and the boat driver watched him disappear into the murky depths in a stream of bubbles. With a single tank of air and such a deep dive, Jose could only stay down at the bottom for less than ten minutes. Ricky waited and counted the minutes.

When Jose didn't come up at the appointed time, Ricky started to panic, wondering what had happened. He asked how deep it was, and the driver said it was 240 feet. But when Ricky looked at the boat's depth gauge, he was shocked to see how deep they were. "It turned out that when we figured out where he went down finally, the bottom depth was 340 feet!" He yelled at the driver. "'Read the damn thing.' He looked at it and said, 'Oh, my God.' The depth finder had been on the wrong scale. He didn't know that…Jose went down, thinking it was 250, but it was really 340. So he probably went off into the deep and just passed out." At that depth, nitrogen narcosis causes a diver to experience a kind of euphoria and lose consciousness. Since the depth gauge on his wrist only registered 250 feet, Jose Angel probably had no idea what was happening when he passed out and slipped into a state of bliss.

Meanwhile, back on the surface, Ricky was desperate, praying against all odds his friend was still alive. "We did ever-widening circles down current looking for him, hoping he would surface. But after about an hour, it was pretty obvious he wasn't coming up. At that point, we radioed the Coast Guard, and a bunch of boats and airplanes came out. We stayed out a good part of the day, and we were afraid to go in because his daughters were down on the dock. When we came in, the older one looked at me, and she said, 'Why didn't you go down for him?' She didn't understand." Ricky says that it would have been suicide to go down after him, "like jumping off a ten-story building." He not only wouldn't have survived such a deep dive, but he never would have been able to find his friend's body with the 2-3 knot current that was running. But Jose's daughter Shelly couldn't understand what had happened to her father and why Ricky couldn't do anything to help him.

Devastated by the loss, especially after his disappearance three weeks before, Mozelle suspected that he had gone down with no intention of coming back up. She says he had insisted on taking the two eldest girls to

162

Maui with him. "He begged me to let the older girls come over. Shelly, my oldest, said that Dad said to her, 'I'm going for one last dive and I'll see you around noon.' And then the boat didn't come in, didn't come in, didn't come in…I think he couldn't have done it without the two of them there. But then we don't know—maybe he was just careless again. He'd had the bends three or four times during his life. He lived right out on the edge." But this time, he had finally crossed over.

Ricky maintains Jose's last dive was not a suicide mission, even though he had been courting death for years. "If you knew Jose like we did— I was his buddy and diving partner—he'd reached a point in his life where he was doing things that were very reckless, and he didn't care. He figured if he died, then so what. It was worth taking the risk because the best part of his life was over. He had little to lose." Jose may have thought that the best part of his life was over, but it's difficult to believe he felt that way about his family. However reckless he was, Ricky insists it was still an accident. "He didn't do it intentionally. I know he didn't do it. It was just an attitude of taking huge risks because he felt, 'If I'm going to die, I might as well have a great time doing it.' Seriously, if you think about how most people die, it's in total destitution and misery. They're holding on, and they're suffering, and everyone around them is suffering. Jose just took the total opposite approach to his life by going out in the biggest possible way. He probably got to the bottom, and he saw an area that he had been wishing to see his whole life, which was the ridge at 340 feet, one of the most beautiful sites there is to see diving in Hawai'i or maybe the world. And that's where he passed out. What more romantic way to end your life?"

Peter believes Jose's death was a tragic accident but a natural consequence of the risks he was taking. "My feeling is that it was a mistake, but he may have thought, 'This is my last one' because he was going very deep. It wasn't a typical easy dive. But I don't think it was intentional." He remembers that the whole surfing and North Shore community was upset by Jose's death, especially because he once seemed so invincible and full of life. Peter says Eddie took his loss hard and wanted to do a special tribute to his memory. "So when Jose passed away, it was Eddie and myself that kind of put on that memorial. I just can't believe the hard work Eddie put into preparing that memorial service…Eddie was very instrumental and he got the permit to stage it at Waimea Bay because he was the lifeguard there. We had a mike set up, and everybody talked about Jose and gave the typical eulogies you would have at a service."

Eddie became the spokesman that day, leading the ceremony. Wearing a traditional *maile* lei and standing on the same beach that his ancestor Hewahewa once ruled, Eddie spoke in his thick pidgin accent about his love and admiration for Jose. Kimo Hollinger remembers Eddie leading the crowd in a moving prayer. "He just took it higher and higher, and I didn't know where he was going with it, but somehow he brought it all together. That guy would have been a helluva preacher. It made a real heavy impression on me." After bidding Jose farewell and aloha, his friends paddled their boards out to the lineup where he used to surf and formed a circle. Holding hands, they shared memories and stories about him and then threw their leis into the center of the circle.

When the service was over, Peter invited everyone up to his house for a reception. Like the parties they used to have in the old days, they had a feast of Hawaiian food and music, which Jose would have loved. Eddie and Clyde performed for the gathering, their throats aching as they sang in memory of their friend. "The irony of the whole thing," Peter says, "is that not too much longer we did the same thing for Eddie. And the two disappeared out in the ocean. No sign of them at all." Mozelle was so torn up with grief that she confuses Jose's memorial with Eddie's two years later in 1978. "I went to it, but I don't remember one single thing. My loss was on me for two years before the real loss set in…I've got Eddie and Jose's day intermingled. It's the same spot in my mind."

The poet Dylan Thomas once wrote, "After the first death, there is no other." More than his own life, Eddie feared losing those who were closest to him. Still reeling from Gerald's death two years earlier, he was probably reliving the pain of his brother's passing. Jose's loss must have been like a reincarnation of that grief.

CHAPTER 10

Hokule'a and the Hawaiian Renaissance

"Ua mau ke ea o ka 'aina i ka pono"

"The life of the land is perpetuated in righteousness."
— *Kamehameha III*

With the slow demise of his marriage and the sudden death of Jose that summer, Eddie struggled to overcome the waves of sadness that kept pushing him under. Like Butch Van Artsdalen, he began drinking too much and staying out late, sometimes not coming home at all. He and Clyde would hop from party to party all around the Island. Though Clyde admits to doing most of the girl-chasing, Eddie was known to stray on occasion. Rumors about other women hung in the air of their home like a strange perfume. He and Linda drifted further apart. But Linda says that their marriage "went downhill not over another woman but because of his brother's death. For almost a year he was a different person. He slept up at Punchbowl at his brother's grave more than once that year. It was an emotional and terrible time for me because everyone was worried about him. I spent a number of nights looking for him on the North Shore when he didn't come home."

Retreating into a cocoon of suffering, Eddie became depressed and withdrawn. He took a long look at his life and wondered where to go from there. Restless and ready for a change, he toned down his drinking and began looking for help. He became deeply spiritual and began seeing a Catholic priest to talk about his troubled marriage. He would say prayers and cross himself each time he went surfing in big waves, as if the ocean was his outdoor cathedral. According to Clyde, he was going through some "heavy personal trips." He had also grown increasingly interested in his cultural heritage. After being suppressed for most of the century, a revival of Hawaiian culture began to flourish in the early '70's. Looking back at the history of his people, Eddie and many Hawaiians experienced mixed emotions. They rediscovered a lost pride in their heritage, but they also became enraged over their cultural oppression.

Eddie was no history scholar, but he had known enough to be skeptical of the version of history offered at his high school. Like most students of his day, he and his siblings had not been taught about the legal maneuvering of the Great Mahele of 1848, which slowly but effectively deprived most Hawaiians of their land. Nor had he been taught about the Bayonet Constitution, which had barred them from voting and holding office if they didn't own a certain amount of land or earn a substantial income. Nor did he learn about the overthrow of the Hawaiian government by a committee of American businessmen when Queen Lili'uokalani tried to reverse the Bayonet Constitution that had been forced upon the monarchy. "In the public and private schools, all of us learned in the books that there was this wonderfully smooth transition of power," Hawaiian lawyer and activist Beadie Kanahele Dawson recalls. "I didn't really know the facts of history that surrounded the overthrow." But when historians in the late '60's and '70's began uncovering the details of what had taken place, Beadie says the Hawaiian Renaissance was born. "The Renaissance was a rediscovery of what had happened to us."

Beadie Dawson goes on to say that traditional Hawaiians didn't believe that owning the land was possible or important. "What was of importance was the 'ohana, the family. Hawaiians are basically a very inclusive people," she says. "We have been from day one. We never chased anyone from our shores—we welcomed everyone, and we still do. The tradition of hanai is typical of the way Hawaiians welcome people, not just to the Islands but into our homes, into our hearts and into our families." Gerry Lopez says that's exactly how the Aikaus lived. "That was the true aloha spirit," he says. "I guess that's what happened to the Hawaiian people—they gave and gave until it was all gone. It's kind of sad."

In the Makaha Sons' song "Hawai'i '78," Israel Kamakawiwo'ole captured the sad spirit of his people during this time:

If just for a day our king and queen
Would visit all the Islands and saw everything,
How would they feel about the changes of our land?

Could you just imagine if they were around
And saw highways on their sacred ground,
How would they feel about this modern city life?
Tears would come from each other's eyes
As they would start to realize
That our people are in great, great danger now.
How would they feel?
Would they smile, be content?
Or cry?
Cry for the gods, cry for the people,
Cry for the land that was taken away,
And then yet you'll find Hawai'i.

As people learned about the overthrow of the Queen and the annexation of the Islands by the U.S. government in the late 1890's, they began to understand how the new Republic had slowly disenfranchised the Hawaiian people. Unlike the direct attacks and genocidal killings of the Native Americans, the leaders had just slowly taken away their culture. In time, the government banned the Hawaiian language and shunned cultural practices like surfing, hula and chants. For several generations, only persistent elders and isolated communities on each island kept the language and their oral history from dying out completely. Hawaiian writer Alani Apio referred to this kind of cultural oppression as a "thousand little cuts to genocide."

Along with their political and cultural disenfranchisement, the Hawaiian people had suffered catastrophic mortality due to foreign diseases. They had been been reduced to a small fraction of their original population before Cook's arrival. Less than 1 in 20 survived the epidemics of cholera, influenza, mumps, measles and smallpox, and many Hawaiians were also victims of severe psychological depression. *"Na kanaka kuu wale aku no i ka uhane—The people freely gave up their souls and died,"* one Hawaiian lamented. Like the Aikau's home, their land had been transformed into a graveyard. Many Hawaiians became homeless or were herded together on homestead lands like nearby Papakolea, where they lived in cheap housing and often squalid conditions.

Until the Civil Rights movement erupted on the Mainland, most local families like the Aikaus had downplayed their Hawaiian roots and hoped to integrate into the mainstream culture. Like Native Americans, they had been made to feel ashamed of their racial heritage. During this time, Hawai'i's landscape was changing dramatically. Waikiki had become a booming tourist resort, with new hotels sprouting up like giant weeds. Modern developers had taken over where the sugar and pineapple planters had left off, and plantation field hands migrated to the city to become hotel workers. Rampant construction transformed the landscape and disrupted ancient burial sites as the skeletons of tall buildings began rising up around the city. With so much new development, locals joked that the construction crane was now the state bird.

Marginalized by mainstream society, many Hawaiians had turned their anger inward and sought to numb their rage with drink and drugs, resulting in high rates of alcoholism, addiction, crime and domestic abuse. Eddie and his family could see these problems first-hand in some of the poorer areas of Papakolea. Skeletons of stripped cars and broken beer bottles littered vacant lots, and violent arguments and fights ripped through the night. But just as the Civil Rights movement had energized African-Americans and other minorities on the mainland, a growing racial pride began to inspire Hawaiians. They started fighting for their rights and demanding restitution for the lands that had been taken from them. Along with political demonstrations and marches, local leaders began emphasizing the need to rediscover their cultural heritage. Unlike his older friend John Kelly, Eddie was not a political activist, but he was eager to participate in the movement. When he heard that a small group called the Polynesian Voyaging Society had built a replica of an ancient Hawaiian canoe, Eddie decided to get involved with the project.

With so much social upheaval and cultural awareness springing up around him, Eddie began to emerge from his cocoon. Though still in love with Linda, his heart was restless. He wanted a new start. Searching for something to rejuvenate his life, Eddie found a new mistress. Her name was *Hokule'a*. He spoke of the canoe as if it were a woman who embodied the spirit of the Hawaiian Renaissance. He had read about her in the newspapers, but it wasn't till he saw her that he fell in love. Eddie had first set eyes on the twin-hulled, sailing canoe in 1975 when she was launched from Kualoa. He had driven to this remote area on the Eastern shore of O'ahu just to see *Hokule'a* set sail for the first time. The place was so sacred to ancient Hawaiian sailors that they would lower their sails whenever they passed by. Eddie joined the enthusiastic crowd gathered on the beach to witness the birth and blessing of this voyaging canoe.

After years of planning and nine months in the making, *Hokule'a* was finally ready for her first sea trials before attempting to sail to Tahiti the next year. Dressed in traditional robes, the *kahu* chanted an old Hawaiian blessing, and a Hawaiian wearing a *malo* (loin cloth) held the *pu* to his lips and blew into the conch shell, filling the air with its low, haunting sound. Then, the flower-covered *Hokule'a* slid down the logs on the beach and splashed into Kaneohe Bay. The crowd cheered. Seeing the vessel move through the blue-green waters, Eddie fell in love with her. With her traditional Polynesian crab-claw sails billowing in the wind, the 60-foot canoe seemed to sail right out of his past and into his future. She was beautiful. A living artifact, a time machine, a work of art. Eddie could feel the pride of his people suddenly awakening after centuries of sleep. But the making of the canoe and its early voyages were anything but smooth, and they had left a wake of racial tension.

Ironically, it was the *haole* anthropologist Dr. Ben Finney who had originally proposed building the Hawaiian voyaging canoe *Hokule'a*. After working on a similar vessel at the University of Santa Barbara, he had come to the Islands to teach anthropology at the University of Hawai'i. More than a pale scholar, Ben was an active surfer and sailor who was well known in academic circles and among the surfing tribe. With his blonde hair and tan skin, he looked like he spent more time in the ocean than in the library. He led a kind of double life: when he surfed with locals like Eddie, he was simply known as Ben, but when he presented papers about his research at universities across the country, he was known as Dr. Finney. His anthropological treatises on the history of surfing and Polynesian voyaging had created waves of controversy in the academic world.

Based on his studies of "accidental" versus "purposeful voyaging," Ben wanted to prove that the ancient Polynesian sailors had not accidentally drifted to Hawai'i but had purposely sailed there to colonize the Islands. So he created a model of a Hawaiian canoe to test his theories. Ben says *Hokule'a* was a form of "experimental archeology, where you recreate an artifact and then you use it in realistic conditions to give you an idea of how it worked in the past, to shed light on the past." A bold innovator with a touch of intellectual arrogance, Ben set about creating a replica of an ancient voyaging canoe. He also wanted to include Hawaiians in the project. But what started out as a scientific experiment soon evolved into a cultural revival.

No one embodied the spirit of the Hawaiian Renaissance more than Herb Kawainui Kane. Born and raised in Hawai'i, Herb had moved to the Mainland for college to pursue his career as an artist. After studying at the Art Institute of Chicago, he had found commercial success as an advertising designer, creating such memorable characters as the Jolly Green Giant. But he was unfulfilled as an artist and longed to rediscover his heritage so he returned to the Islands and immersed himself in every aspect of Hawaiian culture. He began studying the history, archeology, anthropology and traditional navigation of his ancestors. Having done extensive research into the subject of Polynesian voyaging canoes, he worked on a series of architectural drawings of these canoes and paintings of the ancient voyages. In one of those extraordinary instances of fate, Herb eventually met Ben, and together, they decided to build a replica of an ancient, sailing canoe. With the help of waterman Tommy Holmes (no relation to Lynne), they formed the Polynesian Voyaging Society (PVS). The trio threw themselves into the project, putting in thousands of hours planning and building the canoe.

In building a replica of an ancient canoe, the PVS crew had to compromise in a couple of areas due to financial and time restrictions. Instead of using stone adzes to carve the two hulls out of solid trees, they used modern tools to create a plywood frame, which they covered in fiberglass. Though the original canoes were lashed together with cording made from coconut husk fibers, the builders chose to use synthetic rope. Except for these two changes, they followed the original design of the traditional Polynesian voyaging canoes. The amazing thing is that they didn't use a single nail— the crossbeams, the deck, the two masts, and every part were lashed together with miles and miles of rope. Initially, the three PVS founders worked well together, but they came from very different backgrounds and approached the project from divergent perspectives that would eventually tear them apart. "Ben was more interested in the scientific questions," Herb says. "Holmes was interested in the adventure of it. I saw cultural possibilities for the canoe to help stimulate a cultural revival."

Finney, Kane and Holmes may have had different ideas about the canoe, but they shared a passion for the ocean, Polynesian voyaging and Hawaiian culture. They continued to work together and began recruiting native Hawaiian sailors to join the first crew. A handsome, young Hawaiian named Nainoa Thompson was one of their first recruits, and the experience changed his life. He and Eddie would eventually become fast friends. They too came from different backgrounds and their time together was short, but their influence on each other and Hawaiian history would last a long time.

Raised on his grandfather's chicken and dairy farm in Niu Valley, Nainoa was born into a well-connected local family. He grew up in the peaceful countryside, surrounded by lush, green mountains. But after his first fishing trip when he was five, he knew the ocean was his home. Like Eddie, he loved the bigness and wildness of the sea, along with its constantly changing conditions. He found an exhilarating freedom there that he could not find in the sheltered serenity of the mountains. During his youth, Nainoa became an avid fisherman, paddler and sailor, and these childhood experiences would help prepare him for his later role as a deep-sea navigator. His father, Myron "Pinky" Thompson, encouraged him to follow his dreams, but he found many of his teachers at Punahou School to be exactly the opposite. Instead of nurturing his natural interests, Nainoa felt like they were task-masters who told him what to learn and how. When he didn't follow their instructions, he was often punished and was later labeled a difficult child. An intelligent boy with a will of his own, Nainoa felt his teachers stressed competition and conformity over cooperation and originality. He soon became disillusioned with school.

In an article called "The Ocean Is My Classroom," Nainoa later said, "Learning should be something very special, very exciting. Rather than learning eagerly, I found that I was spending my energy avoiding bad grades. School should be relevant, exciting and interesting. I used to ask, 'Why are we reading this book? Why are we reading about dead people in faraway lands?'" But when it came to learning about the ocean and Hawaiian culture, he and Eddie would prove to be eager students. After graduating from Punahou, Nainoa didn't know what to do with his life. In the meantime, he did construction work and drove dump trucks, while fishing and paddling as often as he could. Just as Eddie found his mentors outside of school, Nainoa found his in the sailing world. In a stroke of luck that would change his life forever, he met Herb Kane one day after paddling practice.

"At that time, Herb, Tommy Holmes and Ben Finney were designing *Hokule'a*…Then, one day, Herb invited two of the paddling coaches and me over to his house. Herb's house was filled with paintings and pictures of canoes, nautical charts, star charts and books everywhere! Interesting books! Over dinner, Herb told how they were going to build a canoe and sail it

2,500 miles [to Tahiti] without instruments—the old way. 'We're gonna follow the stars, and the canoe is gonna be called after that star,' Herb said, pointing to the star Hokule'a (whose scientific name is Arcturus). This voyage would help to show that the Polynesians came here by purposely sailing and navigating their canoes—not just happening to drift here on the ocean currents or driven by winds." Many Western anthropologists like Thor Heyerdahl, of *Kon Tiki* fame, had implied that the first settlers didn't have the technology or know-how to sail all the way to Hawai'i. Instead, they insisted that the settlers had landed on its shores through "accidental drift," not by design. But Nainoa knew they couldn't have "accidentally" drifted 2500 miles on many different voyages! Like Ben and the others, he wanted to prove these so-called scholars wrong by sailing to Tahiti in the old way. "The voyage would do something very important for the Hawaiian people and for the rest of the world."

"In that moment, all the parts connected in me that had seemed unconnected in my life," Nainoa remembers with that original excitement. "I was 20! I was looking for something challenging and meaningful! I had a hard time finding that in the four walls of the school. Here it was—in the history, the heritage, the charts, the stars, the ocean, and the dream…there was so much relevance in that dream. I wanted to follow Herb; I wanted to be part of that dream. Herb told us what the requirements would be to sail to Tahiti. We would have to go through a training program in which we would learn all about the canoe and how to sail her, and there would be physical training and training in teamwork. They would select the best 30 from the several hundred who participated in training. When *Hokule'a* was completed in Spring of 1975, I participated in the training and was assigned to the return crew!" Because so many people wanted to sail, the PVS selected two different crews to sail to and from Tahiti. The training had been difficult but Nainoa knew it was worth the effort. "If I want to do something, I can be very disciplined. My dream was coming true!"

Eddie was only peripherally involved with the *Hokule'a* during the early stages of its creation. After seeing her birth at Kualoa, he had decided to become more involved. Wanting to be a crew member, he started volunteering his time to work and train on the canoe. He soon realized, though, that there was growing tension surrounding the *Hokule'a*. Because it was so immensely popular and symbolic of Hawai'i's past, many local groups wanted to claim the canoe as their own. Herb Kane quickly led the charge in trying to take control of the voyaging canoe and make it a cultural symbol. "It's a shared icon of mutuality and ancestry and a reminder of the courage, intelligence and grit of our ancestors," he says. Herb wrote articles about the canoe and the planned voyage to Tahiti for major magazines like *National Geographic*, which also published some of his inspirational artwork. His paintings showed strong, tattooed Polynesians sailing the first canoes toward Hawai'i's smoldering volcanoes and green-clad mountains. In one article for *Honolulu Magazine* during the mid-70's, he referred to *Hokule'a* as the "Space Ship of Your Ancestors." He compared the ancient voyages across the Pacific to modern forays into space. The comparison works when you consider that these explorers were sailing thousands of miles into unknown territory and using the stars as guides. Years later in 1992, Hawai'i astronaut Charles Lacy Veach would make radio contact with Nainoa Thompson aboard the *Hokule'a* from the space shuttle *Columbia* as they both crossed the equator. As the shuttle floated through space thousands of miles above, orbiting toward the future, the canoe sailed below, trying to rediscover the past.

Before *Hokule'a* could sail all the way to Tahiti, she had to prove that she and her crew were seaworthy so they began a series of inter-island sails. Local sailors were selected for each leg of the voyage, and Eddie was chosen to sail from O'ahu to Kaua'i. "A cruise through the Islands was necessary both for a hard shakedown and to introduce the canoe to the entire community and see if Hawaiians would accept her as their own," Herb says. More than accept the canoe, some crew members began to act as if they owned her. But their lack of experience would hurt them. Though he was not a sailor by training, Herb had basically designed the canoe so he became the "unelected default captain" during the inter-island voyages. The sail to Kaua'i had been a smooth one, but crew member Kimo Hugho remembers that Eddie seemed "distant and detached." Was it because one of the crew members had shared his dream that the canoe would sink? "Dreams played a heavy role with the canoe," says Kimo, who would eventually back out of the voyage to Tahiti, due to his own premonitions. Eddie had enjoyed sailing on *Hokule'a*, but he felt relieved when he flew back to O'ahu. During the return sail from Kaua'i, one of the canoe's hollow hulls took on water during the night and swamped in the rough waters of the channel the next morning. Stranded ten miles from the coast of Kaua'i, *Hokule'a* was slowly sinking. The dream had come true. The inexperienced crew argued what to do. Finally, Tommy Holmes, a strong paddler and waterman, volunteered to paddle his surfboard toward the island for help.

Meanwhile, back on O'ahu, Ben Finney heard about the accident, and in a panic, he boarded the next plane to Kaua'i. Once there, he found out that an inter-island hydrofoil vessel, the *Kamehameha*, had spotted the canoe. The ship radioed the Coast Guard for help and stopped to pick up some of the crew members. On their way back to port, they also found an exhausted Tommy Holmes still paddling toward the island. He said he probably could have made it to shore but kept falling asleep. The canoe was towed into harbor a few hours later. In his book *Hokule'a: The Way to Tahiti*, Ben writes that she was a "sad sight" to behold. "The starboard hull was down, completely submerged except for the tips of the prow and stern, while the port hull was thrust up and canted over to one side. The deckhouse was gone, and the crew left on board was clinging to the rail along the port hull."

Suddenly, the bright prospects for *Hokule'a's* future voyages seemed dim with the negative media attention that followed. After reading about the incident in the papers, Eddie was relieved that Tommy Holmes and the others were safe, but he was disheartened by the in-fighting and controversy that followed. Tommy blamed Herb for poor leadership as Captain, and Herb in turn accused Tommy of being negligent since he was on watch that night when it happened. In order to avoid a public scandal about who was to blame for the accident, Ben Finney knew he had to take action. "So at the Polynesian Voyaging Society Board of Directors meeting the following week, against much opposition, I quashed all discussion of the swamping and instituted a formal board of inquiry" to investigate the cause of the accident and make recommendations about how to change the canoe and its management. The PVS Directors already knew that the hulls needed to be redesigned to make each interior compartment watertight and the deck needed to be raised and strengthened. According to one sailor, Eddie had noticed these problems before the voyage.

When the report came out several weeks later, it concluded "that *Hokule'a* swamped due to lack of seamanship, an absence of knowledgeable command at sea and the omission of acceptable standards and procedures for all oceangoing vessels." Everyone shared in the blame, Herb Kane as Captain, Tommy Holmes as officer on duty and even PVS President, Ben Finney. After the incident, Herb gradually withdrew from leadership of the voyaging society and resumed work on his paintings and fundraising efforts for the canoe. Ben stepped in to take control. This was a dark moment for the group, but the report had called the swamping a "very fortunate accident" because it had brought necessary attention to the canoe's deficiencies in design and leadership. If the accident had occurred during the trip to Tahiti, in the middle of the Pacific, it could have been fatal. This would later prove to be an ominous prediction.

John Kruse was a young Hawaiian recruited to sail on the *Hokule'a*, and he was eager to learn more about traditional voyaging. Like Eddie's brother Gerald, he had served as a soldier in Vietnam and had become disillusioned with the war and American politics. What exactly had they been fighting for, he wondered bitterly when he returned. Back in the Islands, John began exploring his own cultural roots as a Hawaiian. He let his hair grow long and curly, and a thick beard covered his rugged face. When he heard about the *Hokule'a*, he signed on to help build her and later trained with Nainoa and Eddie during the inter-island practice sails. Everywhere the canoe went, proud locals gathered to see it. But John says the Kaua'i incident was part of a series of events that caused a lot of tension between the crew members and the PVS. "After the canoe sank off of Kaua'i, we went back and had to rebuild it. And we did it with no money. Nobody was getting paid. All of the money that was supposed to be used for paying the different crew members was now being used on the canoe."

Besides the lack of pay, there were conflicts between the *haole* leadership and the mostly Hawaiian crew. After stating their plan "to make it a cultural revival and scientific experiment," Ben Finney recalls that the PVS directors immediately encountered resistance. "People on the scientific side said, 'Forget it, you can't include the general public.' And then after we actually built the canoe and launched her, a lot of Hawaiians said, 'What's this *haole* science stuff?' So we got flak from all sides." The sailing canoe had become such a powerful symbol that people on both sides sought to claim her as their own.

After the swamping near Kaua'i, John Kruse recalls that the conflict over *Hokule'a* only escalated. On one end of the spectrum, radical natives felt like it was theirs to control. One local faction wanted to make a political statement by sailing the canoe to Kaho'olawe in order to protest against the U.S. Navy's bombing of the Hawaiian island for target practice. On the other end, conservative *haoles* criticized the PVS's inability to control its more radical crew members and wondered if they could actually make the voyage all the way to Tahiti. "The tension was building," John says. "You know, we hadn't done this in 800 years…At the time when the canoe was being rebuilt, everyone was saying, 'Hey, those guys are crazy—those Hawaiians can't do stuff like that. They're never going to do it. Look, the Hawaiians are always fighting. Several of us on the canoe had gone into the service and went to Vietnam. Maybe that's our lot in life: nothing comes easy. You've got to fight for everything. You know Hawaiians and Polynesians, they're fierce people, they're warriors."

While working with Wally Froiseth to rebuild the canoe, John remembers Eddie talking about wanting to sail on the *Hokule'a* to Tahiti. "He said, 'Hey, I'm going to do this for my family. I gotta go on this canoe.' He was really into his family, always consulting with Mom and Pop and asking his brothers and sister, 'Hey, what do you think about this? You think this is a good thing?'" But with the in-fighting between the crew and PVS leaders, Eddie began having second thoughts about sailing on the canoe during that first voyage. "I was thinking Eddie was supposed to come down with Nainoa to be on the second crew to go home [from Tahiti]," Kruse continues. "But he just kind of backed away from that first whole trip because he was probably having some conflict within himself—you know, 'Hey, even though I want to do this for my family, maybe the time ain't right because all this stuff is going on.'" Eddie was a proud Hawaiian and had scrapped with *haole*s before, but he was tired of the racial tension, sick of the arguments and resentful mumbling. He had become fed up with what one crew member called "*hukihuki*," which literally means "pull-pull," referring to the divisive tug-of-war between the sailors and the leaders. After intense deliberation and discussion with his folks, he decided it wasn't his time to go, so he withdrew himself from the selection process. It was a painful decision, but he vowed to be on the next voyage.

"People had different ideas of what this canoe was going to do for them," John says. "I was doing it because this was a good thing to do, we had good people, and I wanted to learn navigation from Mau Piailug." One of the last wayfinders left in the world, Mau was a small, quiet man from the tiny Micronesian island of Satawal. Just like his ancestors, he sailed all over Micronesia, using only the stars and sea birds as his guides. Because Finney and PVS wanted to sail to Tahiti, using no modern or Western instruments of navigation, they had to find a traditional wayfinder to guide them on their voyage. The problem was that master wayfinders were hard to find. Most had died without passing on their unique knowledge to the younger generations who had embraced more modern, Western navigational techniques. In his research on Pacific Island voyaging, Finney had met Mau years before and was greatly impressed with his skill in non-instrument navigation and his ability to work with people from different cultures. He was a master canoe builder, known for his courage and calm under extreme conditions. It was said he had survived two hurricanes at sea. But when he agreed to lead the crew of *Hokule'a*, he wasn't prepared for the whirlwind of racial conflicts and fierce emotions that would arise during the voyage to Tahiti.

Mau became concerned that some of the crew members didn't have enough sailing experience and weren't prepared for the rigors of the upcoming voyage. They were excellent watermen, in terms of paddling, surfing and diving, but he felt their brief training as sailors was not enough. Only a few of them had made any ocean crossings. "Today's Hawaiians are world renowned for their surfing, but few of them ever sail," Finney wrote in his book *Hokule'a*. "In Hawai'i yachting is mostly a *haole* pastime, too expensive for most Hawaiians and not popular among those few Hawaiians who can afford to purchase yachts. If Hawaiians do go out to sea, they typically just go offshore in an outboard skiff to spend the day fishing for their table. It was not always this way. As late as the middle of the last century, Hawaiians were recognized as being expert deep-water sailors—so expert that New England sea captains would sail out to the Pacific with a minimum number of hands, and then head straight for Hawai'i where they would hire Hawaiians to serve for the duration of their long whaling and trading cruises...Mau realized the dilemma of the young Hawaiian crew candidates: wanting to learn how to sail, to recapture some of the glory of their seafaring ancestors, yet woefully lacking in seamanship and discipline." What they lacked in sailing skills, they made up for with their passion to be a part of the voyage. But these passions would often get the best of them.

When the day finally came to set sail, Eddie and thousands of people from all over the Islands gathered on shore to see them off and wish them well. With sixteen sailors aboard the 60-foot canoe, the diverse crew set sail for Tahiti on May 1, 1976, using only the wind, waves and stars to steer by. Because it was the year of the American Bicentennial, the *Hokule'a* was Hawai'i's contribution to the Independence celebrations. In order to document the journey, a cameraman and a writer from the National Geographic Society had joined the crew. Although they had an escort boat follow them for safety reasons, the navigators had no access to Western equipment or modern technology. No radar, no maps, not even a compass. Only the vast desert of ocean with its dune-like swells. But with Mau's intimate understanding of the night sky and the help of veteran navigators, they would map their course by where certain stars rose and set each night on the horizon. In this way, they hoped the heavens would help guide them all the way to Tahiti, the ancestral homeland of Hawai'i's people.

During the voyage to Tahiti, tension flared between the *haole* leaders and the Hawaiian crew members. David Lyman was a first mate on the voyage and remembers the conflicts well. A descendant of New England missionaries, Lyman looks mostly Caucasian, but he is also part Hawaiian and can speak pidgin like the locals. He was known as Dave to his *haole* friends and Kawika (David in Hawaiian) to his local buddies, and he often got caught in the middle of intense racial diatribes. "On the one hand, I'd get the Hawaiian guys saying, 'Hey, Kawika, ya' know what da' *haoles* are doin' today?' And on the other hand, I'd get the *haole* guys saying, 'Hey, Dave, you know what those Hawaiian guys are doing?'" *Hokule'a* was initially supposed to be more of a scientific experiment, but the Hawaiian crew members resented the rules and regulations of the *haole* leadership and insisted the canoe belonged to their people. "This became the tail that wagged the dog," Lyman laments. The local sailors didn't like being told they couldn't smoke their *pakalolo* (marijuana) or listen to the radio they had smuggled on board. Ben Finney tried to explain that these things would jeopardize the legitimacy of the scientific experiment, but the Hawaiians just looked at him with anger in their eyes. Meanwhile, they continued smoking and listening to the portable radio at their end of the canoe as if waiting for a showdown. They even grumbled and laughed about "throwing the *haoles* overboard."

Tensions mounted throughout the trip, especially when they hit the doldrums at the equator and drifted aimlessly for days under the fierce gaze of the sun. Near the end of the voyage, the underlying tension exploded. In a heated argument, some Hawaiian crew members started blasting the *haole* leaders for telling them what to do during the whole journey. Like a mutiny at sea, they confronted the Captain—Elia "Kawika" Kapahulehua—and Finney against the starboard rail and started listing their grievances. As they argued, the pressure grew until it finally erupted into a fistfight. Suddenly, the big Hawaiian lifeguard Buffalo Keaulana lost his temper and slugged the Captain. Then, he jumped on Ben Finney and began hitting him. Dave

Lyman tried to pull Buffalo away from Ben. Mau, the canoe's unspoken leader, stepped in and sternly said, "Buff, stop!" And the violent brawl ended as quickly as it started. Afterward, Buffalo came up and offered Ben his hand in the form of a wordless apology, and it was clear he felt bad about what had happened. Dave later explained that Buffalo had been suffering from an infected sore on his foot and was in a lot of pain so he just snapped. But the damage had been done, and the internal wounds would take a long time to heal.

John Kruse remembers how the fight and dissention infuriated Mau and eventually drove him away from the project. "On the trip, Mau said your problems on the canoe when you do deep-sea voyaging, those little problems that everyone takes for granted and that we can always walk away from on land, those little problems become big problems at sea. So you have to think as one big family, and if you make it, you're going to make it as a family; and if you die or get lost at sea, you're gonna die as one family. Some guys get stir-crazy when they can't see the land. The ocean can be unforgiving." After sailing together for almost 2,500 miles, they had made it as a family of sorts, but it was a bitter and divided one. Before reaching their destination in Tahiti, Mau told Finney that he wanted to go home and wasn't going to sail back with the new crew to Hawai'i. Ben tried to convince the wise, old wayfinder to stay, but Mau had made up his mind to leave. The tension on the canoe had taken a heavy toll on everyone involved, especially its founder. When they finally landed in Tahiti, Ben's family was there to greet him, and they were shocked by what they saw. By the end of the voyage, he had lost considerable weight and had a black eye. The strong *haole* looked weak and dazed.

Despite the racial conflicts aboard the canoe, the mission was basically successful. More than a month after leaving Honolulu, the *Hokule'a* had completed its first voyage to Tahiti. On a beautiful morning, the canoe sailed into Papeete Harbor. In anticipation of the occasion, the Governor of French Polynesia had declared their arrival day, Friday, June 4, 1976, as a public holiday. In jubilant response, almost 17,000 people, more than half the island's population, had turned out to greet the twin-hulled, wooden vessel. Hundreds of canoes and boats from other islands sailed out to greet her. Mobs of natives tried to climb aboard, almost capsizing her with their enthusiasm. "We saw this multitude of people," John Kruse says excitedly. "They were ten feet in the water, standing there in their clothes, waiting for the canoe. We came up to this place, and all these kids came up to the canoe, and the next thing you know, they get on the canoe. At one point, there were so many people on the canoe that it sank right at the water's edge. I mean, it was stuck on the beach!"

Frightened by the number of excited Tahitians at the port and also worried about the political reaction against the French government, authorities soon realized the futility of trying to control or even patrol the huge gathering, and a massive party ensued. "The French police were there, the gendarmes," John remembers. "They cordoned off this area for dignitaries, all the big wheels. All these people charged that barricade and knocked it down. One guy said, 'You can't go down there,' and this old lady remarked, 'Hey, outta my way, I'm going to see my canoe.' They saw this as an extension of their past, and we hadn't done this in 800-plus years. All of a sudden, they saw this thing on the horizon, and it was like 'Whoa, man, this is history!'"

Named after the zenith star of Hawai'i, which had once guided intrepid Tahitian voyagers across the Pacific centuries before, *Hokule'a* suddenly became an international symbol of Polynesian pride. The voyage helped prove that they were some of the greatest sailors and explorers in history, settling an area that covered more than a million miles. Stretching from New Zealand in the South to Easter Island in the East and Hawai'i in the North, the Polynesian Triangle formed what even Captain Cook had recognized two hundred years before as the "most extensive nation on earth."

For the journey back to Hawai'i, Nainoa and the new crew members had looked forward to studying with Mau to learn the art of wayfinding and celestial navigation. But with his abrupt and bitter departure, they were forced to rely on traditional, Western navigational instruments like the compass, quadrant and sextant. But they would still be aiming for the zenith star, Hokule'a. During the voyage, Nainoa tried to memorize as many constellations and stars as possible, measuring their slow course across the night sky. Though there was still some lingering tension from the trip down to Tahiti, the voyage back home was much more positive. It was a younger, more mellow crew, and the burst of support for the *Hokule'a* in Tahiti had buoyed the sailors' spirits. Even the weather seemed to be on their side. Unlike the grueling experience of sailing downwind and getting stuck in the doldrums, the conditions for the return trip were much more favorable. Whereas it had taken the first crew 34 days to reach Tahiti, the voyage back to Hawai'i took only 22 days. Scanning the horizon, they finally saw the summit of Mauna

Kea, Hawai'i's highest volcanic mountain, looming in the clouds.

When Eddie heard about *Hokule'a's* triumphant return to Hawai'i, he convinced his friend David Bettencourt to take him up in his private plane to see her sail the final leg back to O'ahu. A lawyer by trade but a pilot at heart, David Bettencourt loved anything that had to do with flying. Over the years, he had flown all kinds of planes and had even taken up the dangerous sport of hang gliding. He had once broken his back in a terrible hang gliding accident, and Pops took him from the hospital to the graveyard and nursed him back to health. Since then, he had become like a *hanai* son in the Aikau 'ohana. While David was obsessed with flying, he says Eddie became obsessed with sailing on the *Hokule'a*. "He bugged me for weeks to make sure that we would be up there to see that boat come in. We flew out to meet the *Hokule'a* off on the Moloka'i Channel [between O'ahu and Moloka'i]." Flying in the air like a great bird hundreds of feet above, Eddie felt an intense connection to the canoe as she sailed through the blue water. Looking down at the timeless vessel, which seemed to have sailed out of Hawai'i's ancient past, he renewed his vow to be a crew member some day. "I knew from that first plane ride that Eddie would stop at nothing to get on that boat," David says. "It was very clear that the next time that boat sailed anywhere, he would be on it." After landing at the airport, Eddie had David take him out on a friend's boat to meet *Hokule'a* when she arrived in Honolulu Harbor. Sailing by the canoe, they joined a fleet of sailboats, powerboats, and canoes in welcoming the canoe home. They threw cans of cold beer to the crew members and shouted, "Aloooohaa!"

After witnessing the reception in Tahiti, Herb Kane and a local celebrity, Gilbert 'Zoulou' Kauhi [a regular on the TV show *Hawaii-Five-0*], had helped organize an equally impressive homecoming for the *Hokule'a* and its crew. "When the subject of a reception in Honolulu came up at a meeting one night at Bishop Museum, 'Zoulou' offered to take over that task," Herb says. "He had been the last person on shore to release the line when the canoe left Hawai'i. He had seen the outpouring of affection in Tahiti. Now, he brought together, on his own dollar, responsible execs from the County, State and Military, all at a restaurant called Sir John's. After a free lunch and open bar, he gave them a pep talk about *Hokule'a's* return, pointing out that we could not come in second best to the staggering reception given in Tahiti. Pointing to an officer from County Parks, he said, 'I want a reviewing stand set up at Ala Moana park where the crew can come ashore.' To the governor's rep, he said, 'Governor Ariyoshi must be there.' To the Air Force he said, 'I want a fly-over by a squadron of jets.' To the State Harbor Patrol, he asked for the fireboat with all pumps going. To the Army, he asked for the cannon to go off from Fort Ruger as the canoe sailed by. The Navy was asked to send out a destroyer. The Coast Guard was asked to send out an all-girl crew. And so on. There was no way anyone there could respond negatively. Everyone got into the spirit of the thing. A huge assembly of watercraft greeted the canoe off of Diamond Head. The Customs inspector, wearing a *malo* (loincloth), leaped from a power boat, was hoisted aboard *Hokule'a* and cleared the canoe before it landed."

From that day forward, Eddie did everything he could to be on the next voyage of the *Hokule'a*. He came from a race of people who had sailing in their blood and were equally at home on the sea as they were on land. Though Eddie hadn't done much sailing before, he knew that it was something he had to do. When PVS announced plans for the next voyage, he began seriously training as a sailor and asked for time off from his lifeguard job.

Jim Howe, Chief of Lifeguard Operations on O'ahu, believes that Eddie's cultural roots as a Hawaiian helped shape his instincts as a sailor, surfer and waterman. "We may live in America, but socially and culturally, we live in Polynesia, and Polynesian culture centers around the ocean. They were the greatest water people in the world. And for them to be here in Hawai'i meant they were the best of the best because this was the farthest island chain they had to travel to. Before the Hawaiian Renaissance these ocean skills were devalued, but people like the Aikaus kept up those traditions and made a bridge to the past. For me, it goes back to this tradition through thousands of years of trying to understand the ocean. It's this huge body of knowledge that's passed on from generation to generation. It's a knowledge of the most dynamic environment on Earth since the ocean is always changing its moods. That's the essence of being a waterman, having the knowledge and confidence to do anything you want in the ocean. There's a lot of signs if you know what to look for."

Along with the changing moods of the ocean, Eddie also learned to read the shifting moods of his own people. The euphoria of the *Hokule'a's* homecoming united Native Hawaiians across the Islands, but the canoe's triumphant return had also awakened a sleeping giant. They took intense pride in the vessel and the renaissance of their culture. The native population suddenly felt empowered as a people, but it was a thin line between power and violence. And Eddie was about to see the dormant pride of his people erupt into an outpouring of anger and political protests.

The continued bombing of Kahoʻolawe was an additional source of intense outrage for many Hawaiians who considered the island to be sacred. The next year, a group from the Protect Kahoʻolawe ʻOhana (PKO) illegally occupied the island for months in a demonstration against the U.S. Military. But the bombing continued, and the protestors were running out of food, water and time. Fearing for the lives of their friends, political activist and musician George Helm and his cohort Kimo Mitchell were dropped off near the island with surfboards and a load of supplies. When they didn't find their friends and the pick-up boat failed to arrive, they decided to paddle their boards to the island of Maui seven miles away. But the seas were rough, the currents strong and the men exhausted. After foundering off the small, crescent-shaped island of Molokini, they were never seen again and presumed to be lost at sea. George Helm became a martyr to the cause of Hawaiian sovereignty. Eddie was moved by his sacrifice, and in many ways, his life would reflect George's fate.

Eddie and PT—Australian Peter Townend—at the 1977 World Cup Finals when PT became the first World Champion.

Chapter 11

Hawaiian Rage

"Rage, rage against the dying of the light."
—*Dylan Thomas*

Along with fistfights aboard the *Hokule'a* and political protests on Kaho'olawe, Hawaiians began to show their rage and frustration in the surf too. In one issue of *Surfer*, the magazine ran two editorials about the increasing tension between *haole*s and Hawaiians. In the first piece called "Paradise: Bunkum and Propaganda," an embittered Californian surfer wrote that locals were not very welcoming to people from the Mainland. "They don't want anything to do with the *haole*s or anyone else. For all their preaching about brotherhood and intermixing, they are prejudiced, very unfriendly and sometimes downright violent. How many white surfers have been threatened by some fat local with a good punch in the mouth when he drops in on them?"

In the second editorial called "*Haole*, Go Home," an anonymous Hawaiian surfer responded by trying to explain his anger. "Why do I feel like stomping the *haole*? Well, look at my side of things. Suppose I came over to your house and said you weren't dressing right, and you weren't living right, and this and that. You'd get mad and sock me too. It's a lot deeper than that, I guess, but that's the way we feel. You mainlanders come over here and try to run the show, and we are supposed to be your servants. The trouble is, we are slaves to your system. You've taught us to need your money and your conveniences, but we'll never respect you. I get plenty burned up when I think of what's happened to my brothers. But we still have our pride."

With the increasing number of pro surfers migrating to the North Shore each winter from all over the world, the competition for waves, media attention and prize money became intense. Eddie wasn't into the media hype or the cut-throat competition, but he did resent those outsiders who invaded the North Shore and acted like they owned the place. A rebellious, Australian surfer named Wayne "Rabbit" Bartholomew led the charge in 1975 along with fellow Aussies Ian "Kanga" Cairns and Peter "PT" Townend. Together, they introduced a more radical style of surfing and showmanship to the sport. Their pictures appeared in all the surf magazines, and their names headlined the contest results. When Rabbit returned to the Islands from Oz in the winter of 1976, he hoped to continue the previous year's hot streak and establish a reputation for himself in the newly emerging arena of professional surfing. "The North Shore was the place," he says. "It was the proving grounds, the testing grounds—if you didn't make your name on the North Shore, you were nothing."

Rabbit made a name for himself that winter, but he came close to having it inscribed on his tombstone. In trying to prove his surfing prowess, he alienated many of the North Shore locals and almost got killed in the process. Rabbit says that if Eddie hadn't stepped in to save him, there's no telling what would have happened.

A talented young surfer with a brash attitude and quick wit, Rabbit had written an infamous article called "Bustin' Down the Door" for *Surfer* magazine in 1976. Bursting with raw energy, his piece boasted about how the new generation of Aussie and South African surfers had fought for recognition and eventually dominated the North Shore surf scene the year before— and they were planning to continue their domination that winter. "The fact is that when you are a young, emerging rookie from Australia or Africa," he wrote, "you not only have to come through the backdoor to get invitations to the pro meets, but you have to bust the door down before they hear you knockin'." Like his surfing, the article was edgy, original and over the top. But Rabbit would soon discover that some angry Hawaiian surfers had some problems with his article and his attitude. And they were just waiting to tell him so—to his face.

Wayne Bartholomew was a skinny, long-haired Aussie who had been given the moniker Rabbit as a kid because he used to play several pinball machines at once and would bounce back and forth quickly between each machine like a rabbit. When he arrived back in Hawai'i that winter at the age of 22, he couldn't bounce quickly enough to escape the wrath of the locals who were sick and tired of him and his loud-mouthed buddies. He sensed old friends distancing themselves from him. One day on the North

Shore, a shaggy-haired, older surfer named Owl Chapman tried to warn him. The former big-wave legend looked like a burnt-out doomsayer, and he was practically yelling, "You don't know what's coming down! It's all coming down!" But Rabbit ignored the bearded, wild-eyed prophet, thinking he was just ranting or tripping out on drugs. During one of his first surf sessions at Sunset Beach, Rabbit was already tearing up the waves. Sitting in the lineup, waiting for his next wave, he saw the other surfers paddle in to the shore all at once. Stoked to have the waves all to himself, he watched a group of thirty local boys on the beach and wondered what they were up to. Three of them began paddling his way. It wasn't until he saw the anger in their faces that he suddenly realized they were coming after him!

Before Rabbit could paddle away, a fist landed in his face. The three Hawaiians descended on him with a barrage of angry words and heavy blows. One held him under water while the other two pounded him in the back of the head—then, they would bring his head up and pound his face. Bloody and bruised, he lost several teeth before blacking out. They slapped him awake and told him to swim in. Barely conscious but fearing for his life, he managed to swim back in to shore where the other Hawaiians were waiting for him. Luckily for Rabbit, a busload of tourists suddenly pulled up and started taking pictures of the gauntlet of locals surrounding the bleeding wreck of a man. Seizing the moment, he turned and slowly limped down the beach. He went back to the house where he had been staying, but his housemate, a surfer from South Africa, said he couldn't stay there anymore. "I feel sorry for you. It's really crazy what they're doing to you…really heavy, but can you move out straightaway? Otherwise, they're going to burn the house down tonight." Still stunned by the intense anger of these locals, Rabbit gathered his meager belongings and took up residence in some bushes down by the beach. This became his hiding place and makeshift home for the next few days.

Soon after the vicious attack, some of Rabbit's Australian friends showed up and took him to the Kuilima Resort on the far, eastern end of the North Shore. They gave him the word that he was a wanted man so he better lay low if he valued his life. A few days later, his mentor and unwitting partner in crime Ian "Kanga" Cairns arrived on the North Shore and discovered that he too was in trouble. When Rabbit told him what had happened and how there were death threats out on the both of them, the two Aussies decided to hole up for a while until the storm passed. As stubborn and aggressive as a kangaroo, Cairns was a North Shore veteran and not easily intimidated. But when he saw how badly beaten Rabbit was and heard the rumors that angry locals were going to do the same to him, he felt the fear. One night, Rabbit got a cryptic phone call from an anonymous source who warned him not to go to the Proud Peacock, his favorite bar, because there was going to be trouble. Sure enough, a gang of locals showed up that night, and their drunken rage suddenly ignited in an explosion of violence. The next day, Rabbit heard that a visiting Australian film director who looked like him had been severely beaten at the same bar—they found the director "face-down in a glass ashtray and a pool of blood." The man survived, but he ended up with a gruesome gash across his face and a painful memory of Hawai'i. From that point on, Rabbit and Kanga dug in like badgers and remained in hiding at the Kuilima Resort.

As the hostility and anger on the North Shore escalated out of control, many of Rabbit's own Australian friends and fellow surfers kept their distance from him in order to protect themselves. Even local corporate sponsors like Jack Shipley backed off. After working at the Hobie Surf Shop, where he helped Eddie get his first board, Jack had gone on to become part-owner of Lightning Bolt Surfboards with Gerry Lopez. He ran a successful business and sponsored Rabbit and many other Australian surfers—until he was told to stop. "I was giving all these Aussie guys free boards…but it was made pretty clear to me that it wasn't a good idea to give these guys any more boards. Some of this hostility toward these Australians was in a way jealousy. These guys were getting all the media attention; they were getting all the pictures in the magazines; and they were just drop-in guys who were ruling the North Shore by their deeds and by their mouths. The Hawaiians were pretty much willing to accept their deeds but not their mouths."

Besides being the local owner of Lightning Bolt, Jack had recently become one of the first international surfing judges. A stocky *haole* who grew up in Hawai'i, he was sensitive to local racial issues. Yet as a judge who had traveled around the world, he understood the Australian style of showman-ship in competition. Caught in the middle, Jack could see the issue from both sides. He knew that Rabbit and the Aussies had created their own controversy by bragging about being the best surfers in Hawai'i, but he also knew that the hostilities had gone way too far. Unfortunately, there was little he or any other *haoles* could do to stop the rising tension. "Aussies are very aggressive by nature, and they were just being themselves, having a good time, getting incredible rides and doing the Mohammed Ali stuff, talking the trash," Jack laughs. "The Aussies were so aggressive and so good they had every reason to be cocky. But in Hawai'i that type of attitude didn't fly." The hostilities escalated fast, Jack says, and there were guys trying to kill Rabbit. "There was a hit out on him, and it got pretty intense there for a while. It was basically decided among the local community that they were not going to take the brashness of these guys. The local guys were determined to see these guys get the hell off the Island."

But Rabbit wasn't going to run. "That winter it got really bad, and we were banished from the North Shore and in all kinds of trouble," he recalls twenty-five years later, shaking his head with regret. "The big realization was that if we ran, we would still be running. We couldn't run—we had to face the music. The easy way out was a Qantas flight back to Australia, but that would be the end of our dreams too." Motivated by vociferous athletes in other fields, Rabbit had been dreaming about turning surfing into a popular professional sport like boxing or tennis. "It was at a time when there was a lot of high-profile athletes, like the 'Rumble in the Jungle' with Ali and Frasier. We were taking a leaf out of their book and others like [tennis star] Jimmy Connors. And my nickname 'Mohammed Bugs' didn't help! We felt like surfing needed to do something to make the growth and birth of professional surfing a reality in our time. As it was, we were too early anyway. But we felt like time was running out on our generation, and we wanted this dream to materialize for professional surfing and a world tour."

In 1975, Rabbit had seen a glimpse of his dream when surfing entrepreneurs Fred Hemmings, Randy Rarick and Jack Shipley formed an organization called the International Professional Surfers. The IPS attempted to establish a global circuit of contests, as well as a rating system and unified set of rules. Yet the intense localism in Hawai'i threatened not only the safety of foreign surfers like the Aussies but also the success of the world tour itself. Fortunately, Clyde shared Rabbit's vision of professional surfing, and this connection may have saved his life. "I got to meet Clyde before I met Eddie, and I got on really well with Clyde." Rabbit says, "Some people thought we were being disrespectful just by the new way we were surfing," but Clyde liked the new approach. Moving beyond the traditional style of soul surfing that Eddie and many Hawaiians had aspired to, Rabbit and his fellow Aussies introduced the new "rip, tear and lacerate" school.

The essence of this new, radical style centered on creating the most speed and carving as many sharp cutbacks and S-shaped maneuvers as possible. Like the movement itself, a cutback consisted of suddenly changing direction in the fastest, most fluid way possible, creating a wall of spray. Surfboards became like spray cans, and in their wake, surfers painted an elaborate signature across the face of the wave—many saw it as a new art form, while others looked at it like a kind of disrespectful graffiti. Eddie fell somewhere in between: he respected the way the Aussies surfed but not the way some of them bragged about it. Because Eddie had traveled to Oz and seen them on their home turf, he was more accustomed to their aggressive yet playful style, in and out of the surf.

Like Eddie, Aussie surfer Peter Townend was caught in the middle of the building racial conflict. "Just as they were proud to be Hawaiian, we were proud to be Australian," PT says. But he also knew that the aggressive behavior of the Aussies had gone too far. "To be honest, we weren't as humble as we could have been," Peter admits. "In the sportsworld, there's always an element of trash-talking, and sometimes people take it too personally. It's not personal. Sometimes, it's just to throw your opponent off." Tough competitors and rivals, PT had beaten Eddie in the '76 World Cup when he became the first World Champion. Though Eddie looked like an "intimidating guy," PT knew that he was really a "peace-maker." The two remained on friendly terms during this volatile time. After all, they had mutual friends in the Holmes family and had gotten drunk together on swipe, which was akin to smoking the peace pipe. While the graveyard had been a safe haven in the past, the Aussies hoped Eddie could bring that same aloha to the escalating racism on the North Shore.

Angry locals complained these young radicals and foreigner surfers were going against the ocean's natural flow. Traditional Hawaiians preferred a more mellow style and a less competitive attitude. "But Clyde was really into it," Rabbit says. "He thought it was a cool thing. I think we had a sympathizer in Clyde because he kind of understood what we were trying to do with this dream of professional surfing. Eddie and Clyde saw that what we were doing wasn't bad, that we were just trying to talk it up." But their cocky attitudes had inflamed the locals, and Rabbit realized their arrogant comments had come to symbolize yet another insult to the Hawaiian people. "I had no idea of the history and heritage of Hawai'i and how everyone— from the early traders, to the missionaries, to the modern-day real estate developers—had always come and taken from them. But I must have appeared as the absolute enemy trying to steal the last vestige of their heritage—surfing." But this insight didn't occur to Rabbit until Eddie came and gave him the lesson of his life.

Rabbit and Kanga were corralled at the Kuilima, waiting for the inevitable showdown. "Suddenly, we had been disrespectful to the whole Hawaiian culture. It had just gotten blown out of proportion, and I was in a lot of trouble," Rabbit remembers. Justifiably paranoid, they realized their lives were in danger and literally took turns doing guard duty with bats and tennis racquets. After "bustin' down the door" the year before, they had been reduced to hiding behind the door and fearing for their lives. "At that time, we didn't get visitors. Australians had given us a wide berth—no one came to visit us. It hurt, but it was understandable. Our own tribe had abandoned us and were looking after their own skin. There we were, me and Cairns out there, hiding out, locked up, locked in and locked down, doing eight-hour watches. One of us was always awake." Then, one night during the height of the tension, they heard a loud knock at the door. They grabbed their bats, ready for anything.

Peering outside, Rabbit saw a familiar face. "It was a shock to open the door and see Eddie Aikau there. My heart was pumping so hard it was unbelievable. But I also knew that Eddie and Clyde were really decent guys. And Eddie basically sat us down and said, 'I'm a proud Hawaiian, and I don't dig what you, Rabbit and Ian, have done. But it's gone too far, and my family has stepped in to try and calm the waters.' He said, 'But I'm not even sure we can do it.' My heart was sinking," Rabbit recalls. "But he did sit down and tell us all about Hawaiian heritage. He talked for hours and hours that night, and it really drew us close together. He taught me an incredible lesson, and for the first time I saw what I had done. He told us that Hawaiians were losing their land and their culture was being taken from them by the white man, by Western society. Surfing had been something that was done by the kings and the royalty, and this was their last bastion of nobility—and we were seen as the edge of the wedge and that we were going to take that too. I mean those words resonated with me, and I can still clearly remember him sitting there and telling us that, word for word."

At the end of the evening, Rabbit remembers, "Eddie gave us the word and told us that it had gotten completely out of control, that it had gone way beyond the North Shore to the other side of the Island. There were some heavy people who were coming out to get us. He told us to stay indoors until he came back. Ian Cairns and I were focused on staying in one piece, and he was focused on trying to rein in the general animosity. There's no doubt that the intervention of Eddie and the Aikau clan turned the situation around." Exiled at the resort and abandoned by most of his friends, Rabbit couldn't believe he was being rescued by this local legend. Though Eddie didn't mention it, he had been in a similar situation when he was abandoned by his friends and fellow surfers in South Africa in 1971. "Eddie saw that we were really isolated and in big trouble," Rabbit recalls.

Eddie and his family helped set up a meeting of all the local surfers and the Hawaiian community so they could air their grievances against the Aussies and ease their anger. They arranged to have a public meeting at the Kuilima Resort. In old Hawai'i, this kind of meeting was called *ho'oponopono* (to make right), and community leaders were trying to bring back this traditional forum of open and honest discussion. Rabbit was open to discussion, but it seemed more like a trial in his eyes. The whole thing began to take on a surreal, Kafka-like atmosphere. Still, he knew his future in Hawai'i depended on the outcome.

When the day of reckoning finally arrived, Eddie came to their hotel room to escort Rabbit and Ian to the meeting. Rabbit remembers the scene vividly. "Hey, man, it was in a conference room, and they were all there—everybody who had a beef about anything was there. It was an unforgettable gathering. There was me and Ian, and we were at a table. Eddie chaired the meeting and made [Aussie surfer and future world champ] Mark Richards come and sit with him at the front table. That's how diplomatic he was. Mark Richards was absolutely petrified, but Eddie made him do it because they liked Mark—he had that good guy image and didn't have the brashness. It was a stroke of genius." Eddie knew that having a popular Oz surfer on stage with him would defuse some of the hostilities toward the Australians.

During certain moments, the meeting seemed more like a public stoning. The two Aussies bore the brunt of hundreds of years of pent-up Hawaiian rage. "It was a tribunal," Rabbit says, shaking his head in disbelief. "There were specific charges laid against us: disrespect, dropping in, outspoken claims in magazines, irreverent interviews on TV, some very ill-timed quotes, my article 'Bustin' Down the Door' and a litany of other charges. Put it this way, they built their case, bitch by bitch," Rabbit says, his 'bitches' sounding like 'beaches.' "And for each one of them I was guilty. Eddie would then always come to us and let us have our say, and I would get up and give our explanation. I was really scared, but one calming factor was Eddie Aikau. For a while there, I didn't take my eyes off him. He was my saving grace, and I figured somehow he was going to keep me alive. My whole world depended on Eddie Aikau. That's a fact because it could have gone bad. There were some angry people there. There was one point where I actually lost it, unfortunately, and got up and went, 'Look, I can't understand what I've done.' I was really naïve. Then, this big Hawaiian guy came roaring through from the back of the meeting and came up and stood right in front of me. He just pointed at me and said, 'I'll *tell* you what you did!' I was just sinking down in my chair, and at that point, I just wouldn't take my focus off Eddie. Every time it got really heavy, I would just focus on Eddie." Veteran North Shore photographer Bernie Baker says, "Only someone of Eddie's level, with that kind of diplomacy, would be able to step into a fire fight and squelch the fire. He could take a tense situation and calm things down."

Finally, the meeting came to an end. Rabbit and Kanga were told they could stay at the Kuilima and surf in front of the resort and in the upcoming contests. But as for surfing at the other spots on the Island, they would have to do so at their own risk—there were still angry locals out there who might strike out at them on their own. According to his son Brian, Buffalo Keaulana calls these violent, Hawaiian radicals "coconuts" because they are "brown on the outside and white on the inside." As a lifeguard trainer, Brian tells his young Hawaiian counterparts to avoid this kind of reverse racism and hypocrisy. "Make sure you practice your culture before you start preaching to someone else."

As grim as the situation still seemed, Rabbit realized that the meeting had probably saved him from being beaten or killed so he was grateful. Still holed up at the Kuilima, the two Aussies continued playing tennis and occasionally surfed at the most popular beaches where there was safety in numbers. But Rabbit didn't perform well in the contests. "I didn't do too well that winter. But I tell you what, I developed a good backhand! It was a blessing in disguise. I learned to play tennis, and to this day, it's my second sport. I couldn't surf the North Shore for months so that's when I learned to play."

Rabbit can laugh about it now, but it was a tense time in his life. He had lost more than a few teeth—he had lost his nerve and confidence. Later that winter when the tension finally eased, Rabbit forced himself to go out socially and deal with his fears. "Eddie gave us word that there was going to be a party on Sunset Point, and he thought it was a good idea that we come to the party. I, of course, did not think it was a good idea, at all. It was pure fear and loathing. But we went, and it ended up being a good thing 'cause we shook hands with a lot of people and a lot of things were said. That was when I could tell that it was all over. We had passed the test, and they could see we were remorseful. We paid our dues, we took our lickings, and we were still there. That was the beginning of the healing of the wounds." Good music and Primo beer went a long way toward resolving old hostilities on the North Shore.

Later that year, Rabbit even got a chance to reciprocate the kindness the Aikaus had shown him on his home turf on the Gold Coast. In February of '77, Eddie and Clyde flew to Australia for the Stubbies Contest at Burleigh Heads, which was part of the first world tour. On the flight to Oz, Eddie sat next to Bernie Baker. Bernie had shot pictures of him surfing, but he knew Eddie was more than just a surfer. "He could talk about things on a higher plane than others. He had a low-key thirst for knowledge." Bernie says that many people thought Eddie was a loner, "but that was far from reality. He was just quiet, focused and always thinking."

After word got around about Rabbit's harsh treatment in the Islands, he began to wonder about a possible Aussie backlash against the Hawaiians. "I started worrying there was going to be some kind of tit-for-tat thing, but I knew that wouldn't happen. Australians love sport, we're a sporting nation. And I knew that when Eddie and Clyde came to Australia, they would win the people over with their spirit. They would surf hard and then go drink with the Aussies. And that's what happened. There was some healing going on there. Between the tribunal and that, it was like a different world, like night and day. I could actually see the dream of professional surfing happening. Clearly, Eddie and Clyde were there to party, and they partied hard. I kept hearing all the time that they were performing at parties, busting out their guitars and drinking beer with the best of them and just generally endearing themselves to the Gold Coast community." The rift between the Aussies and Hawaiians had mended. "I made my own path after that," Rabbit says, "I made my peace." But for other surfers, the trouble was just beginning.

South African surfer Shaun Tomson would also become a victim of local hostility. "After 1977, the North Shore became a very different place," he says. "Gangsterism began to rear its ugly head, and dope became a big problem. The overall spirit of the North Shore changed. I had a really bad experience with a group of guys who felt like I had maligned Hawaiian surfers, which was absolute rubbish—I've never said a bad word about those guys. I was told to leave the Islands or I would die. I was threatened in the lineup and cold-cocked several times. I had to buy a 12-gauge shotgun and sleep with it under my bed. I had to meet with the North Shore surfers, many of whom stood behind me. This would never have happened if Eddie had been around—one phone call, and he would have taken care of it."

While in Australia, Eddie and Clyde had gone to visit Lynne and the girls. By this time, her marriage had fallen apart. Her husband Darryl had always been a heavy drinker, but he usually kept it under control. Now, alcohol was taking control of his life, and Lynne refused to be held hostage to his violent mood swings and extended absences. Darryl eventually moved back to South Africa to start a new surfboard business. Though they never talked about it, Lynne could tell that Eddie's relationship with his wife was also coming to a close. "He and Linda were already in trouble at that stage. But nothing was said. The talk then was all about training for the *Hokule'a*." Lynne remembers that he couldn't wait to get back home so he could start training. Despite their deep feelings for each other, Eddie and Lynne never pursued a romantic relationship. Though friends suspected they might end up together one day, that day never came. Neither wanted to jeopardize their friendship or betray Linda. Besides, Eddie had already made a commitment to sail on the *Hokule'a*, and his heart was set on the next voyage. He was also determined to win the Duke Contest.

After returning to Hawai'i, Eddie continued surfing in the contest circuit. He was never a great competitive surfer; nor was he naïve enough to think he could make enough money in professional surfing to support himself and his wife. But he kept entering the Duke Contest year after year because he loved the challenge of competing with his friends for the biggest waves and best rides. More than money or prestige, Rabbit believes that Eddie wanted to win the contest for one reason. He sought to honor his family, his people and the Duke. In the winter of '77, Eddie and Rabbit would later find themselves competing head to head in the finals of the Duke, one of the most meaningful contests of their careers.

Looking back on that time, Rabbit says Eddie really shaped his life and career as a professional surfer and promoter. "Eddie helped me become a man and a true professional. I think more than anything, I wanted to become an ambassador for the sport after all that. That's what he instilled in me. He was an ambassador for his Hawaiian culture, the surfing nation, and he wore it well. And I aspired to that in the sport. We wanted this dream of professional surfing, to make a living out of something we loved doing. But we didn't have a great image. We were looked at as bums that didn't work. I wanted to change that image. I had this vision of us being part of a respected sport, where I could walk down the main street of my hometown with my head held high and say, 'I'm a surfer.' That was something that burned deep inside me."

Two and a half decades later, Rabbit can proudly say that he has helped promote professional surfing around the world and improve its image. Sitting on the deck of his friend's North Shore home, Rabbit is staring at the final rounds of the 2000 Pipeline Masters, the last contest on the Association of Surfing Professionals (ASP) Tour. While he talks about Eddie, he watches as Jonah-like surfers disappear into big, blue tubes the size of whales rushing toward the shore. As the current president of the ASP's international circuit, he returns every year for the Triple Crown of Surfing, the final three contests of the tour. "I've still never missed a winter. This is my 29th in a row. It took a while, but I was accepted." Rabbit heads up a $6 million dollar tour with contests all over the world, and the Pipeline Masters is the most prestigious of them all—the jewel in the Triple Crown. The prize money is paltry compared to the inflated incomes of most pro athletes today, but Rabbit and Eddie were never in it for the money.

Rabbit can still vividly remember the night Eddie came over to talk to him at the Kuilima Resort because it was a turning point for him. "Every word he said to me that day I will remember for the rest of my life because it changed everything. I think my life turned around that night. The whole experience over that winter changed me. It was a bit of a ritual of manhood. I grew up. That night I wanted to get to know the Hawaiians, and I wanted them to get to know me how I really was. In the tribalism of surfing, we were really similar but obviously poles apart in our respective heritages. Hawaiians were scared of losing their heritage, and this was the beginning of the whole sovereignty issue. I believe that if Eddie was with us now, he would've been a foremost figure in the sovereignty movement in Hawai'i. He had such respect in the community that transcended the sport."

CHAPTER 12

Victory and Defeat

"The thoughts of man are like
caves whose interiors one cannot see"
— Hawaiian proverb

By the time Eddie was 31, he was known among locals as the "King of Waimea Bay," a strange moniker for such a shy and humble guy. As the head lifeguard and best big-wave rider, his name was synonymous with the Bay. He practically lived at the beach, his home away from home. Flattering articles about his lifesaving rescues appeared in the "Our Quiet Heroes" column of *The Honolulu Advertiser*. Epic pictures of him dropping down huge North Shore waves showed up in the surf mags, boggling the minds of young surfers everywhere. The man was slowly becoming a myth, but only his closest friends and family understood his hidden hopes and fears.

A decade after making his big-wave debut at Waimea in 1967, Eddie continued to surf the biggest swells to roll through the Bay in the winter of 1977. He would take off on the deepest and steepest part of the wave. In fact, the spot where he caught these giant waves came to be called "Eddie's bowl." When the deep-water swells hit the reef and rocks along the cliff, they would suddenly jack up to twice their size and form a bowl-shaped face sometimes forty feet high. To get a feel for the horrifying immensity of such a wave, imagine sitting in a movie theater and seeing the screen suddenly become a huge wall of water that crashes down on you at 25-30 mph. While many big-wave riders just dared to surf on the safer outside shoulder of the wave, only Eddie and a handful of brave souls put themselves in the most dangerous and critical spot. Even ballsy surfers like Ken Bradshaw and James Jones said they were blown away by Eddie's fearlessness in such deadly waves.

What drove Eddie to put his life on the line, knowing that one bad wipeout could be the end? "He was not trying to risk his life or defy death," Linda says, still trying to understand her enigmatic husband. "It was a way for him to feel worthy. He wanted to achieve something for the Hawaiian people." With surfing's growing popularity around the world, other countries like Australia began to attract more media attention and professional contests. By surfing such enormous waves, Eddie and other locals brought recognition back to Hawai'i, where the sport originated. On a more personal level, Linda adds that Eddie "never graduated from high school so maybe this was a way to make his mom and dad proud of him." Eddie not only made his parents proud, he became an icon in the Islands. Young surf rats would follow him like the Pied Piper down to the waterline and watch in wide-eyed awe whenever he paddled out into big waves at Waimea or Sunset. World champion Shaun Tomson remembers surfing with Eddie as a kid at Sunset Beach. "Sunset was considered the greatest wave in the world but also the most difficult," Shaun says. "I used to follow him around like a little puppy because he was the big dog out there." Women would flirt with Eddie at parties when he performed; parents would thank him for looking after their *keiki* in the ocean; and local aunties would say what a good Hawaiian boy he was at family luaus. But Eddie's biggest fan was Big Bill Pierce.

Surrounded by memories of Eddie, Bill now lives in the same old one-bedroom plantation-style house that the Aikaus used to rent for their regular stays on the North Shore. The little house faces Hale'iwa Beach Park, where the brothers used to surf together, and the place seems haunted by their memory. Just as Mom and Pops took Bill and many others into their home, Big Bill has adopted every stray cat in the neighborhood. The graceful, feline creatures wander around freely in his little cabin, brushing against the leg of this towering man. The messy den is like a shrine, with posters of Eddie all over the walls. Each one comes from a different year of the Quiksilver big-wave contest, and they show how Eddie's image has evolved over the years. In an early poster, there is a large photo of his ruddy face, hooded eyes and shaggy hair, and he looks like an intimidating local. In a later poster, an artist has rendered Eddie in glowing colors with perfect skin, bright smile and smooth hair—in the myth-making eyes of the artist, he looks more like a saint than a surfer. And in Bill's mind, he was a kind of Hawaiian martyr. He treasures everything Eddie ever gave him like sacred relics, including a pair of Quiksilver shorts Eddie brought as a gift from his trip to Australia and the red bandana he used to wear around his head.

Big Bill was scared to death of big waves. Yet like the drunken wannabes in Spain who jump into the ring with the bullfighters or run with the bulls, Bill wanted to experience the thrill of riding huge waves. He asked Eddie and Clyde to show him how. "These guys had way more skills than I did, but I learned from them." He remembers going surfing at Waimea Bay for the first time during a relatively "small" day when the swells were about 20 feet high. Eddie had loaned him one of his boards and promised to watch over him. With his heart in his throat and fearing for his life, Bill paddled out and saw a monstrous beast charging toward him. "And Eddie said, 'Go, Bill, go!' And I went, and, boy, I still remember that ride, one of the most fantastic rides of my life. I took off, and it's like you're on top of a precipice, and you're going straight down like an elevator drop. And I made it down to the bottom and to the channel. And I came in because I wanted to quit while I was ahead," Bill says, laughing. "Each time, Eddie was showing me where to go. Not just me—he's taught so many people. Just ask Ken Bradshaw."

One of the converts to tow-in surfing, wave warrior Ken Bradshaw has ridden some of the biggest waves on the planet. In fact, there's a famous poster of him surfing at an outer reef break, and the wave towers some seventy feet above him like a mountain of moving water. "The largest wave ever ridden on Oʻahu," he states proudly. But he becomes more humble and reflective at the mention of Eddie. Ken says Eddie taught him all kinds of things about Waimea, like how to take off on the inside section of a wave that looked like it was going to annihilate him. Miraculously, Ken discovered he could still make the drop, barely escaping the exploding wall of whitewater just behind him. "It was so neat to have a mentor like that at Waimea, basically to show me where to line up, which waves to go for. So I will always have so much respect for him."

Though Eddie was considered the "King of Waimea," he had yet to score a major victory on the professional tour. And though he had performed well in almost every Duke Contest over the last decade, he couldn't seem to win the event, the only one that really mattered to him. Bill had followed Eddie's surfing career for years and often coached him before contests. Having watched him rise through the ranks of professional surfing, he was frustrated that Eddie couldn't seem to capture the title. In 1977, Bill knew better than anyone how much his friend had always wanted to win the

Duke. "I can remember that winter before the contest, when we would sit on the porch, and he would say, 'What, Bill, you think I got a chance? God, I hope I win this time.' He had so many close calls. The reason he wanted to win was to honor the Duke, not to honor himself. I always thought of him as the modern Duke Kahanamoku because wherever the Duke went, he spread aloha. And Eddie kind of personified that for me."

Before the Duke Classic in 1977, Bill talked with Eddie about his strategy during the contest and urged him to take more chances. "It's not the '60's anymore—you've gotta do more maneuvers so the judges notice, like snapbacks and round-house cutbacks." Bill mentioned the 1976 World Cup, when he came in third behind Aussies Ian Cairns and Peter Townend. Although Eddie had caught some of the biggest and best waves that day, he had been content to take the high line and just cruise all the way across the wave. But that wasn't enough after the Australian surfers introduced their own radical style of surfing which included the "off the lip." For this maneuver, surfers would snap their boards off the top or lip of the wave, the most critical section, and float there for a second before coming down with the whitewater. "I used to tell him that he needed to hotdog more on the wave, doing more snapbacks. But he just liked to cruise…So I said, 'God, man, you just can't live in the past, you gotta snap, crank the turns, come straight up and snap it back down.'"

When the Duke Classic came around in December, Eddie was ready. Although the contest had changed dramatically over the last ten years, becoming more commercial and aggressively competitive, he felt his time had come. Eddie was never a cut-throat competitor, but as a contest veteran, he knew what the judges wanted to see. And he was going to give it to them. On the day of the contest, a northwest swell pumped in solid 8-12 foot waves at Sunset Beach. An offshore wind was sculpting the faces of the waves, making them clean and hollow. Perfect conditions. The sun was shining, the cameras were poised, and a large crowd was gathered on the beach for the big event.

Bill stood on the beach with the Aikau family and watched as Eddie made his mark that day. From his first heat on, he seemed to be on fire. "All of a sudden during the Duke, everything just fell into place. It was like a transformation! I couldn't believe it. I said, 'Goddamnit, he's doing it. He's snapping, he's going straight off the lip. He was doing all of those things and making it through the preliminaries and the quarters and the semi's. During the semi-finals, he got barreled a couple of times." Surfing against radical young Australians like Rabbit and veteran Hawaiian pros like Reno Abellira, Eddie used his experience to pick out the biggest waves and then went for the deepest tubes he could find. "During the finals," Bill said, "he was getting deep barrels, the kind of deep barrels where you give up—'Oh, God, he got creamed.' And then all of a sudden, wham! Way down the line, he comes out of the whitewater!" This kind of magical disappearing act was just what the judges loved.

Covering the event for ABC's *Wide World of Sports*, competitor-turned-promoter Fred Hemmings gave a running commentary of each surfer's ride. The former world champion was now a worldly media mogul, working for the nation's top TV networks. During the finals, he described some of Eddie's top-scoring waves. "In the slow-motion replay, you can see that he is really going for it. He's taking a bigger wave. His potential to gain points is greatly increased by the wave selection. This wave has a lot of juice or power, and he wants to get inside it. There, he's in tight. He's going for the tube ride. Look at how that water explodes behind him! He just escapes getting nailed!" The hardest part of tube-riding is escaping before the wave implodes like a collapsing tunnel.

Meanwhile, two local surfers were giving Eddie a run for his money, a young Hawaiian named Dane Kealoha, who was fast becoming a top competitor, and an older *haole* surfer named Bobby Owens. But then Eddie caught the wave of the day, barely making it out of the tube as the crowd on the beach roared. Impressed with his old rival, Hemmings described the moment with bravado. "Here comes Eddie Aikau on the outside. As we said earlier, Eddie's been around a long time. He's got great judgement. He's waiting on the outside and getting the big waves, and here he is. Look at that tube ride. Fantastic! Let's look at it again in slow motion…he knows he wants to go for that tube ride. He knows he needs to do something outstanding to gain points. So he stalls, he's waiting, he's letting the wave build in front of him, it's throwing out over him. He stalls back right in the tube. Look at that. You cannot get any further back in the critical section than that! And how he pulls himself out of there, I don't know. That is going to score a lot of points for Eddie Aikau."

Getting 'tubed' inside the powerful vortex of a wave not only racks up points, but it is a mystical, almost primordial experience. When the silver curtain of the wave encloses you in this glass tunnel of spiraling water, time suddenly slows down. For a few moments, the outside world just falls away, eclipsed by the ocean's green wall. The other competitors, the judges, the crowds on the beach, they all just disappear—so do the fears, worries and concerns that weigh on your mind on land. Everything is suddenly cleansed away by the roaring water. Nothing is left but you, the wave and the daylight at the end of the tunnel. Crouched inside, you keep your eyes on this light, making sure you don't get sucked up the face of the wave or axed by the lip. Psychedelic surfers of the era compared the feeling to going back to the womb or seeing a glimpse of the afterlife. This exciting yet serene experience is what surfers live for. When he finally emerged from the tube during the last minutes of the finals, Eddie must have felt a profound sense of peace as he burst out of the darkness and into the light.

While the judges tallied their scores, all the surfers stood around the contest platform. A large crowd gathered on the beach around the competitors to await the results. Although the Hawaiians had done well in the contest, the judges still seemed to favor the Australians' more radical style. As one of the judges at the contest, Randy Rarick remembers how Eddie finally used his years of experience to outmaneuver the other surfers. "There were better surfers in terms of performance, but that's where his knowledge and experience of being on the North Shore paid off," Randy says. "Perhaps, the other surfers scored better on individual waves, but his ability to pick off the biggest sets and ride the longest distance and basically play the rules to the hilt gave him a leading edge that day."

When the final scores were calculated, the emcee announced, "Third place belongs to Dane Kealoha, and second place goes to Bobby Owens. So you can hear the cheers of the Native Hawaiians for their man, Eddie Aikau!" Ten years after entering his first Duke Contest and placing in the finals almost every year since then, Eddie had finally won. Pops gave him a proud hug, as the rest of the family gathered around. In a photo taken at that moment, Eddie looks both exhilarated and exhausted, with tears in his eyes as his father holds him. It was an emotional moment, the culmination of a long-held dream. Friends showered Eddie with champagne, and leggy girls in bikinis presented him with flower leis. When they handed him the microphone, he shyly said, "Aw, man, the surf was really good. The best waves you can have for one contest." Then, after a pause, he said, "I would like to dedicate my win to my brother Gerry and my family. Aloha." Surrounded by friends and fans, Eddie and his family took a moment in the midst of their celebration to remember Gerald, who had died just days after Clyde had won the Duke in '73. Holding his trophy, Eddie must have recalled the moment when he and Clyde had placed their Duke statuettes in Gerald's coffin.

ABC announcer Jim Lampley interviewed Eddie that day. Looking out over the ocean, the shy Hawaiian said, "I wanted to win when Duke Kahanamoku was alive, but I just couldn't. I think I'm the oldest timer in the Duke Contest today, and I've been trying for years to win it. I thank God for giving me the honor today in taking first place. And I did it for all the Hawaiians, man, all for the Hawaiians. Aloha."

As Big Bill said of his performance that day, "He just cut loose, and it all came together for him. It was totally his day all the way through," from the prelims to the finals. Rabbit Bartholomew competed in the final heat but says he didn't stand a chance against Eddie. "The '77 Duke final was a one-man show. Eddie Aikau dominated the larger sets. He caught at least a dozen 12-footers, taking off deep on the north peak and backdooring the west bowl at incredible speed…He was in his own space and in his own time. It was like he was in one final, and we were in another. It was an inspiring hour in his surfing career because it was the Duke Kahanamoku Classic, and he was surfing as though he were the only one out there. He embodied the spirit of the Duke…It was an honor to be in that final. At the presentation of the awards, we were the finalists, standing up there with Eddie when he had his moment. He only wanted to win the Duke, and now he was a happy man." Normally a very intense competitor, Rabbit was excited for Eddie. Most of the pro surfers on the beach that day shared his excitement.

"The more I got to know Eddie," Ken Bradshaw says, "the more I realized how much he revered the contest and the Duke and all that he stood for." It was Bradshaw's first Duke, and though he didn't do well, he would win the event six years later in 1983. Despite his poor performance, he was stoked for Eddie. "He was on such a roll. He could paddle so well, and he had such good judgement. He caught all the good waves and made them all. When it's your day—like it was my day six years later—nothing can stop you. You're going to catch all the right waves." Ken joined the other surfers in congratulating Eddie, who seemed overwhelmed by all the attention he was suddenly receiving.

For the first time, the Awards Banquet was held at the Polynesian Cultural Center that year, instead of at Duke's or some other swank club in

Waikiki. Randy Rarick felt this was a step down from the glamour of previous years. "It was beginning to lose some of its luster," he says of the Duke, "but it still was an honor to be invited and to win this event." Defending champ James Jones says, "The Duke had been surfing's highest honor up to this point. But this year they were trying to downplay the importance of the Duke because they wanted to favor the small-wave contests outside of Hawai'i," which were part of the newly formed International Professional Surfers (IPS) tour. James had won the contest during its prime in '72 and then again in '76, the years before Clyde's and Eddie's victories. "I always said it would take an Aikau to beat me," he quips. "I was really glad the Aikaus won because it was much better to be beaten by a friend."

Disgusted by the growing decadence of professional surfing, James remembers the banquet as a crass affair. Many of the surfers were too drunk and stoned to follow the speeches so they sat there cheering and heckling the speakers. "We sat in the bleachers of this amphitheater, and they just called out the winners who received their awards and then said a few words as they received their trophies. Michael Ho got up and said what he said every year: 'We need more money!'" But Eddie brought a certain level of class to the affair, according to James, who remembers him wearing a rented tuxedo and giving a very emotional and prophetic speech. After receiving his trophy, he stood at the podium in his black tux and colorful leis and looked around at his friends and family in the audience. "Then Eddie started to speak. 'What is more important in life is not competing against each other. It's your family and loving each other.' He had tears in his eyes, and he was crying." James says many people didn't really hear or understand what Eddie was saying because they were too caught up in their own drunken conversations and thoughts. But others were clearly listening, moved by Eddie's speech.

Unlike his rival James Jones, Ken Bradshaw remembers the banquet and the audience's reaction in a more optimistic light. "When he won, I don't know who cried the most. Everyone was so elated, so happy. That was probably the happiest I ever saw Eddie. It was so emotional for me at the time. I was overwhelmed by it all. It was a beautiful speech." Bradshaw and Jones rarely see eye to eye, and they have come close to scrapping a few times over the years. They are very different—James is thin and lean like an Asian panther, while Ken is big and muscular like an American bear. But they both looked up to Eddie. In fact, when tension erupted between them a few years before, Eddie had stepped in to resolve their differences.

"There was one day when I was all pissed off and raving about James Jones and how he had burned me," Ken Bradshaw remembers. "And Eddie said, 'Hey, Bruddah Brad, get in the truck—I want to talk to you.' We drove around for an hour until he finally actually parked at Laniakea. He told me his whole interpretation of what 'aloha' was and respecting other people. 'Just bite your tongue on this one and be more humble and accept James Jones as a good surfer who has been around for a long time,' Eddie said. It was really neat how he took me in and put a bridle on me really, in a real articulate, concerned way that only a Hawaiian could do. He made me feel really important and humble too. It was a real good lesson.

"I have nothing but the highest regard, the highest respect for Eddie and what he stood for," Ken says in a soft voice. Most people don't associate that kind of sensitivity with this intimidating bear of a man. He has been known to break the fins off of people's surfboards if they were foolish enough to drop in on his waves; once he even took a bite out of a guy's board when he cut him off on a ride. But as Eddie spoke that night, he brought out a gentler side of Ken. "He even taught us to be more loving and understanding of each other…In the beginning, I'm sure he was like all of us—he was young and arrogant and wanted to make a name for himself and the Hawaiians. He always stood up for the Hawaiian people. And when you're young, you tend to do it more aggressively, but as you get older, being a diplomat works much better. He became so much more of a diplomat. And sure, he got pissed off occasionally—he was human, but it was usually a just cause." But at that point in his life, Eddie's scrapping days had come to an end. Looking into his tired eyes, Ken could tell that he had seen too much violence and anger over the years.

For a waterman like Eddie, Ken says, "You face the elements of nature so much that you realize you're kind of insignificant to the big picture and therefore, all you can do is contribute positive things because it's going to go on, with or without you. That's what the ocean finally teaches you. I think being a lifeguard and rescuing so many people, it makes you realize that life is short." Though he was only 31 that night, Eddie had stared death in the face many times. He had buried his brother Gerald and lost his good friend Jose. He had suffered horrendous wipeouts when he ran out of air and barely escaped drowning. And he had saved countless drowning victims by breathing air back into their lungs.

Mesmerized by Eddie's speech, James vividly remembers his last words to the crowd because they were so prophetic. "None of us know how long we are going to be on this earth. We have to love each other and take care of each other 'cause you never know when your time is going to come." Both James and Ken agree that Eddie seemed to sense that his own death was imminent. As a lifeguard at one of the most dangerous surf breaks in the world, Eddie dealt with life and death situations on a daily basis. Even though he had rescued hundreds of people on the North Shore, Eddie had a hard time dealing with the fact that he hadn't been able to save his own marriage.

Though they were separated at the time, Linda had come to Sunset Beach to watch him win the Duke Contest that day. She was also there that night when he gave his speech. Though it was a happy occasion, Linda knew better than anyone about his enduring sadness over Gerry's death. "He didn't handle it well, and he couldn't move on, and it affected our relationship. The grief for his brother totally overwhelmed every aspect of his life, and I just didn't know how to get him out of it. He lost his desire to take care of himself…I guess it had been coming for a long time. Then, things started to get better, and he seemed to come around and be himself again. He stopped drinking so much." Thinking about the *Hokule'a*'s next voyage gave him something to look forward to.

"Everything seemed to be going well, and then, I found out that he had been seeing someone else," Linda says. "It seemed to be over—that's what he said—but I was devastated, and I probably should have left then and put some space between us. But I didn't, and it kind of drove a wedge between us. I had a lot of resentment when I found out he had an affair. Things were never the same, and I started to drift away from him. I just started to withdraw and establish a life outside of the family. And we just grew further and further apart. And he realized the longer he tried to keep me at the graveyard, the more I pulled away from him. It wasn't that I didn't forgive him. I did. But I guess I just needed to step back from the whole thing. I moved out and got my own place. We would talk on the phone." Eddie continued going to the Catholic church downtown to see the priest who was helping him deal with their separation.

Saddened by the demise of his marriage, Eddie turned to the two things that Linda says always gave him comfort: "Water and music. The ocean always had a calming effect on him, and music had a tendency to do that too." So he surfed and played his slack-key guitar and tried to come to terms with the changes in his life. Although Eddie had realized his dream to win the Duke, he had lost his wife and was depressed by the prospect of divorce. Restless and ready for a change, Eddie decided it was time to embark on a new journey. Eddie was eager to start training for the *Hokule'a's* next voyage so he asked the Lifeguard Service for time off from work so he could focus on making the crew. "I think at that point he was able to focus 100% on the *Hokule'a*," Rabbit observes. "He had won the Duke. He was Mr. Waimea. He had climbed his Mount Everest." Yet as excited as he was about the prospect of making such a long voyage, Eddie was still haunted by nagging doubts and dark premonitions. What fears he felt or visions he saw, Eddie didn't say, but he seemed to have a dark foreboding about his future.

Eddie aboard Hokule'a *on the fateful day of departure, March 16, 1978.*

CHAPTER 13

Premonitions

"E pule wale no i ka la oha make a'ole e ola."
"Prayers said on the day of death cannot save one."
— *Hawaiian proverb*

When the Polynesian Voyaging Society announced they were
seeking crew members for the next trip to Tahiti, Eddie was one of the first
to sign up. He joined hundreds of people trying out for only twelve positions.
Marion Lyman also wanted to be a member of the crew. Besides being the
captain's sister, she had the advantage of having worked on *Hokule'a* during
its construction. But she had to go through the training and sailing trials like
Eddie and everyone else. A tall woman with sandy blond hair, Marion
practically lived in the water and had grown up surfing, sailing and paddling.
After a two-year stint in the Peace Corps in Micronesia, Marion had recently returned to Hawai'i and was eager to sail on *Hokule'a*. She remembers
seeing Eddie for the first time at one of the training meetings and being
shocked by his size. Marion had been expecting to see a huge, burly surfer,
"this great thick bull of a guy," she says. "But he was small, like 5' 8" and
160 pounds or so, a very wiry guy. Obviously, a full Hawaiian. Definitely, a
man's man. He was very shy around women. I don't think I ever got more
than five feet near him or five words out of him. I was looking forward to
getting to know him, and that didn't really happen."

Eddie didn't know much about deep-sea voyaging, but his reputation
as big-wave rider and lifeguard carried some clout. "I had heard of Eddie
before," Marion's brother Captain David Lyman recalls, "but I didn't really
know him. He had not done much sailing, except a little bit on Hobie Cats.
But he was really quick to learn and understand. He was a natural, and I

could tell when I first met him that this was the kind of guy I wanted on the crew. I have a sense of who is going to enjoy himself living so close to the ocean, sleeping in the hull six inches from the water, being wet for three days…It's just a gut feeling." During their training sails, off-duty crew members slept in the hollowed-out hulls which were as cramped and dark as coffins. But Lyman could tell that Eddie didn't mind the uncomfortable conditions.

After the intense racial conflicts on the first voyage, Dave Lyman insisted that he make the final selection of sailors to make sure everyone was capable of making such a long and difficult journey together. He even had the candidates take a Myers-Briggs Type Indicator Test to see if they were compatible. With his mixed *haole* and Hawaiian heritage, Dave had been caught in the middle of the conflicts in '76 and wanted to avoid that kind of racial tension on the next voyage. Seeing how hard Eddie worked on the canoe and how well he got along with the other sailors, Dave knew he would fit in with the crew. In spite of his fame, he was surprisingly shy and quiet. Many pro surfers have egos bigger than the waves they ride, but Dave found Eddie to be very humble. "A lot of the guys were more in awe of Eddie, but I didn't realize what a legend he was. When I was talking story with him about going to Roosevelt and I asked him what year he graduated, he looked down, kinda shamed, and said he didn't graduate from high school because he dropped out to pursue a surfing career." But unlike so many other drop-outs, Dave says, "he really did it; he became one of the top surfers in the world."

Eddie also played "a mean slack-key guitar," Dave remembers, and he carried it around with him everywhere, even on the canoe. "We would sit around and sing after our training sails. Nainoa was looking forward to learning slack-key from Eddie." And Eddie looked forward to learning all about wayfinding from Nainoa Thompson, the navigator. "That was why he went on the *Hokule'a*," Linda says, "and that was why he learned slack-key, which was a lost art." If selected as a crew member, Eddie planned to share his passion for Hawaiian music with the rest of the crew. In their phone conversations, Linda says his comments revolved around the canoe, the upcoming voyage and his music, the things that defined him as a Hawaiian.

Of all the potential crew members, Nainoa recalls being most impressed with Eddie. "He wanted to know everything about sailing the canoe. But we had no time to train him," he laments. Though he was young, Nainoa was a natural leader who had several years of experience sailing on the canoe and studying the stars. This gave him a sense of purpose and direction beyond his years. Like Eddie, he had a quiet but powerful presence. The two men had become friends after talking at one of the crew meetings. "That's where we built our short but very deep relationship," Nainoa says. "How could it not be deep with a man of such intensity? He could step through both windows of time: he could participate in the modern world as well as anyone, but his soul was deep and old." During their brief training period, Nainoa could see how dedicated Eddie was to the mission of the *Hokuleʻa*: "He was so full of life. The way he talked, you could see it in his eyes. He said, 'I just want to see Tahiti come out of the ocean.' That whole image that we can bring the island out of the sea is powerful stuff," Nainoa says. He is referring to a mystical belief of Polynesian wayfinding that suggests that if you visualize your destination and stay true to your course, the island will come to you.

As part of their training, aspiring crew members had to attend night classes about sailing and visit the Bishop Museum's planetarium. Inside the planetarium's darkened theatre, Nainoa and Dr. Will Kyselka projected constellations of light onto the dome-like ceiling to show what each night of their journey would look like. The University of Hawaiʻi professor and the young navigator taught the sailors the basics of astronomy and wayfinding, showing them how to steer the canoe by following certain stars as they rose and set on the horizon. The crew tried to memorize the stars that would guide them. At first, they all looked so similar, but slowly the scattered pinpoints of light took on distinct patterns. At night on the training sails, Nainoa would then point out the key stars and constellations. He showed them how they could figure out their latitude and direction by using the North Star and Southern Cross as reference points.

During their daytime, inter-island practice sails, Captain Lyman taught the crew about swell direction, wind patterns, course headings, weather conditions and the infinite variables of deep-sea sailing. Riding the draft from the sail, boobie birds would follow them, as if they were pets. When returning to port, the crew had to navigate around buoys, channel markers and other ships. On one occasion, they had to sail right in front of a huge barge on their way into port. But they gained too much speed coming toward the concrete dock. Lowering the sails didn't slow them down enough, and it was too late to turn. Seizing the moment, Eddie volunteered to swim ahead of the canoe and tie her down before she slammed into the concrete.

He dove into the water and swam to the dock, clambering up the rocks like a crab. A crew member threw him the rope, and he quickly tied it around a cleat. The canoe glided to a stop before any damage was done. The stunned crew looked at Eddie, who waved his arms like a baseball umpire and shouted, "Safe!"

The training period only lasted a few months. According to Marion, it seemed rushed, and the conditions weren't very challenging. "Every time we went out on a training sail, there was hardly any wind. I don't think it ever blew more than five or ten knots." When it came time to select the crew for the voyage, Nainoa had serious reservations about the readiness of the sailors and canoe. "I told the President of the Board that we weren't prepared for the trip." But PVS President Mike Tongg and his board assured him that Captain Lyman and his veteran first mates, Leon Sterling and Norman Pi'ianai'a, were ready and able. "I was 24, and these were guys who had their Master Pilot's licenses and were commanding the thing…I was told if we trusted these guys, everything would be okay, but it wasn't okay."

When the time came to make the final crew selections, all the candidates gathered in a crowded conference room to hear who made the cut. Everyone was anxious because they all wanted to go, but only twelve would be chosen. Eager to be picked, they still feared the prospect of spending a month at sea, away from their families, in search of a small island chain almost 2500 miles away. Just before they announced the names, Eddie asked to play a song he had written about the *Hokule'a*. "I know we don't know who made the crew yet, but I just wanted to sing this song that I wrote for all of you since we've spent so much time working and training together," he said. Cradling his slack-key guitar in his arms, Eddie sang about what the canoe meant to him and his people:

> *Hawai'i's pride she sails with the wind*
> *And proud are we to see her sail free*
> *Feelings so deep and so strong*
> *For Hoku, Hokule'a*
> *The stars that shine to guide her straight path*
> *Across the sea, down to Tahiti*
> *Then back to Hawai'i she sails*
> *For Hoku, Hokule'a*

"I don't think there was a dry eye in the room when he finished," Marion recalls. It was as if he had captured the spirit of the canoe and given a voice to all those who believed in her. Yet there was also a strange sadness in his voice, as if he were saying goodbye. This was offset by the good news to come. When they announced who made the crew, Eddie's name was at the top of the list. The others clapped and congratulated him. "It was unanimous to have him on board," Nainoa recalls. Eddie's dream of sailing to Tahiti was about to come true. It should have been one of the happiest times of his life, but something seemed to be bothering him.

Eddie asked Linda to meet with him to take care of some final business. Although he had been opposed to the idea of divorce and still had strong feelings for her, Eddie knew it was time to let go. "Up until he got accepted to go on the *Hokule'a*, he was fighting the divorce every step of the way," Linda says. "But once he found out he would sail on the canoe, he said we should go ahead with the divorce." He had David Bettencourt file the papers and arrange a discrete and amicable settlement between them. In spite of their separation, Eddie kept in close contact with Linda just prior to leaving. She says Eddie was really excited about going on the voyage, but he seemed preoccupied with vague fears. "He came to me and wanted to talk to me about what he would like to happen if something happened to him." He asked her if his parents could have their house at the graveyard if he didn't come back, and she agreed. In turn, "he wanted them to treat me as his wife, no matter what our legal status was." Though their divorce was close to being finalized, Linda says they still loved each other. Not wanting to leave any loose ends untied, Eddie made sure everything was taken care of before he left. "He did a lot of things like somebody preparing for their own death. But it didn't dawn on me at the time. You just get swept up in all the stuff that is happening." As the day of departure loomed closer, Eddie began to act as if he would not be coming back.

Six days before leaving, Eddie drove to Makaha on O'ahu's western shore to talk with his old mentors and surfing buddies Buffalo Keaulana and Boogie Kalama, who had sailed on the first voyage in '76. "I just had to come out and see you before we sail," he told them several times, as if seeking their advice. Boogie told him to be strong and "know who the captain is." Eddie also shared his fears about being so far out at sea. Sensing an unusual reluctance in the young surfer and lifeguard, Buffalo told him he didn't have to sail if he didn't want to. But when he realized Eddie was going to go anyway,

Buffalo reassured him: "No worry. I give you all of my aloha." Then, the men embraced in the darkness, and Eddie drove off into the night.

In response to rumors that Eddie foresaw his own fate or had some kind of death wish, Clyde insists that Eddie was just being cautious. After all, he had learned as a lifeguard to anticipate accidents before they happened. "I understand Eddie went to see Buff and Boogie before he left and talked about maybe not coming back, but it's just a part of who he was. I guess he always anticipated the worst. In 1978 the *Hokule'a* was still new stuff. It was just a twin-hulled canoe lashed together with some string. I mean who knew how strong it was and how it would hold up? The whole concept was still in its infancy." Although Peter Cole had spent his life in the ocean, he shared Clyde's hesitations about making such a long voyage. "Going in a little boat all the way to Tahiti was the last thing in the world I would ever do. It's a big difference being along the coast than in the middle of the ocean. I never go out further than I can swim in."

During that last week, Eddie asked Sol's wife Ricky if she would cut his hair in the graveyard. She sits in the graveyard 25 years later, her long blonde hair having turned gray, remembering their last conversation together. "I remember he asked me to trim his hair out there, and he said that he had a feeling that he wasn't going to come back. I'm quite sure he had a premonition—it was like fate." Eddie also made a strange request, asking her to gather a lock of hair from his three nephews and niece. "He wanted to take the kids' hair with him. I had no idea why he wanted to do that but what an honor. He loved the kids. He was such a good man." Eddie braided their hair together, wrapped it in a piece of white cloth so he could wear it as a necklace on the voyage. Like many Hawaiians, he believed that the hair of loved ones possessed a powerful *mana* that might protect him.

The day before *Hokule'a's* departure, Eddie, Captain Dave Lyman and fellow crew member Kiki Hugho did a radio interview with Ron Jacobs of KKUA about the upcoming voyage. When RJ asked how this voyage differed from the last one in '76, Dave said, "The main difference is the fact that we'll be going without an escort vessel." The PVS leaders were so confident about the upcoming voyage that they decided not to have an escort boat follow them—the crew would be on their own out there, just like the Polynesians of old. Referring to the "hell on the high seas" incident in '76 when crew members duked it out on the *Hokule'a*, he went on to say, "I expect it to be a little mellower. It's not quite as intense as it was before, and one thing we're not faced with is the big question of 'Will she make it or won't she?' She's already proven herself. We already know she can make it."

After hearing from Dave, RJ opened up the interview to questions and comments from listeners. One local woman who called in said, "I just wanted to say I think the decision to have Mr. Eddie Aikau on the canoe was an unreal decision because I think the Aikau family is so full of aloha. They do so much for everybody, and he's a great man. And I'm so glad to hear that he will be on the canoe, and I'm really grateful for him." RJ then asked Eddie to share his thoughts about the *Hokule'a* and play his song about the canoe on the air. "I put the feelings of what I felt and what my people felt into music and words, and this is what I came up with," he said in his poi-thick voice. "And I would like to dedicate this song especially to my mom and dad and my family; and secondly, to the family of the *Hokule'a* and all of Hawai'i."

Eddie sang his song in a strained voice full of raw feeling, and the people of Hawai'i listened in their cars, at home and at work. His lyrics showed how proud he was to be part of the voyage. But when the song ended, Eddie sounded nervous talking about the upcoming trip and the pressure to leave. "Right now all the crew members and the leaders of the *Hokule'a* that will take her down to Tahiti have been pressured from the media and all the families coming in, and I feel something like this as a crew member…See, we have to get out there because the pressure is unbelievable from all over. Once we get out there, we will be all right," he said, as if trying to convince himself. When RJ asked about superstitions and the spiritual aspects of the journey, Eddie said, "I'm proud to have *kahuna* blood that links back to Hewahewa…As a crew member myself, I'll just be trying my best to help take everybody down safely."

That afternoon, Pops threw a small party for the departing crew members. Eddie's friend Liko Martin flew in from a neighbor island, but he was in no mood for a party. A high-strung Hawaiian with an intense mystical streak, Liko was a family friend and a talented musician whose hit song "Waimanalo Blues" had become one of Eddie's favorites. He had played guitar with Eddie for years and taught him a great deal about slack-key, and their friendship revolved more around music than words. But when he went to the Aikaus' party at the Chinese graveyard, Liko brought an ominous message. He took Myra and Pops aside and told them his wife had had a premonition about Eddie the night before. In her dream, she had seen the

215

Hokuleʻa capsize and Eddie lost at sea. "He came here and begged us not to let him go," Myra says, recalling the wild look in Liko's eyes. "He was a rebel, and you would think he was a little *pupule* (crazy). He said, 'Something's going to happen, and one person is not coming back. And, Myra, that's your brother Eddie'…I'll never forget those words." When Pops heard what Liko had to say, he was tempted to warn his son, but he didn't want to spoil his dream of sailing on the *Hokuleʻa*. "I cannot go into that room after Eddie has trained so hard for this and tell my son he is not allowed to go," he said. "That would be insane."

The whole family agonized over whether to share Liko's dark warning with Eddie and eventually decided against it, knowing he would go anyway. "When Eddie decided to do something, he did it," Linda says. "There was no talking him out of it once he made up his mind about it. He usually put a lot of thought into what he was doing." Though determined to go, Eddie had been struggling with his own doubts and demons. "Maybe he himself had a premonition," Linda wonders. "In the end, the night before he left, he had me come over to the house to talk with the family so that if something should happen, his parents would get the house and I would still be part of the family. He took the time to express those feelings, and not many people do that…Before he left, he set a lot of things in order, things that I was kind of surprised he was doing." Along with paying off all his debts, Eddie wrote out a last-minute will that night. He gave the will to David Bettencourt, who informed him that his divorce papers had just been finalized that day.

On the day of their departure, March 16, 1978, more than 10,000 people gathered at Magic Island to take part in the big celebration and send-off. The Polynesian Voyaging Society hosted a traditional *ʻawa* ceremony. Sipping from coconut shells, each sailor drank the muddy juice of the bitter *ʻawa* root, just as Polynesian sailors had done centuries before. Then, the state's two most powerful leaders and political opponents, Governor George Ariyoshi and Mayor Frank Fasi, came together to present each crew member with leis and wish them well. The ceremony blended ancient traditions with a modern setting. Dressed in traditional robes, the *kahu* chanted Hawaiian blessings. Hula dancers told stories of legendary voyagers with their hands and hips. The politicians droned on in their speeches, and photographers swarmed around the crew, taking their pictures. In the photos, Eddie was wearing several leis, a gold cross and the cloth necklace with the locks of hair from his nephews and niece. Looking back on the pictures from that day, Marion recalls a strange detail: "We were all wearing the same T-shirt that we had made that had the crab-claw sail on it and the words *Hokule'a 'Elua* (two). But Eddie was wearing a different shirt; he was the only one not wearing the same shirt." In another ominous picture taken that day, he is wearing his trademark bandana and paddling a surfboard away from the canoe.

During the day, the already gusty winds picked up, and the seas grew even heavier. "I don't think the canoe had been out in that kind of weather," Marion says. "If she had, it certainly wasn't under those circumstances with a fully laden canoe with enough food, water and equipment for 16 people and 28 days." Captain Dave Lyman had already asked the crew to unload 1200 pounds of food and supplies because the canoe was too heavy, especially for the rough conditions. Worried about the weather, the Captain and crew debated whether they should postpone their departure. But crew member Kiki Hugho recalls that the Polynesian Voyaging Society "had set a date months earlier, and they stuck to that date." With all the politicians, reporters and friends who had come to watch their departure, there was mounting pressure from the PVS directors to leave that day. Neither the captain nor the navigator wanted to set sail, but they eventually gave in. Going against their instincts and reservations, Dave Lyman and Nainoa Thompson made the controversial decision to set sail—in spite of gale warnings, gusty 35-40 mph winds and stormy 8-10 foot seas in the channels. It was a decision that would haunt them for years.

"My belief is that we were destined to get in trouble once we decided to leave," says Kiki Hugho, "and I was trying to stop the voyage from happening that day." Kiki is a pilot boat operator, sign maker and self-proclaimed "messenger of God." A mystical man like his brother Kimo, who bowed out of the '76 voyage because of a premonition he had, Kiki believes in natural signs, and that day he sensed the weather was trying to tell them not to go. Though the direction of the wind was what they needed to sail through the Kealakahiki ("the way to Tahiti") Channel, Hugho says everything else was wrong. "There was no reason for us to leave that day, not in that kind of storm. The attitude and mood of the crew was really down. A lot of people knew something was up. I felt it, and even Eddie knew that something was wrong. But Eddie and I were just two Indians with one feather in our caps, and we were just taking orders from the chiefs."

When the hour of departure finally arrived, the sky was already turning red as the sun began to set. Crew members said tearful goodbyes to their loved ones, exchanging anxious hugs and salty kisses. Just as they had done for centuries, native Hawaiians held large conch shells to their lips and sounded their mournful salute as the canoe prepared to leave. With thousands of friends and family members waving from shore, the *Hokule'a* departed from Magic Island just before dusk, setting sail in what the Coast Guard would later call "questionable conditions." Cutting across the whitecaps, the heavily laden canoe flew toward Diamond Head and out to sea, followed by a fleet of other sailboats. "As soon as we got out past Diamond Head, the wind picked up, and the flotilla of boats that were out there to watch us leave kind of got left in the dust," Marion recalls. "We just went so fast…Those of us who weren't on watch were told to get some rest."

Instead of having an escort boat track them for navigational and safety reasons, the Captain decided to have an Instrument Navigator aboard. He chose a veteran seaman named Norman Pi'ianai'a to monitor Nainoa's sailing direction, using only a quadrant, compass and timepiece like they did in Captain Cook's day. He would not share his measurements with anyone else on the crew, unless the canoe went dangerously off course. Norman was also in charge of the emergency beacons, radio and inflatable raft in case something went wrong. But unless they were in a dire situation, the radio was not to be used, and the sailors were basically on their own until they reached Tahiti. For the voyage, the canoe's leaders had set up two rotating shifts of seven crew members with Captain David Lyman in charge of one shift and Chief Mate Leon Sterling in charge of the other. Non-instrument navigator Nainoa Thompson would remain on deck most of the trip, plotting their course and taking occasional cat naps, while Instrument Navigator Norman Pi'ianaia would track his progress.

Hungry and tired, the off-duty crew decided to eat and then get some sleep. "Pops Aikau had made a whole big batch of fried chicken, and we had rice. We were hungry because we hadn't eaten all day during the ceremony," Marion recalls. "After we ate, we went into the *hale*, this thatched little house in the middle of the deck, to get some sleep. Eight of us, seven guys and me were stuck like sardines in this little *hale*. So we crashed." As she drifted in and out of sleep, Marion could feel *Hokule'a* climbing each swell. "I could hear the canoe creaking and groaning. I had helped build the canoe, and I had every confidence that she was seaworthy."

The voyaging canoe made good time that night as it rose and fell with each swell. But when Captain Lyman had the crew check the hulls for water-tightness, they found several inches of water in each compartment of the hulls. He had the water pumped out, but the choppy seas kept pouring over the hulls and leaking into the compartments through the hatches which hadn't been properly sealed. After the swamping off of Kaua'i, the canoe's open hulls had been sealed and divided into water-tight compartments with hatches to cover each opening. Because space was tight on such a small canoe, crew members used the compartments for sleeping and storing their gear. Before leaving, Dave had asked that rubber gaskets be used to seal the hatches, but he had been talked out of it at the last minute. Referring to the small O-ring which caused the Space Shuttle *Columbia* explosion, Captain Lyman would later say their fate hinged on a rubber gasket.

As they sailed across the windy darkness, the Captain had the crew check inside the hulls periodically to keep an eye on the water level. During one check, two of the hatch covers were not replaced correctly in the darkness. As the heaving ocean poured over the hulls and water gushed into the compartments, the canoe began listing heavily. By the time Captain Lyman realized that it was not the heavy wind tilting the canoe but excessive water leakage, it was too late. He checked the hulls again and found the starboard side filling with water. The canoe had suddenly become sluggish with the added weight. Fearing they might capsize, Lyman shouted, "All hands on deck!"

"When we got into trouble and the shit hit the fan, there were only seven of us on deck, with 15-foot swells and 35 mph winds. Eddie and I were right there," Kiki recalls. "There was a window of about two to five minutes when we could have saved the canoe, and Eddie and I saw it, and then we saw it close." The sleeping crew members stumbled out of the cramped *hale*, and Marion and Dr. Charman Akina immediately became seasick. Captain Lyman ordered the sailors to start bailing out the starboard hull, but the water was coming in faster than they could bail it out. The crew was told to put on their life jackets and to clear the compartments of any gear to help make bailing easier. Several crew members searched for emergency equipment, including flares, a hand pump for the life raft, a Gibson Girl radio and the Emergency Radio Beacon (EPIRB), which would broadcast a distress signal when activated. But in the howling darkness, they could only find the flares and radio. Captain Lyman and Navigator Thompson decided to fall off the wind to ease in bailing, but as the canoe changed course, the starboard hull suddenly began to flood, with waves breaking over the gunwales. The crew was ordered to jettison all equipment on the starboard hull and to sit on the port side to compensate for the 15 degree list tilting the canoe sideways. "At this time the vessel was dead in the water with the sails full," the Coast Guard report stated later.

While several crew members tried to take down the sails, waves kept hitting the vessel and she tilted even more. "Within five or ten minutes of hearing 'All hands on deck,' a huge swell swamped us," Marion recalls. It was about midnight when the rogue wave hit the windward hull and a gust of wind pushed on the sails until it began to turn over. In a dizzying rush, the canoe capsized, plunging the sailors into the dark, windblown water. Coming up for air, the crew immediately did a head count. The crew was stunned and disoriented, but they were all there.

"When it flipped over, everybody was trying to help each other be calm and hang onto the canoe," crew member Snake Ah Hee remembers. "It was late at night already. The captain was saying, 'Just hang on! Let's keep everybody warm!' Everybody kind of held on to each other." As shivering crew members floated in the water, they huddled together and held onto the overturned hull, while wave after wave splashed over them. They tried to salvage as much as they could, but the emergency EPIRB and much of their food and equipment had been lost when the canoe capsized.

"So here's the dilemma," Nainoa states twenty years later, his eyes bloodshot and his face strained, as if part of him were still out there in the ocean. "We're upside down, the EPIRB's gone and the radio is drowned. We have no communication with anybody." That night, as they clung to the overturned hull, crew members took turns cranking the handle of the useless radio, trying to transmit an emergency message. They also fired flares at passing planes but no one spotted them. "Right after we went down, Eddie said, 'Let me go for help,'" Marion says. Eddie volunteered to paddle his surfboard to the distant island of Lanaʻi to get help. He had brought the board to surf in Tahiti, but now he hoped to paddle it across miles of raging ocean toward the shimmering lights of Lanaʻi. He had to do something to help. But the Captain refused his request, saying it was too dangerous and they should wait until morning. Cold, wet and scared, they held on to the hull, calling out to each other in the darkness to make sure no one was washed away by the 8-10 foot swells which battered them all night long.

"I remember during the night, you could see the Lana'i airport from the distance," Snake says. "It's way on top, like in the middle of the island. To see the airport, we must have been far, far out because when you are close to Lana'i, you cannot see the airport. You could see the light, the greet light on the tower." As they watched the faint light pulsing in the distance, it glowed like a beacon of hope through the long, dark night.

By sunrise, the crew realized how far they had drifted out to sea and how sick some of the sailors had become. Both Marion and Charman had been violently seasick and appeared to be suffering from shock, dehydration and exposure. The Captain wondered if they could survive another night. "I was seasick the whole time, and I was just miserable and weak," Marion recalls. "I was the smallest member of the crew, being the only female, and so I was just out of it...You know what they say about being seasick: at first, you are afraid you are going to die—and then you are afraid you won't."

Early that morning, crew members took turns paddling the surfboard around the canoe, looking for food or equipment that had floated away. Some dove under to search the sunken compartments for anything they could use. Frustrated that he couldn't do much to help, Snake Ah Hee decided to paddle the board toward the nearest island for help. Like Eddie, he was a quiet and intense man who did what needed to be done. He had the same dark skin, bright eyes and bold courage. Without asking the Captain's permission, Snake paddled about a mile and a half away until he sighted what looked like a rescue plane flying overhead. "When I looked back to where they was, everybody was kinda small. When I seen the Coast Guard plane, I figured maybe they had seen us so I was happy to paddle back." But by the time he made his way back to the canoe, it was clear the plane hadn't spotted them.

Hopes of rescue began to fade as the canoe drifted farther out of the flight pattern of the planes flying between the Islands. Not wanting to wait another day, Eddie knew what he had to do. Again, he asked the Captain for permission to go. As a lifeguard, he couldn't just stay there and do nothing—something had to be done. Fearing for the fate of his crew, Captain Lyman consulted with his officers. After much heated debate, they all reluctantly agreed: Eddie should go. Their decision went against the cardinal rule of never leaving the ship, but the captain and the others believed Eddie was their only chance for rescue. The island of Lana'i was now more than twenty miles away and the ocean was seething with gale-force winds and high seas, but Eddie insisted he could make the journey. "If you were to ask me if I could make it, I would say no," Nainoa admits. George Helm didn't make it when he tried to paddle seven miles to Maui, nor did Tommy Holmes when he tried to reach Kaua'i ten miles away. "But Eddie was godlike," Nainoa continues. "When I look at myself in long-distance, one-man paddling contests, there's absolutely a factor of exhaustion. You get so tired that you just try to stay on without getting knocked off [the board] by the waves. When you get to that point, trying to get some place is secondary." But the crew was depending on Eddie, and he knew it.

Wearing his yellow foul weather pants and jacket, Eddie was given a bag of sugar cubes for energy, a knife, a whistle and a strobe light. Although he didn't want to wear one, the captain insisted he wear a life jacket around his waist. They wanted him to take a bag of oranges with him, but he said they would get in the way and ate two before he left. At approximately 10:30 am on March 17, 1978, Edward Ryan Aikau prepared to leave, and the rest of the crew gathered around to say goodbye and wish him luck. "We all held hands and said a prayer that he make a safe journey," Marion says. "In my mind, I remember chanting, 'Go, Eddie, go.'"

If Eddie was frightened, he remained calm and confident in front of his crew mates. "He wasn't afraid of anything," Nainoa says. "He had very strong convictions, very strong beliefs that drove not just his intellect but all of his instincts." The day remains an emotional blur, but Nainoa cannot forget the moment Eddie went. "He put a lifejacket on and then he paddled off. And I swam out to him. I was so conflicted with this idea. We're tired, we're somewhat in shock, we're in denial. Emotionally, it was an extremely draining situation. But he was like a miracle man—he could do anything. So if he says he could go to Lana'i, he's gonna go. I remember grabbing his hand and holding his hand real tight. We weren't that far from the canoe, but we were significantly far away, and he said, 'I'll be okay. Everything will be okay.'"

It was an emotional moment when Eddie stroked away on his 12' surfboard, heading toward the hazy outline of Lana'i. Watching as he crested each wave, several crew members saw him stop about fifty feet from the canoe and take off his orange life jacket. "I was probably one of the last guys to see him," John Kruse says. "He was far away, and I remember him turning around and looking at me. I looked, and I saw him take off the vest and throw it away. He had the kind of confidence like, 'See ya. No worry, brah, I get 'em.' I think maybe he took off the vest so he could paddle better because it was so bulky." As Eddie paddled away, he rose and fell with each wave until he disappeared in the distant whitecaps.

Clinging to the overturned hull of the *Hokule‘a*, the other crew members continued shooting off flares whenever they saw a plane passing overhead, but no one spotted them. That afternoon, they saw a white ship sail in their direction. They shot off flares and screamed at the large vessel, but it veered away without noticing them. From a distance, the overturned canoe probably looked like a piece of driftwood in the vast ocean. Their hearts sank as the ship disappeared on the horizon. They suffered through a long, hot day of watching the horizon, followed by a long, chilly night of waiting for help. They saw planes flying in the distance, but none seemed to notice their fading flares, and they wondered if they would ever be found. Later, after most of the inter-island flights had finished for the evening, the crew saw one last plane headed toward Honolulu so they fired off their remaining flares—bright flashes in the immense darkness. For a moment, it looked like the plane would continue on like all the others. But then it suddenly banked and circled the canoe, coming so close that crew members could see Japanese tourists in the plane snapping photographs through the portals. The plane circled the canoe one last time, blinking its landing lights before flying on to Honolulu Airport.

Less than an hour later, a C-130 plane flew over the capsized *Hokule‘a*, circled around and dropped phosphorescent lights in the water to light up the area. Then, Coast Guard helicopters could be seen scouring the ocean with a bright search light. The copter hovered above the canoe and lowered down a metal cage to rescue the crew members. Inside the basket was a radio wrapped in plastic. Captain Lyman grabbed it and told them about Eddie, yelling above the beating of the helicopter blades. But he got no response. "Realizing that it was a one-way radio, Dave told them to blink their lights once if they could read him," Marion recalls. "The lights blinked once—affirmative. Then, Dave asked if they had heard from Eddie Aikau. The lights blinked twice—negative."

Captain Lyman then reported that a crew member had paddled off for help around 10:30 a.m. toward the island of Lana‘i. Nainoa was the first to crawl into the wire cage and be hauled up into the belly of the helicopter so he could help organize the search for Eddie. Then, the sickest crew members were loaded into the basket and lifted up into the copter's blinding light. As Kiki swam Charman Akina over to the basket, he said the man was "hours away from dying. He was already in shock and barely conscious." Kiki says he saw sharks below him in the spotlight, circling like vultures.

Another Coast Guard helicopter returned and transported four more crew members to Honolulu airport. Then, the first copter returned for the remaining sailors. But Captain Lyman told them that he and his officers Leon Sterling and Norman Pi'ianai'a would remain with the *Hokule'a*. He asked that a ship be sent out to tow the damaged canoe back to port. Four inflatable rafts were dropped into the water, one for each man and one to store any equipment they could salvage. After alerting Captain Lyman that the USCG Cruiser *Cape Goodwin* was on its way, the chopper returned to Honolulu, scanning the water for any sign of Eddie Aikau.

What happened to Eddie that night remains a mystery. Though he was a strong surfer, he probably didn't make much progress through the Moloka'i Channel. With the high winds and deadly currents being funneled between the islands of O'ahu and Moloka'i, it is one of the most dangerous channels in the world. Paddling against the currents would have been like trying to go upstream in a whitewater raft. By that evening, he had been without sleep for almost two days and nearing exhaustion. Stroking toward the faint green light of Lana'i's airport, he struggled to stay awake and afloat on the surfboard. The 35 mph winds would have blinded him with saltwater spray, as the 10-12 foot waves washed over him. Sharks probably surrounded him as he clung to his board, his strobe light pulsing like a fading heartbeat in the howling darkness.

CHAPTER 14

The Search

*"Missing me one place search another,
I stop somewhere waiting for you."*
— *Walt Whitman*

Once the Hawaiian Airlines plane spotted the *Hokule'a* and the Coast Guard began their rescue operation, news of the capsized canoe hit Honolulu like a severe storm front, covering the city with a dark pall. Compelled by the dramatic nature of the story, the media jumped on it immediately. Working as a TV reporter at the time (before becoming director of the Polynesian Voyaging Society), Elisa Yadao recalls the moment she heard about *Hokule'a's* fate and Eddie's disappearance. "I was working in the newsroom in '78 when the canoe swamped, and I can remember standing there in tears as the story was developing. It was such a tragedy…He was a man of great accomplishments, Hawaiian to his core; he was a very giving person…so completely selfless."

After being evacuated during the rescue operation, Nainoa wanted to begin the search that night, as they were flying en route to O'ahu. But the Coast Guard crew in the helicopter was under strict orders to bring all the *Hokule'a* sailors directly back to Honolulu. Besides, Marion and Charman needed medical attention because they had been so seasick and dehydrated. Seeing the city's burning lights in the distance and knowing what a media firestorm awaited them, Nainoa dreaded having to explain to Eddie's family what had happened. "When we got in, Mom and Pops Aikau were there. I don't know how she knew," he says. But he could tell by the look on her face that she knew her son was missing.

John Kruse was one of the last crew members to be evacuated. He remembers landing at the airport, seeing "the vans roll up, with all the video cameras" and sensing that this was a bad situation for the family. The crew had been told not to talk to the press, but he knew they were hungry for the story. "There was this camera guy from Channel 9, and he was right at the Aikau's van. Myra said, 'Get these guys outta here.' The TV guy says, 'I want to show the emotion of the event,' and Pops gets up and says, 'Brah, I'll show you some emotion!' He hits the side of the camera—Boom!" The cameraman quickly scampered away, realizing how emotionally raw and volatile the family was over Eddie's disappearance. From then on, reporters and cameramen kept a respectful distance.

As word of the capsizing spread, the extended Aikau network was notified about Eddie's disappearance. Calls went out to family members and friends who were stunned by the news. As a close friend and pilot, David Bettencourt was one of the first people contacted late Friday night. He was at home in bed with a cold when he got the call. "I was really sick when the boat capsized," he recalls. "Sol called me up and told me the boat had gone over, and then I got a call a couple hours later, saying that everybody had been rescued, except Eddie. I calculated that night where I thought the *Hokule'a* would be the next morning." Based on where the canoe had capsized, David began plotting flight patterns and working with family members to organize the rescue effort for Eddie.

Meanwhile out at sea, Captain Lyman and his officers had spent a long night in the water with the overturned canoe, waiting for help. The next morning, the Coast Guard's cruiser *Cape Goodwin* arrived on the scene and picked up the officers. The leaders of the Polynesian Voyaging Society came out in a 50-foot saipan called the *Imua*, to bring back the overturned voyaging canoe. After righting the vessel, the *Imua* began to tow the badly damaged *Hokule'a* back to O'ahu. During the long and torturous journey to Honolulu, news choppers hovered overhead and took pictures of the water-logged vessel. For the people of Hawai'i who had seen news footage of the *Hokule'a's* glorious departure from Magic Island just days before, these images were devastating. Finally, the canoe crawled into Ke'ehi Lagoon just after dark on Saturday night. David Bettencourt says that's when Pops went down to the dock "to ream Captain Lyman a new asshole." As if the capsizing wasn't traumatic enough, the captain had to face the wrath of Pops and the Aikau family, who couldn't help but hold him partly responsible. Meanwhile, he had to deal with the media and the ensuing Coast Guard investigation. But his top priority was helping to coordinate the massive search that was just getting underway.

"It was probably one of the most intensive land and air searches ever conducted," Captain Lyman says. "There were some of us who walked on the beaches on the North side of this Island; there were people walking the beaches along Lana'i and Moloka'i. The Coast Guard, along with private airplanes, were out searching, doing intensive search patterns." Working out of the house at the graveyard which soon became command central, Eddie's brother Sol worked with Pops and David Bettencourt to coordinate the search and organize the many volunteers who wanted to help. "Every morning we would have a meeting and go through the plans for the day," Sol recalls. "We had three helicopters at the time. That guy Zoulou, who used to work on *Hawai'i Five-O*, went up looking for him."

During the first day of the search, Sol, Nainoa and David were in the helicopter of their friend Tom Hauptmann, scouring the wind-swept ocean for any sign of Eddie. The conditions were horrible, with gale-force winds blowing the ocean into a frenzy. Each time they thought they saw something, it turned out to be just another whitecap. After searching for about an hour, wondering if they would find anything but still hopeful they would, Sol suddenly spotted what looked like Eddie's board! "First of all, it was just luck that we came across it because you got to remember it was like a storm," Sol says. "It looked like a washing machine. You could see something, blink an eye and then you'd miss it—it's gone. It was hurricane-like conditions. Seeing the surfboard without him wasn't a good sign." Then Sol briefly spotted something else in the distance that looked like a lifejacket, but none of the others saw it.

"Tom Hauptmann was flying," David Bettencourt says. "I remember we were optimistic because it was a five-seater, and we only took four people because we wanted to make room for Eddie. I was sitting in the right front seat when I saw the board. What I did not see and what Sol claims he saw was something orange in the water." Whether it was a lifejacket or a piece of debris, Sol couldn't say for sure; so they concentrated on retrieving the board. Realizing they couldn't retrieve it or do a rescue themselves in such dangerous conditions, they immediately contacted the Coast Guard for assistance. Screaming over the beating of the helicopter's blades, David tried to convey their location to the Coast Guard. "The problem was that we didn't know exactly where we were. We were too low to get a radar fix so we had to pull straight up. I'm talking to Honolulu Center, and they still don't have us on radar. Finally, we get up to about 1500 feet, and they get us on radar. But right at that moment, the helicopter swung, and I lost the board. We never re-established visual contact. We were heart-broken because Sol had seen something orange, like a life jacket, in the water. God, if that was Eddie, he was only a couple hundred yards from the board."

Sol may have seen a lifejacket in the water, but it's doubtful that it was Eddie's. Several crew members had seen him take his off after paddling away from the *Hokule'a*. Some people would even question whether it was definitely Eddie's board they saw that day. Surfboards were often swept out to sea by swift currents when the waves were big, and there was some confusion about the markings on the board. But Sol is sure it was his brother's. "It was one of those big tanker boards that the lifeguards used. I was down at the *Hokule'a* that day they left, and he was paddling around on that board, fixing stuff along the hull." In fact, the picture of Eddie paddling near the *Hokule'a* on the day of their departure appeared in the newspapers. It was a haunting image because it seemed to foreshadow his fate.

After spotting the board from the helicopter, Nainoa says he will never forget the sight of it blowing across the surf like a feather. "It was just rolling downwind, just tumbling because the wind was so strong." After flying back to Honolulu, Nainoa and the others worked with the Civil Air Patrol to give them information to help with the search. "And I remember I was shocked when they asked me what was the color of the surfboard, what was the color of the leash and how was it tied? I was in such pain and trauma at that time," Nainoa says. Though he has replayed the events of that week over and over in his mind through the years, he still can't recall many of the missing details.

One crucial detail the search team centered on was how Eddie became separated from his board when he was supposedly wearing a leash tying the board to his ankle. Several crew members insisted that Eddie had been wearing the leash when he paddled away from the canoe, but Sol speculates that he probably untied it when he took off his life jacket and foul weather gear. "To take off the pants, he would have to take off the leash around his ankle. And Eddie never used a leash in his life. You can't paddle with all that stuff on." However awkward and uncomfortable, the life jacket and leash were essential for surviving at sea. Discarding them seems to suggest that he was determined to make the journey to shore or die trying.

Despite the heart-wrenching sighting of Eddie's board and the fact that he wasn't on it, family and friends continued to look even harder for Eddie. During those first two days of the search, they made five trips out on the helicopter. Meanwhile, Captain Lyman continued to work with the Coast Guard and the family to coordinate their rescue efforts. After each day's search, all the key players would gather together to go over their plans. "What would happen in the evenings is that we would all meet over at Pops Aikau's house and then go over what areas we had searched and what areas would be more likely," Captain Lyman remembers. Angry, confused and frustrated over Eddie's disappearance, the family finally confronted the exhausted captain about why he had let him go when the cardinal rule of seamanship is never to leave the ship. "They put me on the spot one night, and they just wanted to know, 'Did Eddie leave on his own or did you give him permission to go?' And I said, 'I gave him permission to go.' That obviously put it back on my shoulders." Waiting for the blunt edge of Pops' anger to come down on his head, Captain Lyman was surprised by his reaction. Having been in the military and knowing the importance of following orders, "Pops was very proud that his son had listened to his captain. But there was still a lot of resentment." This issue would come up again during the Coast Guard investigation.

Crew member John Kruse was also actively involved in the search and says he heard all kinds of conflicting theories about where to look. Some said the prevailing northeasterly winds and swells pouring through the treacherous Moloka'i Channel would have pushed Eddie back toward O'ahu and even toward the distant island of Kaua'i. Others insisted that there were ocean undercurrents carrying him toward Lana'i or Moloka'i. To cover all possibilities, people searched the coastlines of each island. But as the search wore on, even Eddie's close friends wondered if he could have made it. "As good a waterman as he was," Peter Cole says, "there's a limit to what he can take. In the Moloka'i Channel, he would have been paddling against really high seas and winds whipping at him. The current would have been going away from Moloka'i and Lana'i. It was as bad a situation as you could have out there. I don't think any of us could have made it. I don't think there's a soul anywhere who could have made it."

In spite of increasing doubts and conflicting theories about what happened to Eddie, everyone was united in their determination to keep looking for him. "We'd go back everyday after the search, and Pops was cooking all the food, and everybody was starting to come together," John Kruse says. He remembers the flood of money, calls and letters of support that flowed into the Aikau house each day. "People from all over the world started sending checks because we needed money for helicopter time, search time and gas money. People wrote, 'Hey, I remember Eddie saved my son in the early '70's, and I've heard that he's lost so here's something to help.'" Singer Helen Reddy, in town doing a concert, was so moved by the massive search for Eddie that she donated several thousand dollars toward the rescue effort. Recalling how Eddie had stood up for Rabbit and the other Aussies, surfers from Down Under donated money to the cause.

Clyde had been in Australia for a surf contest when the canoe capsized so Myra had called the International Red Cross to relay an emergency message to him. Jack Shipley was a judge at the competition and remembers when they heard about Eddie's disappearance. "I was with Clyde at the Stubbies Surf Contest in March of '78 when the news came. He got the word—and we all got the word—that Eddie was missing. That's how it came—it wasn't like Eddie was presumed dead—he was just missing. Clyde's reaction to that info was 'I'm outta here!' He was going to find Eddie. He was charged up like a raging bull. His mission was to get home and find Eddie." Clyde boarded the next plane out of Sydney.

Lynne Holmes heard the news as it spread through the Aussie surfing community, and she immediately called Pops Aikau. The night before, her daughter Tracey had had an ominous dream in which she had seen some kind of catamaran capsize in the open seas, and Lynne had been disturbed by her daughter's dream. A strange omen. "I was talking to Pops, and he said it wasn't looking good, and it might be a good idea to get on the first plane out of there and come to Hawai'i." So she borrowed money from a friend and booked a flight to Honolulu the next day. "The weirdest thing was flying all that way and looking out the plane and thinking, Where is he? I mean if anyone could survive in the ocean, it's him. Looking down from the plane, you realize how big that ocean is," Lynne says, recalling that long and anxious flight.

"Myra and Fred picked me up at the airport, and we drove back to the graveyard. There were so many people there it just blew my mind, and yet it was so incredibly quiet. People were just sitting, waiting, talking quietly. The family was all in Eddie's house. They were all in there, and nobody other than family was allowed in that house. I was included, and they took me in. You were dumbfounded because you still had this belief that you would look out the door, and he would be walking down the driveway. There was still hope. I can still see Pops walking outside, and there was a bell hanging outside the door, and he would go and ring that bell, yelling, 'Ryan, get your butt back here!' to break the tension." Pops insisted Eddie was not dead, just lost. So he and the family waited, their hopes rising and receding daily like the tides.

With each passing day, the search for Eddie became more desperate. While the others studied maps and analyzed drift patterns, the captain's sister Marion had sought out a clairvoyant for help. "We heard about this psychic somewhere in Manoa, and we went up to the house. She seemed like a regular person. She didn't look like some fortune-telling gypsy lady. We took a chart of the Hawaiian Islands with us. She evidently had a successful history of finding missing persons. She went into some kind of trance, and I remember her asking us a lot of questions, and we were describing him. We had a piece of his clothing. We described him and the situation he was in and where he was when we went down. Her hand was going around this chart, and then she pointed to this spot. We made sure we knew what the longitude and latitude were so we could search that area."

Captain Lyman says the psychic also told his sister, "A little blond girl knows where he is." Though wary of psychics and their vague warnings, he and the others were so desperate to find Eddie that they would try any-thing. After Liko's premonition came true, they were willing to believe that a young girl might somehow know of Eddie's fate. Sol's daughter Pi'ilani fit that description so they began questioning her, but the young girl had no idea where her uncle was. According to Captain Lyman, another psychic "said something like 'You'll find him somewhere where there are cliffs.' So we were thinking, 'Okay, he's along the southwest shore of Lana'i, where all the cliffs are.' The Coast Guard was ready to call it off, and I called them and begged them, based on the information from this psychic, to take one last fly out there." Miraculously, the Coast Guard heeded Captain Lyman's plea and extended the search for another day. But physical and emotional exhaustion began to cloud the judgement of family and friends who refused to believe that Eddie was dead. "We had all these psychics from California and across the country calling us," Sol remembers, "and they were saying that he is in a cave, he's hurt and he's waiting. Going on what these people were saying, we just concentrated on all the caves we could find." It was like a desperate game of hide and seek, tearing the family apart.

In private, people began speculating about what could have happened to Eddie. "He could have been easily separated from his board by one of those big breakers and not be able to get back to it," Dave Lyman says in a raspy voice. "In those conditions, if he had gotten separated from his board, it would have gone cart-wheeling across the ocean. Then, of course, it's deep; he could have drowned." After several days in such turbulent seas, he would have been completely dehydrated, exhausted and barely conscious—as good a swimmer as he was, it would be impossible to stay afloat for that long without a surfboard or life preserver. There's also the chance that Eddie wasn't alone. "He could have been hit by a shark—there were a lot of sharks out there and around the canoe," Dave concludes.

John Kruse vividly recalls being bumped by something during the night when they were stranded on the overturned canoe. Until he was rescued, he assumed it had been the surfboard bumping into his legs in the darkness. "When I got lifted up into the helicopter, I was looking down, and there was only Dave Lyman, Leon and Norman on the boat because I was the last guy lifted up. They've got fluorescent Willy Petes—phosphorus—lighting up the whole place like it was daylight. Going through all that heavy stuff were these big 10-12 foot growlers." That's when he realized it wasn't the surfboard hitting him against the legs that night. "It was the Bruddah—the man in the gray suit was checking us out. That's probably what happened to Eddie." During the search, John remembers flying over the churning ocean and seeing some commotion in the water that gave them a rush of hope. But flying down to check it out, "we saw a baby whale that was getting chewed by sharks—it was getting thrashed." On the way back to Honolulu Airport, John says, "Everybody kept thinking about that whale. I think Pops figured that was some kind of omen."

Jo-Anne Kahanamoku Sterling also joined the search with her husband Leon, the chief mate. The daughter of Duke's brother Sam Kahanamoku, she was a striking older woman who had trained with Eddie on the *Hokule'a*. He had admired her commitment to the canoe and her connection to the Duke. At the party on the eve of his departure, Jo-Anne says Eddie looked at her and told the crowd, "This is the mother of the canoe." She was both embarrassed and honored. "Then, he came over and kissed me. He was a very intense invidual." During the search, she remembers going out on a boat toward where the canoe had capsized and having a disturbing vision of Eddie. "I was meditating when we were in the Moloka'i Channel. I closed my eyes, and I had this very clear picture of Eddie in red foul weather gear, and he was in a fetal position underwater." When Eddie's mom asked her later what she thought happened to her son, Jo-Anne shared her vision. "Momma Aikau looked at me and said, 'Okay, now I understand,' and that was it—that's when she let go."

In spite of bad omens, the search continued for a fourth day, but it became increasingly hopeless. Physically and emotionally drained, family and friends stumbled through their searches, pushing themselves beyond the edge of exhaustion. The night before, David Bettencourt, who had flown for the Civil Air Patrol, took his plane out to look for the faint pulse of Eddie's strobe light. Fighting off fatigue and a bad cold, he had decided to fly at night because he could spot a light from miles away in the darkness. But David lost track of his flying time, ran out of gas and almost crashed his plane during an emergency landing. Meanwhile, friends continued searching the coastlines. "We were on Kaua'i, and one of our attorney friends Boyce Brown fell off of this cliff and broke his leg," Sol says. "So we had to get him out of there and on top of the bluff, and then we took him to the medical center on Kaua'i." After these two accidents, Sol says the family realized the search had become too dangerous. "After we came home, our parents decided that was it. Somebody had gotten hurt, and Eddie was trying to tell us, That's it." The family decided to have a news conference the next day. Because of all the support they had received with the search, the Aikaus felt like they needed to tell the world that it was over.

Like the lunar eclipse that took place early that morning, Eddie's disappearance cast a dark shadow over his family and all those who had known him. The news conference was held at the Aikau's home later that day. It was decided that David Bettencourt should address the reporters because the family was too distraught to talk. The grassy area in front of the house was filled with cars, vans and a crowd of friends. Inside the house, the family gathered on the sofa, while reporters and photographers stood on the other side of the room. In the surreal atmosphere of that living room, intense personal grief mingled with public curiosity, as tearful faces looked into the cold, glass eyes of the surrounding cameras. Eddie was no longer just a member of the Aikau family—he had been adopted by the people of Hawai'i. Transformed by the tragedy, they now looked at him as their long-lost native son.

Wearing a yellow shirt and jeans, Pops sat on the sofa in a grief-stricken trance. He was asked by one reporter how many people lived in the two houses at the graveyard. Without hesitating, the short, barefooted man said, "My five sons, my daughter, my wife and myself." Although Gerry and Eddie were physically gone, Pops still counted them as living members of the family. Their presence could be felt in the house, and their pictures hung on the walls like holy shrines. When Clyde finally walked into the room, he took control of the situation. Ever since returning from Australia several days before, he had assumed a major role in dealing with the crisis. He gave everyone instructions so the conference could begin. "No more glasses," he told his sister Myra, who took off her sunglasses. "Momma, you should be sitting in the middle," he said as Henrietta moved toward the couch. "Are you comfortable, Momma?" She could only nod as Pops sat down on one side and Bettencourt sat on the other side. "Freddie Boy, you sit here," Clyde said, pointing to a spot on the floor next to him. Crew member John Kruse sat on the sofa behind Pops.

When everyone was seated, David addressed the small gathering of reporters and laid down the ground rules. With his dark skin and wavy hair, the raspy-voiced attorney looked and sounded like he could be one of the family. "We ask that nobody take any photos of people breaking down, please. We don't want to see that on the air. The tears remain here." He also asked that questions be limited to Eddie and his life, not the events leading up to his disappearance. Then, he told the crowd what they already knew: the search was over. David said the decision to end it was "not an easy one, but it's based upon the fact that we have no new facts to give us any reason to believe there is a likelihood of success. The family is satisfied that every-thing that could be possibly done has been done." As these words hung in the air, Myra touched her handkerchief to her red eyes, while Momma sat motionless and heavy-hearted, dazed by the prospect of outliving yet another son. Pops and the boys stared at the floor.

David deflected criticism of the Polynesian Voyaging Society, Captain Lyman and the *Hokule'a*. He went on to say that the family had no ill will toward the crew of the voyaging canoe. "Eddie's love for the *Hokule'a* will not be lost. They hope it will continue to be a symbol of Hawaiian unity and will be used to educate the young." One reporter asked whether or not Eddie should have tried to make such an impossible rescue, a touchy topic for the family. "Anyone who has ever seen Eddie in action on the North

Shore understands why he did what he did," David quickly responded. But in the back of many people's minds, there was still the nagging question of why he had taken off his lifejacket. Some even wondered if Eddie knew he was going to die and had tried to be a martyr.

Unable to sit still and listen to his brother's motives being questioned, Clyde jumped in to defend Eddie's actions. "My brother didn't have to take chances. He told me when we worked on the North Shore, 'Only jump in if you know you can handle it.' When he left the boat, I'm totally sure he thought he could make it. He wasn't trying to be a hero. He didn't have to prove nothing to nobody." The room was charged with an electrifying silence after Clyde spoke, and the family sat still for a few moments, trying to control their emotions. Unwilling to give up all hope, Clyde then looked around the room as if asking for help. "We'd like to call off the search, but…," he paused, choked up. "All I ask for is if you're on a boat and going to Maui, just keep your eyes—just, just look in the ocean, that's all." With those plaintive words, Myra's eyes welled up with tears, and big Freddie stared helplessly at the floor. John Kruse put a reassuring hand on Pop's shoulder as the old man buried his face in his handkerchief. David Bettencourt announced that there would be a memorial service for Eddie at Waimea Bay on Saturday, April 1, and with that, the news conference was over.

Afterward, reporters, friends and guests walked through the house as if it were a museum. They looked at lei-covered pictures of Eddie and the surfing trophies he and Clyde had won over the years. They studied the black and white pictures of the kids, the folded flag from Gerry's funeral and the color photos of the Aikau boys dropping into gigantic waves at Waimea and Sunset. The house was like a holy shrine to mythic watermen whose boards rested in the rafters above. In one family portrait taken on Maui when they were kids, the Aikau clan stands together in their best Sunday clothes while Eddie shyly stands before a *haole* woman in a cowgirl outfit. She is handing him *The Book of Knowledge* that he won at a community fair. In one of the last pictures taken together, the family is gathered in front of the ginger garden they planted in Gerald's memory. The boys wear T-shirts and their hair is longer and wilder. Like his father, Clyde sports a mustache, and he and Eddie squat in front, flashing the shaka sign.

The reporters stared at the photos quietly and respectfully, while Eddie's niece Pi'ilani slept peacefully in the next room. When they finally left, Pops went outside and rang the bell by the door. Friends and fellow crew members who had been talking quietly in the cemetery, reminiscing about old times, slowly made their way to the house. Still unwilling to admit that Eddie was *make* (dead), Pops said, "He'll probably walk in from Maui or Tahiti; or somebody will call and say, 'Hey, he's here!' He's just missing, that's all." Just as Jose Angel had called home from Moloka'i after his first disappearance, Pops still held out hope that Eddie might suddenly reappear. Heading for the coolers, he yelled, "Okay, everybody here, the bar is open! I want everyone to have a beer in his hand." Then, he went back over to the bell and rang it twice. Thus began the somber party celebrating Eddie's life.

Eddie's memorial service at Waimea Bay took place a week and a half later to give the family a chance to grieve and plan for the event. Just as Eddie had taken a key role in planning Jose's memorial at the Bay two years earlier, the Aikaus wanted to make sure his memorial was equally impressive. Lynne Holmes had been helping the family prepare for the service all that week, including arrangements with the Mayor and the Governor to transport hundreds of people all the way from town to the North Shore. On the morning of the memorial, Lynne says, "Everybody met at the graveyard, and it was just a flotilla of buses and police escorts all the way to Waimea, which was just mind-boggling." It seemed more like a funeral procession for a head of state than a local surfer and lifeguard. When they arrived at the Bay, a large crowd of friends and surfers had already gathered on the beach. They had planted a circle of surfboards in the sand around Eddie's orange lifeguard tower like a primitive collection of spears in honor of their tribal leader. He had spent a great deal of time in that tower, strumming his guitar and watching all who swam and surfed in the Bay. But now the tower was empty with only a sign on the side that stated, "No lifeguard on duty."

It was a sunny day, and the wind blew over Waimea's sparkling blue water. Just outside the Bay, mourners spotted a whale playing in the water, breaching and spouting occasionally, as if to buoy their spirits. Then, a Fire Department boat with the word RESCUE on its side pulled into the Bay bedecked with flowers, and the whale disappeared.

Eddie's big, red Hobie board stood like a memorial in the sand. A special altar had been set up on the beach with statues of Jesus and Mary and pictures of Eddie. There was a large portrait of him in Hawaiian clothing, looking like a young chief from ages past. In one photo, he was wearing a *haku* lei around his head that looked like a crown of thorns. The picture was

236

covered in green *ti* leaves and flowers, and people kept bringing more leis and placing them on the altar with the other images of Eddie. The altar revealed the family's devout Catholic beliefs, while also showing their respect for traditional Hawaiian ceremony.

The Aikau family had invited two spiritual leaders to officiate at the memorial service, Rev. Abraham Akaka and *Kahu* Edward Kealanahele. Abraham was a surfer himself and a beloved public figure who had officiated at the funerals of many famous dignitaries, including Duke Kahanamoku. His brother Daniel Akaka would later become a U.S. senator from Hawai'i. Edward Kealanahele was a close family friend and spiritual advisor who, like the Aikaus, incorporated traditional Hawaiian beliefs into his Christian worship. Kealanahele came from a long line of *kahunas* and warriors, and he had left Hawai'i as a young man to enlist as a soldier, eventually fighting as a Green Beret in Korea and Vietnam. But after his grandfather died, his father told him it was time to stop being a warrior and start being a peacemaker so he went to theology school and became a minister. *Kahu* Kealanahele stood on the beach in the native robes of a Hawaiian *kahu*, and Rev. Akaka, who was delayed, would later show up in traditional Protestant vestments.

The people gathered on the beach that morning wore a variety of outfits that reflected the diversity of the crowd. A few government officials showed up in coats and ties, but most of the North Shore locals wore surf trunks and bikinis. After they set up the microphones, the popular entertainer Zoulou, from *Hawai'i Five-O*, announced that Rev. Akaka was running late so the service would be delayed a little while. As they waited, a chorus of musicians began singing Hawaiian songs on the beach, and friends of the family handed out copies of Eddie's lyrics about the *Hokule'a*. They sang "Aloha 'Oe," the sad song of farewell written by Queen Lili'uokulani. Then, above the music, they heard a rhythmic beating coming from across the blue sky. The crowd looked up to see a helicopter hovering over the green mountains. After circling around the blue waters of the Bay, the copter landed on the far end of the beach, and Rev. Abraham Akaka stepped out, his long robes fluttering in the wind. He greeted each of the family members with a warm hug. When the Aikau's extended family and close friends took their seats, the crowd of a thousand or more gathered around them, and the service began.

Speaking in English and Hawaiian, the minister told the story of how Eddie had set out on his surfboard after the *Hokule'a* capsized in order to save his fellow crew members. He said Eddie had been hoping to find "an island or a new tomorrow." Rev. Akaka affirmed that this was a noble desire for anyone's life. "The most beautiful thing for us to do is to keep on searching, and to stop searching would be the worst thing in the world." He then said the words that would resonate in people's minds that day and for a long time afterward. "The open sea is to the Hawaiian people as the desert was to Moses and his people…a place where people go to meet God."

After his speech, the Rev. Akaka led the crowd in singing "Hawai'i Aloha," as he strummed the ukulele. Following the benediction over the crowd, Zoulou read a letter that Eddie's family had written. Immersed in their grief, the family sat together on the beach, unable to speak. The message recalled "his final words to his second family, the crew of the *Hokule'a*: 'Don't worry, everything's going to be okay.'" Still plagued by conflicting feelings and unanswered questions, the crowd joined together to sing Eddie's song about the *Hokule'a*.

"Hawai'i's pride she sails with the wind,
And proud are we to see her sail free."

Despite Eddie's last words, everything was not okay, and the family wondered what had gone wrong. The Aikaus had lost yet another son, a shining light in their lives, one who was always looking out for others. Why him? Listening to all those voices singing his song, perhaps the family managed to see a glimpse of hope through all their suffering. The show of love and support from the crowd offered some comfort. And there was talk of rebuilding *Hokule'a*. Maybe Eddie was right, maybe after all the pain had finally faded, everything would be okay.

"Feelings deep and so strong/ For Hoku, Hokule'a."

In some mystical way, Eddie seemed to have known his fate before leaving on the voyaging canoe. As they tried to sing the lyrics, Myra and the family remembered Liko Martin's premonition that the canoe was going to capsize. Momma recalled a comment Eddie had made about going down with the ship. Did he know he was going to die at sea? Was it his destiny?

"The stars that shine to guide her straight path/ Across the sea, down to Tahiti/ Then back to Hawai'i she sails."

Standing with the family and singing Eddie's song, Linda felt more like Eddie's widow than his ex-wife. Although their marriage had failed, they had affirmed their deep love for each other before he left on the *Hokule'a*. She remembered how Eddie had told Mom and Pops that if anything hap-·

pened to him during the voyage, he wanted them to treat her as his wife and part of the family. And she now stood by them. She even wondered if Eddie had been preparing her for his final departure. "You never know why things happen the way they do. But if I had been living at the graveyard with the family and he went off on the *Hokule'a* like he did, I don't know if I could have handled it. The time I spent apart, I became more independent and stronger."

"For Hoku, Hokule'a/ For Hoku, Hokule'a."

When the song ended, Mayor Frank Fasi addressed the large crowd stretched out across the beach. He proclaimed the day to be "Eddie Aikau Memorial Day." Because Eddie had saved so many lives as a city and county lifeguard on the North Shore, where he was known for his surfing prowess in huge waves, the Mayor declared that there would be a permanent memorial and plaque placed at the park to honor his courage and sacrifice. The announcement was met with applause from the crowd. Michael Tongg, President of the Polynesian Voyaging Society, followed the Mayor and told the gathering that the *Hokule'a* would sail again and Eddie would be with them on their next journey to Tahiti. He said a steering paddle on the port side of the canoe would be dedicated to him.

When David Lyman got up to speak, the crowd stared at the captain, waiting to hear what he had to say. Although the day remains hazy, Dave recalls feeling the eyes of the world upon him because he was the one who let Eddie go. Never shrinking from his responsibility, he says, "I may have reminded people that Eddie was given permission to go because even today some believe that he took off on his own. I remember I said a few words, something like, 'Sixteen of us left, and only fifteen of us came back. It's up to us to decide what to do with the rest of our lives. Eddie is still with us in our hearts.'"

In his eulogy, Peter Cole said the day should be a happy one, a celebration of Eddie's life, because he was such a happy person. Peter recalled the glorious days of surfing giant waves with Eddie when it seemed they were the kings of the wild surf and even the waves seemed to bow down before them. Though they were there to celebrate his life, most were still overwhelmed by his tragic disappearance. Many in the crowd only knew him from a distance as Eddie the legendary surfer or Eddie the heroic lifeguard, and for them he was more myth than man. But his family and close friends who grew up with him and called him Ryan knew another side of the man, one who struggled with his own fears, insecurities and doubts. And for them, it was a double loss because they mourned for both the public figure and the private man whom many people never really knew. But when Liko Martin played the song "All Hawai'i Stand Together" on his guitar, they sang the same chorus together in Eddie's memory. Though he had disappeared at the young age of 32, people knew his memory would last longer than his life.

Using the same conch shell that had been used to herald the canoe's departure from Magic Island weeks before, *Hokule'a* crew member Sam Ka'ai put the shell to his lips, and its mournful sound hovered over the crowd. Following the sad bellow, the air was punctuated by the ceremonial clapping of stones like the sharp sound of rifle fire. Then, *Kahu* Kealanahele gave the final blessing and explained the ancient Hawaiian ritual that would be performed in Eddie's honor. A sacred volcanic stone called a *pohaku* would be taken out to the spot in the Bay where Eddie used to surf. Clyde had selected the *pohaku* from under Eddie's house in the graveyard and then wrapped it in *ti* leaves to place on the ocean floor. When the family members and friends were settled in the outrigger canoes on the beach, they paddled into the Bay's placid, blue waters. Clyde led the way followed by over a hundred surfers on their boards.

"Eddie had always wanted his ashes scattered at Waimea Bay, but there was no body," David Bettencourt remembers. "So this volcanic rock was to be the embodiment of Eddie's *mana*. Clyde says Eddie wanted to be buried at the Bay so he could keep watch over everyone. He swam out to this place on the bottom of the Bay and placed this volcanic rock there, and no one but Clyde knows exactly where it is."

The surfers then gathered in a circle and shared stories and tributes to Eddie. Then, something strange happened. "It was a completely calm day," Marion remembers. "Those guys sat in a circle and threw their leis into the center. And then this set came in from out of nowhere, and Clyde was the only one to catch the wave. It blew everyone away. He was actually sitting in the lineup where Eddie always sat, deeper than anyone else."

While everyone paddled back to the beach, the Fire Department's white rescue helicopter hovered over the Bay, dropping thousands of flower blossoms over the water. Though the sun was still shining, it began to rain. Like Duke's funeral ten years before, the light rain was considered a blessing, a sign that Eddie was an *ali'i*, a royal descendant of Hewahewa. A beautiful rainbow appeared over the green valley and the *heiau*, like a shimmering bridge to another world.

Lynne Holmes remembers everyone leaving Waimea Bay in a long line of buses and vans. "We went back to the graveyard for a celebration of his life. It was huge. They had great music, and a lot of professional musicians were coming by to pay their respects." As she listened to them perform and sing some of Eddie's favorite songs, Lynne remembers thinking about his love of music. "His guitar playing had gone through the roof. He had improved so much. We sort of envisioned as he got older that he would have gone into being a musician. So much of it was coming from his heart—people who play from the heart get that extra sound."

After the service and the gathering at the graveyard, lifeguard Mark Dombroski went home and tried to put the day behind him. But he had trouble moving on and letting go of his friend. Eddie had been Mark's mentor, teaching him all about water safety and Hawaiian traditions, helping him become a lifeguard and a man. Mark can only recall bits and pieces of the memorial because it was so emotional for him. "I just remember a whole lot of people, and it was a really hot, sunny day in front of the tower. I remember kneeling in the hot sand, not really believing what was happening, just crying. There was never any real closure: no body, no board. There was a lot of sadness, but at the same time you didn't want to believe it, you couldn't believe it.

"Every now and then, I still have a dream where I see his face and actually talk to him. I usually never remember my dreams, but these were hard to forget. It was like he was still there, living on the other side of the Island. I still see his face and body. It's a spiritual kind of thing where he's still there. When those dreams come around, you think maybe he's still around; maybe he didn't want to be found."

Just as Mayor Fasi had promised, several months later, the City erected a memorial in Eddie's honor. *Kahu* Kealanahele had told Pops Aikau to find a large boulder above Waimea for the permanent *pohaku*. When Pops asked what to look for, the *Kahu* said, "You'll know it when you see it." After finding a large stone just above the park, the City used a crane to transport it to its permanent site near the bathhouse and behind the lifeguard tower. Reporter Elisa Yadao covered the dedication service for KGMB News. It rained during her report, and looking at the solemn crowd, it was hard to tell the tears from the rain. "A very special memorial ceremony was held at Waimea Bay this morning, a tribute to the late Eddie Aikau, one of Hawai'i's finest men of the sea," Elisa reported. "Eddie's mother unveiled a plaque with her son's name and his story on it. The plaque rests on a huge, black stone, a *pohaku*, that symbolizes strength and character and determination, traits that Eddie Aikau is remembered for."

Despite Eddie's tragic fate, his sacrifice ended up changing the lives of all those who knew him and came in contact with the *Hokule'a*. As it is written on his memorial, "'Greater love hath no man than this, that a man lay down his life for his friends.' (John 15:13)…Eddie Aikau is gone, but his name will live on in the annals of heroism in Hawai'i. His spirit will live too, wherever the *Hokule'a* sails...."

CHAPTER 15

The Voyage Continues

"We shall not cease from exploration
And the end of all our exploring
Will be to arrive where we started
And know the place for the first time."
— T.S. Eliot

The Aikaus and the Polynesian Voyaging Society had tried to discourage people from blaming anyone for Eddie's fate, but the Coast Guard's ongoing investigation kept the issue alive. The *Hokule'a's* voyage to Tahiti had been one of the most publicized events in modern Hawaiian history and a source of great pride for its people. But after the canoe capsized and Eddie was declared missing at sea, the state felt the shame and the loss. Flags were flown at half-mast, and his memorial headlined the morning papers and the nightly news. Friends and strangers across the Islands and on the mainland continued to send letters of sympathy and financial aid to the Aikau family. Yet once the sorrow had sunken in, people began to ask questions and look for someone to blame. Some crew members still feel Captain Dave Lyman became the scapegoat for their frustration and anger.

During the Coast Guard hearing, Norman Pi'ianai'a remembers investigators grilling him with questions. "Well, what would *you* have done?" they asked, knowing that he was a veteran Merchant Marine officer. "I think they probably asked because of my experience going to sea and my qualifications. And my answer was 'I don't know.' There's only one guy who can answer that question, and that guy's the captain. I might have done something entirely different from the start." Norman didn't think they should have sailed when they did because of the weather conditions; nor did he agree with the decision to let Eddie leave the capsized canoe. "I don't remember what I said, but I didn't think Eddie should have gone; everyone should have stayed together. I'm sure we could have lasted a few more days, but who knows? I mean, you're sittin' in the middle of the ocean, it's blowin' 35 mph, and the swells are coming over, and every now and then, they're breaking on you. The wind's howling like hell, you've been in the water for twelve hours, and you're probably thinking, 'Shit, is this it?'"

Recalling the turmoil of being stranded at sea, Norman resented the examiners' condescending questions and judgements. "For a guy to sit in front of a board of review and tell us that we made the wrong decision or that we should have done this or that is horseshit," he exclaims. "They were looking to hang somebody; they were looking to find fault. You know, David is a good sailor. To be a harbor pilot and drive those ships around—sometimes, it's pure terror." Having worked with Lyman on rough seas, he knows first-hand how terrifying it can be to guide a ship safely through stormy, 20-foot seas. As for Lyman's decision to let Eddie go, Norman says there was no stopping the young lifeguard. "Eddie did what he had to do; he did his best to try to go for help. That's his training too. The reality is that it didn't work out like it does in the movies. We lost Eddie—there's no going back."

Even before the Coast Guard report was completed, articles appeared in the newspapers questioning Lyman's leadership. In one article, several yachtsmen were asked their opinions about what happened on the *Hokule'a*. Though they were generally sympathetic, they did criticize the captain's decision to let Eddie leave. "Nobody wants to sit around being an armchair quarterback because everybody makes mistakes out there. It's just that the price isn't often this high…It is a cardinal sin to leave a boat when it's afloat. You never leave the boat. He may have been a fine surfer, powerful in the water and all that, but surfing the North Shore is entirely different from the Moloka'i Channel."

Dave Lyman was quoted in the article as saying that he had refused to give Eddie permission to leave several times before finally giving in. "I was concerned that some of the crew members might not have handled another night under the conditions. I was worried, too, because we were drifting out of the area that planes and ships use, and it might not be a matter of another night, but possibly a week or two." Would Eddie have gone with or without the Captain's permission, as Norman implied? As a lifeguard, that's what his instincts told him to do. One anonymous yachtsman in the article said,

"Sure, it's a basic rule that you don't leave the boat. They teach it in school. It obviously has proven to be a mistake, but how can you argue with a guy who wants to save his buddies?"

When the Coast Guard report finally came out, it said nothing about the captain's decision regarding Eddie's fatal rescue attempt. Ironically, it left that issue alone and instead mentioned that "If Edward Aikau had been wearing a personal flotation device, he might have survived." The report went on to state that "the vessel's Captain, David Lyman III, displayed poor judgement in electing to embark on a voyage under the existing weather conditions before his vessel was ready for sea." To this day, Lyman insists that he was pressured to leave that day over his objections. "I woke up that morning, and I remember turning to my wife and saying, 'I don't think we're going to leave today. I don't want to leave today.'" But he refuses to point fingers at those in PVS who actually made the decision. "Let's just say, I was talked into it. There were a couple of times when I balked, but I was always talked back into it. But the ultimate decision was mine. But there are certain people whose whole tack was to make sure their asses were covered, and they left me out to dry. It was a tough and bitter pill to swallow."

When it comes to Eddie's fate, Dave says, "It was my ultimate decision" to let him go. "It was a decision that was talked about at length, the pros and cons of it, and we decided that if anyone could make it, then it would have been Eddie." John Kruse doesn't blame Lyman for what happened but realizes that accountability comes with the job. "When you're the captain and you lose somebody on your watch, you're responsible. I think to this day David is just coming to terms with it. He still has a hard time thinking about it because Eddie was already an icon before he even got on the canoe." Lyman's sister Marion agrees, saying he still suffers from survivor's guilt. "He took responsibility for Eddie's loss. I don't think he really ever has made peace with what happened. I don't know if that's something that you can ever really reconcile. He was never asked to be skipper again."

Sitting in O'Toole's, a dank Irish pub down by the waterfront where local seamen congregate in Honolulu, Dave smokes a cigarette and sips a glass of whiskey. He strokes his tobacco-stained, handlebar mustache as he remembers that painful time in his life. Steering away from the topic of the *Hokule'a* for a moment, he tries to lighten the moment by joking about his job as a Harbor Pilot. Downplaying his tremendous responsibility as a

245

captain, he says, "I park ships. Think of the harbor as a great big parking lot, and I'm like a valet parker." Yet behind his hardy laugh, he is haunted by memories of that voyage and the decisions that were made. Speaking in a raspy voice from years of drinking and smoking, he talks about the *Hokule'a* and the incident that changed his life. "Some of the crew still back me 100%. But you'll find some people to this day who still completely disavow themselves of any responsibility for the decision to leave and the decision to let Eddie leave. And to this day I accept full responsibility for what happened because I was the captain."

In the end, Lyman weathered the storm of controversy and continues to be a successful Harbor Pilot, but the incident took a heavy toll on his personal life. His marriage suffered, and he and his wife eventually divorced. Looking back on that windy day when they set sail from Magic Island, Lyman cannot help but remember his words to his wife about not wanting to leave in the stormy conditions. In retrospect, he says, "I not only capsized the boat, but I capsized my marriage at the same time."

Suffering tremendously over what happened, Master Navigator Nainoa Thompson also felt responsible for Eddie's loss. More comfortable on the ocean than he is on land, Nainoa seems lost in the city and restless indoors. His dark eyes glisten like deep pools of water when he talks about the fate of his friend. "I carry a lot of guilt about this whole thing, and that's just the way I am." But while Dave dealt with his grief by pulling away from the *Hokule'a*, Nainoa stepped in to take charge, determined to see the voyaging canoe sail again. He wanted to fulfill Eddie's dream of sailing in the old way and seeing the island of Tahiti emerge from the ocean.

"So that vision, that dream, captivated me. If we didn't continue to sail, then that vision and the choices he made in terms of his life wouldn't have value," Nainoa says. "So for me, there was no question as to whether we should continue voyaging or not—the question was *how* are we going to do it. What's our commitment to voyaging? So that was an enormous turning point: for those who chose not to go, everyone respected that choice; for those who chose to go and needed to complete the voyage, I had to commit to a whole new set of priorities. Now, we had to have safety as our top priority."

Raising funds to rebuild *Hokule'a* and trying to regain public confidence after Eddie's tragic loss proved to be difficult. Then, Governor George

Ariyoshi decided to get involved. He invited the crew to his office, gave them his personal support and even offered to donate his own money to help pay for the next voyage. "I basically told them that they were on a very important mission and that they could not stop now," he recalls. "I felt they should do whatever they could to regroup and continue further." The nation's first governor of Japanese descent, he realized that *Hokule'a* could help unite Hawai'i's diverse population and heal the wounds suffered on the last voyages. Governor Ariyoshi also believed that sailing again would be a meaningful tribute to Eddie, who represented "Hawaiian pride" in the eyes of the people.

Rigorous training and planning went into *Hokule'a's* next voyage to Tahiti in 1980. Nainoa managed to convince Micronesian navigator Mau Piailug to return to Hawai'i to help them. Working together, the old wayfinder and his young apprentice spent many nights under the immense night sky, just staring at the stars and identifying the ones that would help guide them to Tahiti. Nainoa also continued studying with Professor Will Kyselka, who trained him in astronomy. He and the professor spent countless hours at the Bishop Museum Planetarium, studying the stars projected onto the dome-like ceiling and memorizing the way they rose and set on the horizon. Blending the ancient Polynesian art of wayfinding with a modern Western understanding of astronomy, Nainoa created his own navigational system called a star compass. This hybrid system was in sync with his own mixed heritage as a *hapa-haole*—part-Hawaiian and part-Caucasian. He still hoped to sail to Tahiti in the traditional way, the way Eddie had wanted, following the same sea roads that their ancestors had sailed centuries ago. But this time, he would also use modern safety methods and leave no room for mistakes. After the painful lesson of the previous trip, Nainoa made sure the *Hokule'a* and its crew were fully prepared, insisting the canoe always sail with an escort boat, a two-masted sailboat equipped with all the modern technology and equipment they would need in case of an emergency.

After two years of extensive repairs to the canoe and many months of training for the 1980 voyage, the *Hokule'a* and its crew were finally ready to sail. When all the preparations had been made for the voyage, the crew came together at the oldest church in O'ahu for the rededication ceremony of the canoe. The service was held at Kawaiaha'o Church, where much of Hawai'i's history had unfolded. Within these coral block walls, Kamehameha III had uttered the memorable words that would eventually become the state motto: "*Ua mau ke ea o ka ʻaina i ka pono*" (The life of the land is perpetuated in righteousness). Here, the kings and queens of Hawaiʻi had affirmed their faith in a Christian God while their land and power were slowly being taken away. And in this church, Rev. Akaka had celebrated Hawaiʻi's becoming the 50ᵗʰ state, saying that the "hopes and fears of Hawaiʻi are met in state-hood today." Now, twenty-one years later, another significant event was taking place: the blessing of the *Hokuleʻa* and its crew on their next voyage to Tahiti. At the end of the service, *Kahu* Kealanahele reminded the sailors and all their families, "Whenever you are sailing on *Hokuleʻa*, another is always present—the spirit of Eddie Aikau."

Almost two years later to the day, the *Hokuleʻa* left Hilo on the Big Island on March 15, 1980, sailing for Tahiti, with an escort boat not far behind. As if replaying the events of the previous voyage, they encountered somewhat stormy conditions after leaving, but this time the canoe and crew were well-prepared for the adverse conditions. *Hokuleʻa* safely weathered the storm and made good progress. At the beginning of the voyage, Marion had become violently seasick again. "But after three or four days, I started to gain my sea legs," she says. "I was like a resurrected person. I had a great voyage. I didn't want it to end." Jo-Anne Sterling, the other woman on board, was excited about returning to Tahiti. She had grown up there with her Tahitian mother before moving to Hawaiʻi to live with her Hawaiian dad, Sam Kahanamoku. "Because of the connection of my family to Tahiti, my God, what better way to go back than in a double-hulled canoe! It was a full cycle for me culturally…The canoe represented a new beginning. It got people back into dancing and doing the hula. It helped rebuild our self-esteem. I still say it's the most important artifact in the Pacific." In spite of the cramped conditions on board, Jo-Anne says, "I experienced infinity and a feeling of being one with the universe on the canoe."

Surrounded by such a vast ocean and sky, Nainoa had to be vigilant in his course or else they would miss their destination entirely. Studying the path of the stars at night and watching the direction of the swells during the day, he stayed on deck for most of the voyage and hardly slept. But he was being watched over by his two mentors, Will Kyselka and Mau Piailug, the professor and the wayfinder. In his book *An Ocean in Mind*, Kyselka talks about how he monitored Nainoa's progress from the escort sailboat *Ishka*. Following a mile or two behind, he measured the canoe's course and kept in radio contact with the young navigator. "It was impressive," Kyselka said. "When he would give us his position, he was usually no more than five miles from the position we had established through instruments. Sometimes he would describe five or six ways of determining his latitude. He's breaking new ground in non-instrument navigation."

Meanwhile, on the canoe, Mau watched silently over his apprentice as Nainoa made his calculations about their location. As crew member Harry Ho put it, "We knew Mau had confidence in Nainoa when he started to sleep twelve hours a day," especially after staying awake for almost the entire journey in '76. "When Mau went to sleep, we'd say, 'The computer is down again.'" They sailed for 33 days, enduring severe storms and windless doldrums, chilly nights and scorching days. Except for the fresh fish they caught, which they prepared in every possible way, the sailors ate mostly canned or dried foods. Drenched in saltwater spray for days at a time, they could only shower when it rained. But the crew remained in good spirits, and when they spotted the first fairy terns circling above, they began eagerly looking for land. A crew member shinnied up the mast, scouring the horizon for the slightest outline of an island. When he finally saw the turtle-like back of an island slowly emerge on the horizon, he alerted the excited crew. Together, they watched as the island emerged from the sea, a sight the sailors would never forget.

Toward the end of the voyage, after so many long and sleepless nights, Nainoa began to recall Eddie's dream. "There was this very powerful drive in me 'to make Tahiti come out of the sea.' Those were his words. For me, that was a quiet drive, a very powerful force. But when the coconut trees came up, it was just so overwhelming, and I went into the canvas-covered hull and just cried." Wanting to be alone after such an intense voyage, Nainoa crawled into his small sleeping compartment in the hull and felt Eddie's presence with him. "It was just this whole feeling of being very close to him in that one single moment and…a sense that everything was going to be okay because that's what he told me on the surfboard: 'I'll be okay, everything's going to be okay.'"

When they sailed into Pape'ete Harbor, hundreds of canoes surrounded the crew and thousands of people gathered on the beach to greet them. As part of the welcoming ceremony, the natives treated the crew like Polynesian royalty and gave them a warm homecoming, throwing them gifts, flower leis and cold beers. Hula dancers performed for the crew, and they were feted by the local leaders. The Prime Minister welcomed them back, as if they were long-lost relatives which in a cultural sense they were. Nainoa was honored as the first Polynesian in modern times to navigate a voyaging canoe across the Pacific, using only the sun, stars and seabirds as guides. With his warm smile and pensive eyes, he quickly became the heartthrob of Tahiti, and the local women kept asking for introductions. His picture appeared in all the local papers, and he was heralded as a hero both there and back in Hawai'i. But it was a bittersweet time for Nainoa, and the celebrations were punctuated by poignant memories of Eddie.

In completing their voyage to Tahiti, the mission of *Hokule'a* had been reborn. In the years that followed, she would eventually sail back and forth across the Pacific to Samoa, Tonga, the Marquesas, New Zealand and throughout most of the Polynesian Triangle. After the first voyage in 1976 inspired a cultural renaissance throughout Polynesia, many of these nations began designing their own sailing canoes, modeled after the *Hokule'a*. Over the next decade, Nainoa and his voyagers helped train many native people in the method of wayfinding so they could sail their own canoes back to Hawai'i some day.

Whenever Clyde heard about the *Hokule'a's* well-publicized voyages throughout the Pacific, he thought about his brother and how he had never finished his journey. It was like his spirit was still out there in the ocean somewhere because his body had never been found. Then in 1995, the Polynesian Voyaging Society organized a fleet of Polynesian canoes modeled after *Hokule'a* to sail from the Marquesa Islands to Hawai'i. Still struggling over Eddie's loss, Nainoa invited Clyde to sail on the *Hokule'a* as a special tribute to his brother. Clyde talked it over with his sister Myra and brother Sol, his only siblings left out of the original six. At the time, Myra was still living in Eddie's old house and working for the City & County as an Ocean Recreation Specialist. Sol flew in from his home on the Big Island, where he owns a horse ranch and breeds horses. In one of their *ho'oponopono* meetings at the graveyard, they debated whether Clyde should go. The ocean had already claimed one brother, and they weren't ready to lose another. Torn and uncertain about what to do, Clyde reflected on his life since Eddie's passing.

When his brother disappeared at sea, it had left an emptiness inside him. Just as Eddie never really recovered from Gerald's loss, his death affected Clyde in the same way. "Me and Eddie was like partners in everything. We would go out and ride the biggest waves, we'd go out and party, we'd go chase girls, we'd play music on Sunset Point. We did everything together, and when he got lost at sea, it was like being all alone. It was a heavy thing on me because I felt like I had to keep up the whole family. Eddie's not here so I felt like I had to step up. It was kinda hard for me at the time because I looked at Eddie as being a god. He was my brother, but at the same time I looked at him as being larger than life. I never told him, but I'm sure he knew that."

Eddie's loss seemed to take a toll on the rest of the family, and the Aikaus were struck by a string of deaths during the next decade. Myra says that her family has suffered like the Biblical character Job, and she doesn't understand why they have had to endure so much loss. Clyde says they have definitely experienced their "fair share of suffering." Heartbroken over having lost two of her sons, Momma Aikau's health declined after Eddie's disappearance. After a long illness, she finally died of kidney failure in 1982. Clyde's oldest brother Freddie was killed by cancer, and just two years later his father succumbed to kidney failure like his beloved wife Henrietta. But before he died, he told Myra, Sol and Clyde that he wanted them to keep Eddie's legacy alive.

Still haunted by Eddie's disappearance, Clyde needed to do something to bring Eddie home and put his memory to rest. After wrestling with Nainoa's invitation to sail on the voyage from the Marquesas to Hawai'i in 1995, Clyde finally decided to follow in his brother's wake and sail on the Hokule'a himself. "It was a voyage to complete Eddie's voyage," Clyde says. "He didn't have a chance to make it so I was going to take up where Eddie left off and complete the journey."

Clyde flew to the Marquesan Island of Nuku Hiva, where he joined the crews from the different voyaging canoes. That night, they met for a final gathering of all the sailors on the eve of their departure for Hawai'i. "During our last day there," he says, "before leaving on our twenty-two day voyage at sea, we sort of had a ho'oponopono thing with all of the tribes, and each member would say something. I got picked as a special crew member, and I felt like I had to explain why I was there…I finally stand up, and I can't say a word. Tears are running down my face, and I'm standing there in a rage of tears. I can't say anything for ten minutes. Finally, I get my first word out and explain to the people who I am and who Eddie was." Speaking to these solemn, tattooed sailors from all over Polynesia, Clyde explained why the voyage was so important to him and his family. "Eddie embarked on a journey that he couldn't finish, and I am here to finish it for him," he told them. "I was all busted up, brah, all busted up. Man, I'm in this far-off Pacific island, and that was a heavy trip for me."

That night, on the eve of their departure, something mystical happened that Clyde and his sailing partner Moana Doi would never forget. "My fellow crew member is sleeping across the room from me," Clyde says, his eyes flashing with excitement, "and she wakes up and sees this person sitting in a chair looking over me, checking to see if I was okay. And that was Eddie. Eddie came to me on this far-off island just giving me his last okay to go on this trip. That was a pretty far-out thing."

Moana, whose name means 'ocean' in Hawaiian, recalls her vision of Eddie as if it were a spiritual blessing. "I just remember getting up in the middle of the night. I opened my eyes, and I saw somebody sitting in the chair between our two mattresses. He had long hair, and a bandana was wrapped around his head. I only saw his back, and he was just looking over Clyde. I wasn't afraid—I just thought it was Eddie sitting there, watching over his brother. And I turned over and went back to sleep." Was the vision just a dream or was it part of what the Hawaiians call 'ike papalua or second sight? Had Eddie's premonitions been just projections of his fears or part of his mana? In the book Nana I Ke Kumu (Look to the Source), psychiatrist E.W. Haertig says, "The Hawaiian is closer to his unconscious than most persons. His unconscious information is more easily accessible." Or as Israel Kamakawiwoʻole once put it, "We Hawaiians, we live on both sides."

When Moana told Clyde about her vision the next morning, he was stoked, burning with a newfound desire to complete Eddie's journey. "It was a chicken-skin moment," she says. "But I think it made him feel really good, and he couldn't wait to tell his family. That was the reason he was there sailing, and it just all came together. The canoe holds such mana in itself. Everybody who touches her gives her strength and power and spirit."

During the voyage back to Hawaiʻi, Clyde says the Hokuleʻa sailed behind all the other canoes from the different islands "like she was watching over the flock." The highlight of the trip for Clyde was riding the ocean swells. "We were sailing, and it felt like a huge surfboard on the waves. That was exciting, brah...like dropping into a huge wave." Then, one morning after almost a month at sea, Clyde heard shouts as one of the crew spotted the majestic peak of Mauna Kea on the Big Island in the distance. It was a beautiful sight watching each island slowly rise up out of the sea, and he imagined what his ancestors must have felt when they first arrived in Hawai'i. Looking out over the water, he thought about Eddie. When the canoe finally sailed back into Honolulu Harbor, Clyde knew he had completed an epic journey. "I feel like I brought Eddie home."

A quarter century after Eddie witnessed the first launching of the *Hokule'a* at Kualoa, the Polynesian Voyaging Society dedicated her 25th anniversary in his honor. On Sunday, March 12, 2000, the voyaging canoe returned to the place of its birth, and sailors from all over Polynesia and the Pacific gathered together with thousands of Hawaiian locals to celebrate the occasion. Eddie's closest friends and family waited on the shore, including Eddie's widow Linda and her adopted daughter Mylinda, Sol's ex-wife Ricky and their daughter Pi'ilani, Big Bill Pierce and David Bettencourt. Sailing on *Hokule'a* for the first time since 1978, David Lyman joined Nainoa, Myra, Sol and a crew of veteran sailors to bring the canoe back home. It was a short journey from the other side of the Island, but it went a long way toward healing old wounds. In the distance, they could see serrated cliffs and a tree-lined shore, crowded with people. As they approached the beach, it was like seeing a glimpse of old Hawai'i and knowing the place for the first time.

When *Hokule'a* landed on the pristine beach of Kualoa, still considered sacred by Hawaiians, hula groups from across the Islands welcomed them with traditional dances and chants. The sad but beautiful sound of the *pu* hovered over the crowd and across the water. Dressed in their traditional garb, representatives from island nations all over the Pacific took part in the *'awa* ceremony and sipped the bitter drink from the same coconut shells. Fierce-looking *Maori* sailors from New Zealand took part in the ceremony, their muscular bodies covered in bold tattoos. Dressed like warriors, these *Maori* men welcomed their Hawaiian brothers by touching their foreheads and noses together, breathing each other's breath in an ancient greeting of peace. There was also a new chant recited in Hawaiian especially for the occasion.

Wearing a loincloth and *ti*-leaf leis, the chanter told how the *Hokule'a* continued a voyaging tradition that dates back centuries to Hawai'i's first Polynesian settlers. He sang of her voyages and how the canoe had crossed more than 90,000 miles of ocean since its first journey in 1976—roughly equivalent to sailing four times around the Earth. Weaving together the past and present, the chanter shared the story of Eddie's sacrifice during the voyage of '78 and how his *mana* had touched the voyaging canoe and all who sailed on her. Like a buoy pulsing in the night, Eddie's memory has become an enduring beacon of light, beating like the heart of the deep.

Follow the Turtles

*"We are from the ocean, and we are water people
who will end up back in the sea sooner or later."*
—Solomon Aikau III

Honoring his father's wish to share Eddie's legacy with the world, Clyde proved his dedication to his brother in 1986, the year of the first annual Quiksilver in Memory of Eddie Aikau Contest. During the waiting period for the contest, a mammoth swell hit Oʻahu's North Shore, flooding roads and destroying two homes. Because the surf was so big and dangerous, officials argued over whether or not to hold the event. While they debated over the safety of the surfers, big-wave maverick Mark Foo looked out into the maelstrom of waves and whitewater and nonchalantly told one camera-man, "Eddie would go." The saying stuck, and it eventually became popular in the Islands and in the international board-riding community.

When they finally decided to hold the event, the early rounds went off in huge waves that continued to build throughout the day. Like the Smirnoff Contest in '74, monster swells more than 40-feet high sometimes closed out the Bay and swept the surfers toward the shore. Sitting out in the lineup with friends and fellow surfers like Ken Bradshaw and Mark Foo, Clyde knew he was competing against the best big-wave riders in the world. Foo was on fire that day, and it became clear he was the man to beat. Taking off on giant waves with vertical drops, Mark pushed all the limits and established an early lead in the contest. Well aware of the dangers of the sport, Mark Foo would later say during an interview with *Surfer* that dying in huge surf would be a "a glamorous way to go" and that "it's not tragic to die doing something you love." Years later, he fulfilled his own prophecy. In the winter of 1995, while surfing with Ken Bradshaw at Mavericks, the epic break located at Half-Moon Bay below San Francisco, Mark Foo wiped out on a wave that broke his board and held his body underwater until he drowned.

During the finals of the Quiksilver Contest, Clyde saw two turtles swimming out beyond the lineup. In the face of such huge waves, they seemed calm and playful, like Eddie and Jose Angel used to be. Staring at the graceful creatures, a voice inside him said, "Follow the turtles." As a Native Hawaiian steeped in *mana*, Clyde believed that animals could take the form of 'aumakua, or spiritual guardians, so he listened to his instincts and followed them. Knowing that positioning was critical in big surf, he paddled toward the turtles way past the lineup. When he was far beyond the other competitors, Clyde suddenly saw the biggest wave of the day rise up on the horizon and swallow the sky. He turned his board around, started stroking for the beast and then dropped more than forty feet down its rushing face. Crouched just ahead of its roaring maw, Clyde rode the wave across the Bay to the inside section until it died out. The crowds on the beach and the overlooking cliff shouted with excitement. When he finally made it back out, Clyde followed the turtles once again. Another set came rolling in, and he rode the mammoth wave all the way in to the shore.

A fog horn announced the end of the heat, and the other contestants came in from the giant surf. While the judges tallied the final scores, everyone speculated as to whether Clyde had been able to overtake Mark's lead. When the emcee announced that Clyde had won the event, a surge of electric energy swept through the crowd. Family and friends swarmed around Clyde, who was so overcome by emotion he couldn't speak. "To have it come out that way," head judge Jack Shipley said, "It was almost too much to bear. That Hawaiian *mana* stuff is pretty awesome." With tears in his eyes and a stammer in his voice, Clyde dedicated his victory to his brother, just as Eddie had done for Gerald during the Duke Classic ten years before. To this day, Clyde still believes the turtles were the guiding spirits of Jose Angel and Eddie—together, they had won the contest.

BIBLIOGRAPHY

Ambrose, Greg. *The Surfer's Guide to Hawai'i*.
Honolulu: Bess Press, 1991.

Bartholomew, Wayne "Rabbit" and Tim Baker. *Bustin' Down the Door*.
Queensland, Australia: Harper Sports, 1997.

Berry, Paul and Edgy Lee. *Waikiki: In the Wake of Dreams*.
Honolulu: FilmWorks Press, 2000.

The Big Drop. John Long, Ed.
Helena, Montana: Falcon Publishing, 1999.

Brennan, Joseph L. *Duke: The Life Story of Duke Kahanamoku*.
Honolulu: Ku Pa'a Publishing Inc., 1994.

Daws, Gavan. *Shoal of Time: A History of the Hawaiian Islands*.
Honolulu: University of Hawai'i Press, 1968.

Doyle, David. *Rescue in Paradise*.
Honolulu: Island Heritage, 2000.

Dudley, Michael Keoni. *Man, Gods and Nature: A Hawaiian Nation*.
Honolulu: Na Kane O Ka Malo Press, 1990.

Finney, Ben. *Hokule'a: The Way to Tahiti*.
New York: Dodd, Mead and Co., 1979.

Finney, Ben. *Voyage of Rediscovery*.
Berkeley: University of California Press, 1994.

Finney, Ben and James Houston. *Surfing: A History of the Ancient Sport*.
San Francisco: Pomegranate Art Books, 1996.

Fornander, Abraham. *Ancient History of the Hawaiian People to the Times of Kamehameha I*.
Honolulu: Mutual Publishing, 1996.

Gabbard, Andrea. *Girl in the Curl: A Century of Women in Surfing*.
Seattle: Seal Press, 2000.

Goodman, Robert B., Gavan Daws, and Ed Sheehan. *The Hawaiians.*
Honolulu: Island Heritage, 1970.

Grigg, Ricky. *Big Surf, Deep Dives & the Islands: My Life in the Ocean.*
Honolulu: Editions Limited, 1998.

Hall, Sandra Kimberly and Greg Ambrose. *Memories of Duke: The Legend Comes to Life.*
Honolulu: Bess Press, 1998.

A Hawaiian Reader. A. Grove Day and Carl Stroven, Eds.
Honolulu: Mutual Publishing, 1959.

Holmes, Tommy. *The Hawaiian Canoe.*
Honolulu: Editions Limited. 1993

Hemmings, Fred. *The Soul of Surfing is Hawaiian.*
Hong Kong: Sports Enterprises Inc., 1997.

Jarratt, Phil. *Mr. Sunset: The Jeff Hakman Story.*
London: General Publishing Group, 1997.

Jenkins, Bruce. *The North Shore Chronicles: Big-Wave Surfing in Hawaii.*
Berkeley: Frog, Limited, 1999.

Kamakau, Samuel. *Ruling Chiefs of Hawai'i.*
Honolulu: Kamehameha Schools Press, 1992.

Kanahele, George Hu'eu Sanford. *Ku Kanaka: Stand Tall.*
Honolulu: University of Hawai'i Press, 1986.

Kane, Herb Kawainui. *Voyage: The Discovery of Hawaii.*
Honolulu: Island Heritage, 1976.

Kyselka, Will. *An Ocean in Mind.*
Honolulu: University of Hawaii Press, 1987.

Lueras, Leonard. *Surfing: The Ultimate Pleasure.*
New York: Workman Publishing, 1984.

Nana I Ke Kumu: Look to the Source, Vol. 2. Mary Kawena Pukui, Ed.
Honolulu: Bishop Museum Press, 1983.

Noll, Greg and Andrea Gabbard. *Da Bull: Live Over the Edge*. Berkeley: North Atlantic Books, 1989.

"The Ocean Is My Classroom," Ed. Gisela E. Speidel and Kristina Inn, Honolulu: *Kamehameha Journal of Education*, Fall 1994, Vol. 5, pp. 11-23.

Olelo No 'Eau: Hawaiian Proverbs and Poetical Sayings. Mary Kawena Pukui, Ed. Honolulu: Bishop Museum Press, 1983.

Surfer's Journal: Great Waves, Vol. 6. Produced by Ira Opper, Opper Sports, 1998. Video.

Surfing For Life. David L. Brown Productions. 1999. Documentary.

Timmons, Grady. *Waikiki Beachboy*. Honolulu: Editions Limited, 1989.

Young, Nat. *The History of Modern Surfing*. Angourie, Australia: Palm Beach Press, 1983.

ACKNOWLEDGEMENTS

Like a voyaging canoe, this book took time and many hands to build, and now, after four years in the making, it is finally ready to sail. It would have been impossible to write the book without the support and assistance of the Aikau family. I want to express my deep thanks to Clyde, Myra and Sol, along with the extended Aikau 'ohana, including Linda Crosswhite Ipsen, Ricky Aikau, Lynne Holmes, Jodi Young, Bill Pierce, David Bettencourt and John Kruse. They have all helped to perpetuate Eddie's spirit.

A big mahalo goes to Peter and Sally Cole for introducing me to the Aikaus and for supporting this book from beginning to end. Sandy Hall was a tremendous help as a writing partner, editor and friend, and her biography of Duke Kahanamoku served as an inspiration for this one. I want to thank Jesse Kornbluth for believing in the book and shepherding it from rough draft to finished product. Mahalo to all those who gave me valuable feedback on the book, including Lori Aki, Beth McDermott, Dan Kois, Katharine Walton, Tai Crouch, Sabrina Civitella, Dotsie Brittingham and Ed & Alex Coleman.

Special thanks to all those who helped support and promote the project, including Nainoa Thompson, the Polynesian Voyaging Society, the Surfrider Foundation, and Donne Dawson, Don King, Baron Stander and Wren Wescoatt.

Because much of the book is based on personal interviews, I am grateful to all those who shared their memories and stories about Eddie, including (alphabetically): Terry Ahue, Mozelle and Johnny Angel, former Governor George Ariyoshi, Rabbit Bartholomew, Ken Bradshaw, Joey Cabell, Mark Cunningham, Beadie Dawson, Darrick Doerner, Mark Dombroski, former Mayor Frank Fasi, Ben Finney, Mark Fragale, Wally Froiseth, Ricky Grigg, Jeff Hakman, Fred Hemmings, Kimo Hollinger, Jim Howe, James Jones, Barry Kanaiaupuni, Herb Kane, Bill Kapuni, Brian Keaulana, Buffalo Keaulana, John Kelly, Sammy Lee, Gerry Lopez, David Lyman, Marion Lyman-Mercereau, Pi'ikea Miller, Greg Noll, Roger Pfeffer, Norman Pi'ianai'a, Randy Rarick, Jack Shipley, Kelly Slater, Jo-Anne Kahanamoku Sterling, Jock Sutherland, Shaun Tomson, Peter Townend, Peter Trombly, Fred Van Dyke and Elisa Yadao.

Many thanks to the design team. Book design and production are by MacKinnon Simpson and Noreen Valente, with input from Greg Laliberte and Wren Wescoatt. Wainwright Piena's petroglyph designs enlivened each chapter heading. The cover design is by Michel Le, based on an image by the late Bob Goodman, who photo-

graphed Eddie in the enormous surf at Waimea in November 1967.
Mahalo to those who contributed photographs, including the Aikau family, Mozelle Angel, Greg Laliberte, Kimo Hugho, Bernie Baker, Tim McCullough, Ricky Grigg, Fred Hemmings, Linda Crosswhite Ipsen, Lorie Goodman, David Brown, Leroy Grannis and Peter Townend.

Additional thanks go to Wanda Adams, Bill Anderson, James Baker, Paul Berry, Michelle Ching, John Heckathorn, Scott Hulet, Sean Marrs, Maile Meyer, Michael Peters, Michelle Shin and David Yoshida. During my research I was also helped by Nick Carroll, Marion Lyman-Mercereau and Weston Yap, whose articles on Eddie helped lay the groundwork for this book.

Special thanks to Frank and Kitty Damon, my hanai family in Hawaii.

Finally, I want to thank the following corporations sponsors for their support: QUIKSILVER, TS RESTRAURANTS and SURFING MAGAZINE.

THE POLYNESIAN TRIANGLE

From Autearoa (New Zealand) to the south, Rapa Nui (Easter Island) to the east, and Hawai'i to the north, the Polynesian Triangle encompasses some ten million square miles, with but one unit of land for every twenty of water. For thousands of years intrepid ocean voyagers in organic canoes spread across the vast watery universe, settling every habitable bit of land within it.

This has been called humankind's most incredible adventure, as some of these islands have more than 2000 miles of uncharted open ocean between them. Hawai'i was the last to be discovered, perhaps as early as the time of Christ by sailors from the Marquesas, then—independently—hundreds of years later by Tahitians.

Eddie Aikau's beloved *Hokule'a* has recreated these voyages and touched each corner of the Polynesian Triangle.

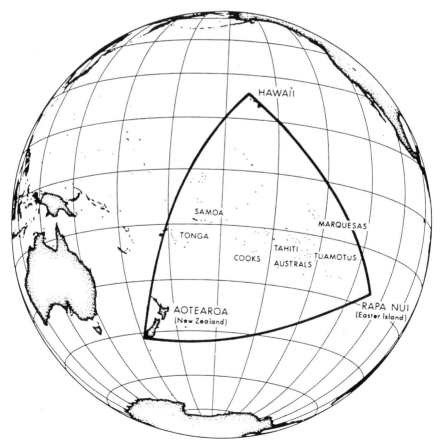

Selected Voyages of Hokule'a

While Eddie trained aboard *Hokule'a* before the first voyage in 1976, he decided before crew selection that he would not compete for a position until the second voyage. The first crews, to and from Tahiti, were:

CREW MEMBERS: HAWAI'I to TAHITI, 1976

Mau Piailug-Navigator, Clifford Ah Mow, Shorty Bertelmann, Ben Finney, Tommy Holmes, Sam Kalalau, Boogie Kalama, Kawika Kapahulehua, Buffalo Keaulana, John Kruse, Dukie Kauhulu, David Lewis, Dave Lyman, Billy Richards, Rodo Williams

CREW MEMBERS: TAHITI to HAWAI'I, 1976

Snake Ah Hee, Andy Espirto, Kawika Kapahulehua, Mel Kinney, Kainoa Lee, Kimo Lyman, Gordon Pi'ianai'a, Leonard Puputauiki, Penny Rawlins, Keani Reiner, Nainoa Thompson, Maka'ala Yates, Ben Young

* * * *

Eddie did, indeed, compete hard to sail aboard on *Hokule'a* on her second voyage to Tahiti, and easily won a position.

CREW MEMBERS: HAWAI'I to TAHITI, 1978

Snake Ah Hee, Eddie Aikau, Charman Akina, Wedemeyer Au, Bruce Blankenfeld, Kilila Hugho, Sam Ka'ai, John Kruse, Dave Lyman, Marion Lyman, Buddy McGuire, Norman Pi'ianai'a, Leon Sterling, Curt Sumida, Tava Taupu, Nainoa Thompson

* * * *

In 1995, seventeen years after Eddie was lost at sea, Clyde was offered a crew slot for the final leg of the voyage *Na 'Ohana Holo Moana*, from Nuku Hiva to Hawai'i.

CREW MEMBERS: NUKU HIVA to HAWAI'I, 1995

Snake Ah Hee, Clyde Aikau, Chad Baybayan, Moana Doi, Pi'ikea Miller, Mel Paoa, Sam Pautu, Mau Piailug, Sesario Sewralur, Gary Suzuki, Tava Taupu, Nainoa Thompson, Mike Tongg, Gary Yuen

THE QUIKSILVER EDDIE AIKAU MEMORIAL SURF CONTEST
"THE EDDIE" WINNERS

February 21, 1986   Clyde Aikau

January 21, 1990   Keone Downing

December 29, 1995 (One heat run. Event never completed)

January 28, 1998 (the "Almost Eddie" cancelled as too dangerous)

January 1, 1999   Noah Johnson

January 12, 2000   Ross Clarke-Jones

January 18, 2002   Kelly Slater

Duke Kahanamoku Invitational Surf Contest
"The Duke" Winners

1965	Jeff Hakman (HI)	1975	Ian Cairns (AUS)
1966	Ricky Grigg (CA/HI)	1976	James Jones (HI)
1967	Jock Sutherland (HI)	1977	Eddie Aikau (HI)
1968	Ricky Grigg (CA/HI)	1978	Michael Ho (HI)
1969	Mike Doyle (HI)	1979	Mark Richards (AUS)
1970	Jeff Hakman (HI)	1980	Mark Warren (AUS)
1971	Jeff hakman (HI)	1981	Michael Ho (HI)
1972	James Jones (HI)	1982	Ken Bradshaw (HI)
1973	Clyde Aikau (HI)	1983	Dane Kealoha (HI)
1974	Larry Bertleman (HI)	1984	Derek Ho (HI)

The Duke contest was replaced by the Billabong Pro in 1985.

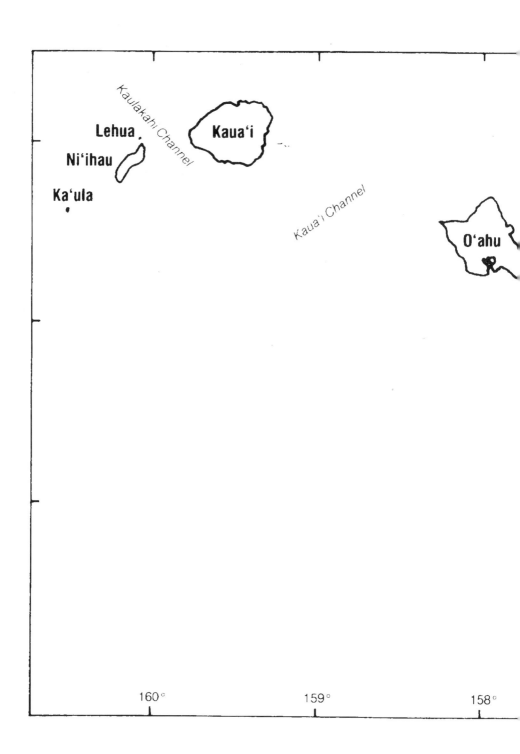

Lehua

Ni'ihau

Ka'ula

Kaua'i

Kaulakahi Channel

Kaua'i Channel

O'ahu

160°

159°

158°

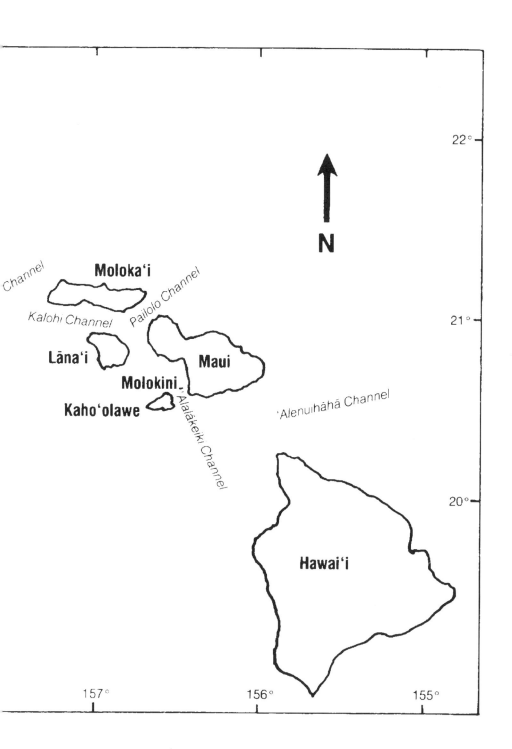

Channel

Moloka'i

Kalohi Channel

Pailolo Channel

Lāna'i

Maui

Molokini

Kaho'olawe

Alalākeiki Channel

'Alenuihāhā Channel

N

Hawai'i

22°

21°

20°

157°

156°

155°